God's Plan *for*
PREGNANCY

From conception to childbirth and beyond

NERIDA WALKER

Scripture quotations are taken from the Holy Bible, New International Version® NIV® Copyright © 1973, 1978, 1984 by International Bible Society unless otherwise indicated. Used by permission. All rights reserved worldwide.

Scripture quotations marked (Amp) have been taken from the Amplified® Bible, copyright © 1954, 1958, 1962, 1964, 1965, 1987 by The Lockman Foundation. (www.lockman.org) Used by permission.

Scripture quotations marked (NKJV) are taken from the New King James Version®. Copyright © 1982 by Thomas Nelson, Inc. Used by permission. All rights reserved.

Scripture quotations marked (NLT) are taken from the Holy Bible, New Living Translation, copyright © 1996. Used by permission of Tyndale House Publishers, Inc., Wheaton, Illinois 60189. All rights reserved.

All dictionary definitions are from Webster's Dictionary for everyday use, copyright © 1988 by Budget Books Pty Ltd, Melbourne in association with Ottenheimer Publishers, Inc. ISBN 0 7323 0375 3. All rights reserved.

1. Pregnancy — Religious aspects — Christianity. 2. Childbirth — Religious aspects — Christianity. 3. Motherhood — Religious aspects — Christianity. I. Title 248.8431

God's Plan for Pregnancy

ISBN 978 981 08 6536 8

20 19 18 17 16 15   10 9 8 7 6 5 4 3 2

© 2004. Nerida Walker — New Life Ministries. All rights reserved.

New Life Ministries — Bringing Life to Barrenness
PO Box 593 Forestville NSW 2087, Sydney, Australia.
Email: contact@newlifeministries.com.au
Web: www.newlifeministries.com.au

Published in Partnership

22 Media Pte Ltd
info@22media.co

Harrison House Publishing
Tulsa, OK 74145

Printed in the United States of America

I give God all the glory for revealing the truths in

His Word regarding my family.

If it wasn't for Him and for the work He did on the Cross,

Shaun and I wouldn't have our children,

New Life Ministries or this book!

Contents

Acknowledgements

I would like to thank the following people who have been a great source of encouragement and support in my life and with **New Life Ministries**.

Thank you first of all to my dear husband Shaun for supporting, encouraging and releasing me in ministry. I also thank him for allowing me to spend copious amounts of time on the phone, the Internet and away ministering to couples all around the world. I also want to thank him for helping me to fine tune what I wanted to say and how I put my thoughts together with the revised edition of this book.

Thank you also to our precious miracles; Kaitlin, Aidan, Aaron and Jesse for being you and for sharing me with others by allowing me to pray and minister when needed.

To all my loving friends and family, thank you for supporting me throughout the years with your encouragement and prayers. It has truly helped me to continue to do what God has called me to do.

To the amazing men and women I minister with in **New Life Ministries**. Your time, gifts, talents, skills, love, prayers and support have been invaluable in my life. Thanks for joining me and helping me to continue the work the Lord has begun. Especially to my prayer partner and dear friend Julie Cantrill for her support throughout the years!

To all my church family, at **RIVER Christian Church**. Your love, prayers and support have been invaluable too. Thanks for releasing me to go where I'm needed to minister to couples around the globe.

Thank you also to Debbie Nolan who edited the revised edition of this book. I cannot thank you and your husband, Sean enough for all your love, support and encouragement.

Thanks also to everyone who allowed me to include their testimonies. I appreciate your support for the vision for this book. Your testimonies continue to encourage others in similar situations throughout the world!

And lastly thank you to the wonderful team at **22 Media** for believing in this book and for your support in helping to spread the truth in God's Word to help many couples worldwide obtain their precious miracles!

About God's Plan for Pregnancy

When Julie, my prayer partner in **New Life Ministries**, attended her prenatal childbirth classes during her first pregnancy, the midwife conducting the course opened the meeting by stating, 'Childbirth is like a deck of cards. The hand you are dealt is the *luck of the draw*. My job is to show you how to manage with what you have in your hand'.

The purpose of this book is to reveal and teach God's promises — His plan for conception, a healthy pregnancy, victory over miscarriage and safe childbirth, as well as caring for your newborn baby. And this doesn't mean that you have to 'manage with what you have in your hand' but instead you can learn to overcome what you might face and walk in victory over it.

During my first pregnancy in 1994 I began to search the Bible regarding what God said on every area of fertility and pregnancy. What the Holy Spirit revealed to me as I studied His Word led me to write the first edition of this book, then called *A Plan for Pregnancy — God's Plan For Conception, Pregnancy, Childbirth And Beyond* with help from Julie. Since its publication at the beginning of 1998, Julie and I have had four more children between us. Shaun and I were blessed with identical twin boys and Julie and her husband had another two boys born two years apart. So I now have four children and Julie has five!

Since the publication of the first edition, God has continued to give me a deeper knowledge and understanding of His will for couples that are either beginning or building on their existing family. This led me to revise and expand my first book and then create this new book *God's Plan for Pregnancy*.

Throughout this book I have outlined what God has provided in His Word for the areas of childbearing and healing. But I have not left you with knowledge alone; I have also revealed how to apply what God has provided so that you can see the fullness of the provision **become a reality in your life**.

It is my heart's desire that you will discover through reading this book, that absolutely NOTHING is impossible and no Word from God shall be without power and impossible of fulfilment (**Luke 1:37 AMP**). Jesus said when you know the truth it will set you free (**John 8:32**). Through the work He did on the Cross, you can overcome any form of barrenness, miscarriage, fertility challenge or any other complication throughout your pregnancy, birth and postnatal period. Like me, you can triumph over your natural circumstances and obtain your victory.

As you develop your trust in God, your relationship and understanding of Him will deepen. I pray that you will receive revelation and knowledge of His '*good, pleasing and perfect will*' **(Rom 12:2)** as you seek His Word regarding His plan for your children.

My Story

*"Worship the LORD your God, and His blessing will be on your food and water. I will take away sickness from among you, and **none will miscarry or be barren in your land**. I will give you a full life span."* **Ex 23:25–26**

To my husband Shaun and I, the scripture above is not simply words on a page but living truth. This has meant that our children Kaitlin, Aidan, Aaron and Jesse could be born into the world. It is the power of God that brought about what man declared an impossibility. In January 1994, after several medical tests and examinations Shaun was diagnosed as being sterile. The tests concluded that he had a non-existent sperm count and that it was medically impossible for him to father a child. The only options offered to us were to have a child using sperm donation or adoption. However, Shaun made the decision to reject the diagnosis as soon as he was diagnosed because **he knew** it was God's will for us to have our own biological children. When Shaun came home and shared the diagnosis with me, at first I was devastated. All my hopes and dreams of becoming a mother seemed shattered. All I could hear in my mind were the words of the doctor that it was 'medically impossible for us to have a child of our own'. Shaun's body needed physical healing but my thinking also needed healing.

I had often prayed in the past for healing from colds and sore throats and I would be healed. That seemed easy for me. But initially I couldn't fathom the miracle that Shaun needed. Essentially this was because back then I had no idea that God had provided answers in this area in His Word. That was until I came across the scripture in **Exodus 23**, which said '*I would not miscarry or be barren*'. If I had not discovered this provision, I may have never known God's will for my life. This scripture was like a shot of life and radically transformed my thinking in a powerful way. With revelation on this one scripture, I now knew **it was God's will** for me to have my own biological children!

God's Word showed that our situation was not impossible. An impossible situation for us was simply an opportunity for God's healing power! I soon learnt how to trust the truth in God's Word regardless of the doctor's words and in spite of the natural facts of the situation. The Word of God had been planted like a seed in my heart. From that time on it was up to me to overcome my natural fears and doubts and continue to water, feed and nurture the seed so it could grow. Shaun and I believed together that the power of God would bring to life what our circumstances declared were dead.

When our doctor recommended more tests to find the cause of Shaun's sterility, we prayed for wisdom and decided to trust our judgement and chose not to follow through with the tests, but to trust solely in God and in what His Word said. We thanked God for healing Shaun's body and for our child.

Initially our circumstances didn't seem to change. However, we supported each other in prayer, because we believed God's Word was true and we spoke words of faith, not words of defeat. And within six months, I became pregnant with our first child! When Shaun told our doctor the news, he wouldn't believe it. He called Shaun into his office and said, 'This is not your baby. It is impossible for you to father a child!' Well, he was wrong! Nothing is impossible with God!

And my testimony doesn't end there. I also faced adverse circumstances such as threatened miscarriages, a threatened ectopic pregnancy and also the threat of a child with Down's Syndrome. However, by placing my trust in God and in what His Word said over my natural circumstances, I had four healthy children within four and a half years! I also 'took' the Word like medicine into my pregnancies, births and postnatal period and was able to overcome complications in all these areas. I experienced healthy pregnancies, and childbirth without trauma, complications or excruciating pain. I enjoyed the blessing of bringing forth new life as well as the whole childbearing experience.

Now It Is Your Turn

I encourage you to not just read the truths in this book but to meditate on them and renew your mind with them and **apply** them to your life. **Hosea 4:6** says, '*My people perish because of lack of knowledge.*' We gain the knowledge of God's will for our lives through His Word. God does not show favouritism (**Rom 2:11**). Anyone who knows and believes Him can receive what He has freely provided.

I believe that, like many other couples around the world, you too will receive your breakthrough!

When you do, make sure to write to me and share your testimony!

Yours Truly,

Nerida Walker

A note to your husband From my husband

'You'll never have any children of your own.' Upon hearing these words from my doctor, I could have reacted in any number of ways. I could have cried out in anguish and despair, or in anger and accusation. I could have blamed my wife, God, my parents, the government, climate change or genetically modified food. Any of these reactions would have been normal and to be expected when someone hears such devastating news. Instead, I received the news with an unexpected calm. I can still remember to this day what I did as soon as the doctor spoke those words — I rejected the diagnosis! I just **knew** that one day I would have a child of my own and whatever 'medical science' said to the contrary was simply not true. As I left the doctor's office, God gave me a vision. I saw myself holding the hand of a small child and I heard a voice say, 'This is your child.' That was it! We would have a child of our own, and nothing any specialist said to me could ever change that fact. I knew that God had said in His Word, '*be fruitful*', and that was enough for me.

The situation will be different for each couple, but in our case, I was the one diagnosed with the problem. Those men like me who have experienced fertility problems can sometimes feel that like they're somehow 'less than a man' because they are unable to father a child. But that's just like saying that a car missing its rear vision mirror is no longer a car! One part not functioning the way it was designed to doesn't make it any less able to be what it was meant to be.

Maybe your wife is the one experiencing a fertility problem. She may also experience feelings of incompleteness or inadequacy. As the spiritual head of the household, you are called to uphold her, strengthen her, pray for her and encourage her in her faith in Jesus. As you join together and walk by faith for your situation you will find that you will grow stronger together as a couple and in your relationship with the Lord.

If you are experiencing fertility problems, then I encourage you to read as much of this book as possible. While it has been aimed primarily at women, with many subjects that can make even the toughest of us guys queasy, it nonetheless contains biblical truths and encouraging testimonies of other couples who have overcome infertility.

It is my prayer that all who read this book will receive the revelation needed to believe for their own family and receive the breakthrough — your own children!

Shaun Walker

It is Finished!

When Jesus hung on the Cross His very last words were '*It is finished*' (**John 19:30**). Three simple words, but very powerful in their meaning. Jesus had completed the work He came to do.

Through reading this book you will discover the fullness of what Jesus purchased through the finished work of the Cross. You will learn that He paid the price in full for EVERYTHING that came into the world as the result of the fall in the Garden of Eden. JESUS DISARMED IT ALL! He bore it ALL on His body, taking it in our place. Jesus is not just our sin substitute but He is also a substitute for everything that came into the world as a consequence of sin.

Before we learn how to apply what Jesus purchased through the finished work of the Cross it is important to know the fullness of what has been provided. This is so that we can confidently know what we have inherited and then begin to live in the fullness of that provision.

> "*His divine power **has given us** (past tense) **everything we need for life and godliness** through our knowledge of Him who called us by His own glory and goodness. Through these He has given us His very great and **precious promises**, so that **through them** you may participate in the divine nature and escape the corruption in the world caused by evil desires.*" **2 Peter 1:3**

Through God's power, glory and goodness, **everything** we need for life and for godliness has already been established! It is through God's precious promises in His Word that we find what has been provided and how to apply it to our daily lives.

When Jesus ascended into heaven He SAT DOWN! His work was complete! So when it comes to what Jesus has purchased we don't need to pray and ask God for these things because they have ALREADY been provided! If you are in Christ then you already have your inheritance. God has done His part for us through Jesus. Jesus is sitting at the right hand of the Father — WAITING FOR YOU to go and possess EVERYTHING He died to purchase for you!

What did Jesus do?
- **He became your sin** — so you have forgiveness.
- **He disarmed the devil and all his works** — so you have deliverance.

13

- **He disarmed ALL sickness and disease** — so you have healing.
- **He gave you His Word** — so you can know who you are and what you have already inherited.
- **He gave you His authority** — so you can exercise authority over your body and your natural symptoms and circumstances.
- **He gave you His power** — so you have power over ALL the power of the enemy **(Luke 10:19)**.
- **He poured His Spirit in you** — so you have His resurrection power by the Holy Spirit who dwells in you **(Rom 8:11)**.

What more do you need?!

God has ALREADY done everything He could possibly do! **IT IS FINISHED!** It is now up to you to KNOW, BELIEVE and ACT on this truth if you want to see it come to pass in your daily life.

How To See God's Power Released In Your Life

When it comes to receiving what Jesus did on the Cross, it's not about praying or asking God to do what He has already done! Instead it is about discovering what has **already been provided** and then learning how to walk in the fullness of that provision. I believe that there are three simple keys to seeing God's power released in your life to change your natural circumstances:

1) Knowledge — *Information*: Knowing what is available to you as outlined in God's Word, the fullness of what Jesus has done and your authority in this world.

2) Faith — *Revelation*: Believing you have received what Jesus purchased through the finished work of the Cross, by meditating on God's Word until what it says is more real and powerful to you than what your natural circumstances are dictating.

3) Action — *Application*: Walking this out, meaning to operate in faith by applying this truth to your life, acting on what you believe and exercising authority over the natural circumstances.

As you read through this book you will learn how to apply these keys so you can walk by faith, not by sight and see God's power released to overcome the challenges you face in every area of childbearing.

So let us begin this journey....

PART I
The Foundations

chapter

God is Good
— All the time!

*"For the eyes of the LORD run to and fro throughout the whole earth, to **shew Himself strong** in the behalf of them whose heart is perfect toward Him."* **2 Chronicles 16:9 (KJV)**

I believe that the key to your breakthrough isn't just knowing what God has provided and how to apply it to your life, but also about knowing who He is to you personally! We need to come to the place where we KNOW that God is good — *all the time!* He is our loving Heavenly Father and when you know this truth and you begin to see Him in this light, then your relationship with Him can be strengthened.

We begin this wonderful journey through Jesus. He is our entry point to a relationship with God the Father. The moment we accepted Jesus' sacrifice on the Cross for our sins and received Him as Lord and Saviour, our relationship with the Father began. And it is because of Jesus that we can come boldly into the throne room of grace to obtain mercy in our time of need **(Heb 4:15–16)**.

We are all at different levels in our walk with the Lord and we may all have different perceptions of who He is. If we have had poor examples of earthly parents then this can shape our view of God and the expectations we have of Him. Any flawed view can prevent us from walking in what He has freely provided. If we judge God through the experiences of our upbringing then we can easily limit His unconditional love and power and reduce it to a poor earthly example. How we view God therefore is crucial to our breakthrough because it can affect how we relate to Him, and how we are able receive what He has freely provided through His Son.

We need to be careful that we don't judge who God is or His will for our lives through the filter of our past experiences or through our natural understanding. If for example, we feel angry, rejected, cheated, abandoned, or that we are going through some trial because God is trying to teach us something, then this incorrect view will prevent us from believing that God is good. Instead we need to measure who God is through His Word because what we experience is not always His will for our lives. It is **through His Word** that we discover what His will is and that His nature and character is always good, constant and unchanging.

> ..."I pray that you may really come to know practically, through experience for yourselves the love of Christ, which far surpasses mere knowledge without experience"... **Eph 3:19 (AMP)**

We need to know the truth: that He is a God of unconditional love who longs to have a daily living and growing relationship with us. He is not sitting on the throne ruling with an iron fist waiting for us to slip up so He can punish us. No! He is a loving Heavenly Father. In fact, He loves us so much that He has even numbered the hairs on our head.

> "Indeed, the very hairs of your head are all numbered. Don't be afraid; you are worth more than many sparrows." **Luke 12:7**

> "How precious and weighty also are Your thoughts to me, O God! How vast is the sum of them! If I could count them, they would be more in number than the sand." **Ps 139:17–18 (AMP)**

I encourage you to grow in your relationship with the Father by getting to know His unchanging nature and character. Meditate on scriptures that outline His goodness and faithfulness and love. This will help you to know Him more intimately and to also know and trust that He is always good!

God Is The Giver Of Good Gifts

God does not lie or change His mind. When He says something He always means it!

> *"God is not a man, that He should lie, nor a son of man, that He should change his mind. Does He speak and then not act? Does He promise and not fulfil?"* **Num 23:19**

> *"a faith and knowledge resting on the hope of eternal life, which God, **who does not lie**, promised before the beginning of times."* **Titus 1:2**

God remains the same. Therefore, if He is the giver of good gifts one day, He is still the giver of good gifts the next day. Depression, anxiety, fear, anger, jealousy, confusion, guilt, phobias, shame, sickness, disease, infertility, miscarriage or pain are **not** good gifts. They never were and they never will be! God wants His children to walk in health and be whole!

> *"Every good and perfect gift is from above, coming down from the Father of the heavenly lights, **who does not change** like shifting shadows."* **James 1:17**

> ...*"those who seek the LORD lack no good thing."* **Ps 34:10**

> *"No good thing will He withhold from those who walk uprightly."* **Ps 84:11b (NKJV)**

> *"Which of you, if his son asks for bread, will give him a stone? Or if he asks for a fish, will give him a snake? If you, then, though you are evil, know how to give good gifts to your children, how much more will your Father in heaven give good gifts to those who ask him!"* **Matt 7:9–11 (Luke 11:11–14** similar)

God Is Faithful

We have just discovered that it is through God's Word that we obtain knowledge of His will and nature. However, sometimes we can become so focused on the Word that we start to put more attention on the promises instead of on the **One** who gave us the promises! Let's look at the example of Abraham.

> *"By faith Abraham, even though he was past age — and Sarah
> herself was barren — was enabled to become a father because **he
> considered Him faithful who had made the promise**. And so
> from this one man, and he as good as dead, came descendants as
> numerous as the stars in the sky and as countless as the sand on the
> seashore."* **Heb 11:11–12**

It wasn't through Abraham's faith alone that he became a father against
the natural circumstances; he didn't consider the promise itself but he
considered the character of the One who made the promise.

The **NKJV** of the scripture above says *'through faith also **Sara herself
received strength to conceive seed**, and was delivered of a child when she
was past age, **because she judged Him faithful** who had promised'*.

When you consider that God is faithful, and that what He says is true, it
will enable you to lay hold of the strength of God to conceive!

I remember a time where I had no rest because I was so focused on 'the
baby'. I lost my peace and joy. However, when I stopped stressing and put
my trust and confidence in 'who God is' and not on 'the promise' that is
when my joy returned and I was able to rest in His peace. It was not long
after that I received my breakthrough and conceived my miracle baby!

> ...*"the word of the LORD came to Abram in a vision, saying, 'Do
> not be afraid, Abram. **I am your shield**, your **exceedingly great
> reward**.'"* **Gen 15:1 (NKJV)**

God is OUR REWARD! Not the baby, not the breakthrough or even the
answer to prayer. Our focus should be **all about Him**. Remember that
God has given you His very best — He gave you HIMSELF. **He gave you
Jesus**. We have everything we need in Him!

> *"If God is for us, who can be against us? He who did not spare
> His own Son, but gave Him up for us all—how will He not also,
> **along with Him**, graciously give us all things?"* **Rom 8:31–32**

Let Jesus be your provision! He is your Jehovah Jireh, your provider; He is your righteousness, your peace, your healing and your reward!

In Him, JESUS, is where you will find your breakthrough. He is the author and perfecter of your faith! Renew your mind with the truth that God is faithful and He will never leave you nor forsake you.

> ...*"be satisfied with your present circumstances and with what you have; for He God Himself has said, I will not in any way fail you nor give you up nor leave you without support. I will not, I will not, I will not in any degree leave you helpless nor forsake nor let you down, relax My hold on you! Assuredly not! So we take comfort and are encouraged and confidently and boldly say, The Lord is my Helper; I will not be seized with alarm I will not fear or dread or be terrified. What can man do to me?"* **Heb 13:5–6 (AMP)**

Therefore seek Him first, worship Him, delight yourself in Him and remember always that...

> ...*"no matter how many* **promises** *God has made,* **they are 'Yes' in Christ**. *And so through him the 'Amen' (so be it) is spoken by us to the glory of God."* **2 Cor 1:20**

The Word of God

"Your Word is a lamp to my feet and a light for my path."
Psalms 119:105

God's Word, the Holy Bible, is not just a history or a story book but a book of life! And when we meditate on the powerful truths contained within, that is when the message becomes real and personal. This is how we begin to see God's power released in our life! The Bible will, however, remain just a book and empty words on a page if it sits on your bookshelf unread, or if you don't allow yourself the time to meditate on it and understand what it is saying.

> *"The Spirit can make life. Sheer muscle and willpower don't make anything happen. Every word I've spoken to you is a Spirit-word, and so it is life-making."* **John 6:63 (Msg)** [**NIV** says *my words are spirit and they are life*].

The Bible is the source whereby God's power can transform your whole life. However, if you read God's Word regarding your situation and you don't comprehend what it says, then it will not be of any benefit to you. It is important then, to spend time meditating on what the Word says until it transforms from mere information and becomes real and personal to you. When this happens then God's Word becomes a source of life to you!

God's Word Is Eternal Truth

Even though the Bible was completed over 2000 years ago, God's Word is still relevant for us today. In fact, His Word will remain this way for all eternity.

> *"Heaven and earth will pass away, but my Words will never pass away."* **Matt 24:35**

> ... *"the Word of the Lord stands forever."* **1 Pet 1:25**

God's Word is eternal. It is the same today as it was when it was first spoken or written. God does not change and it is impossible for Him to lie (**Heb 6:18**). So if His Word says that *'by Jesus' stripes you have been healed'* and that *'none shall miscarry or be barren'* then this is exactly what it means!

> *"Every Scripture is God-breathed (given by His inspiration) and profitable for instruction, for reproof and conviction of sin, for correction of error and discipline in obedience, [and] for training in righteousness (in holy living, in conformity to God's will in thought, purpose, and action), so that the man of God may be complete and proficient, well fitted and thoroughly equipped for every good work."* **2 Tim 3:16–17 (AMP)**

Not only is God's Word our instruction book to demonstrate how we should live our lives, it also reveals the very nature and character of God, and details our New Covenant with Him. It also reveals who we are in Christ, where we are seated and what belongs to us as His children. Most importantly, it tells us how to walk in the truth and see that truth become a reality in our lives.

> *"Sanctify them by the truth; your Word is truth."* **John 17:17**

I have such a passion for God's Word. The more I grow in His Word, the more I grow in my relationship with Him. After all, His Word is all about

Him! His Word has become the foundation of my life. When I discovered the truth in God's Word regarding my life, and I believed and acted on it, that truth set me free! Every breakthrough I have received is the result of taking God at His Word and applying what that Word said to my life.

This began during my first pregnancy with Kaitlin. When a problem arose, I meditated on the truth of what God's Word said until it became personal to me. I then learnt to walk by what that Word said, and not by what the natural facts were and I soon saw victory.

We Have An Inheritance

God has **already** established His Word and Covenant here on this earth. Every provision within it is signed and sealed by the blood of Jesus. This means that this Covenant cannot be broken because it wasn't made between God and men but between God and Himself (**Heb 6:13–18**). When we accepted Christ's sacrifice on the Cross we came into relationship with God and entered into this Covenant. This means that all that belongs to God now belongs to you. He took our sickness, pain, shame, lack and loss and gave us His health, love, acceptance, fruitfulness and prosperity in every area of our lives. Sounds like a great exchange to me!

God doesn't show favouritism by choosing certain people to bless; His blessings **are for ALL** who are in relationship with Him. We are God's children and joint heirs **with Christ** (see **Gal 4:7** and **Rom 8:17**). Not only have our sins been forgiven and we receive eternal life, but we have also received an inheritance. And within our inheritance there is provision for both this life and for the one to come!

> *"For where there is a last will and testament involved, the death of the one who made it must be established. For a will and testament is valid and takes effect only at death, since it has no force or legal power as long as the one who made it is alive."*
> **Heb 9:16–17 (AMP)**

If our earthly parents died and left us possessions in a will then we wouldn't have to pray, beg or plead for them. Those possessions would now belong to us — *we would have inherited them.* We would simply need to go and take possession of our new belongings. And it is the same with our godly inheritance. We don't need to ask for what already belongs to us, we simply go and possess **what God has already provided** through His Son.

> *"My Covenant will I **not break**, nor alter the thing that is gone out of my lips."* **Ps 89:34 (KJV)**

God's Word is **His will and testament** to us! God has bound Himself to His Word. He swore by Himself, so it can never be broken (see **Is 45:23** and **Heb 6:13**). All of the provisions within our Covenant are set out in God's Word. Every area of life is covered so if you want to know what God's will is for a particular area of your life then search His Word to see what that says. If God said it, then we need to believe that He meant it!

God's Word On Fruitfulness!

There are many scriptures within God's Word that cover fertility and the blessing upon the fruit of our wombs, such as:

> *"I will look on you with favour and **make you fruitful** and **increase your numbers**, and I will keep my Covenant with you."* **Lev 26:9**

While God's promises of fruitfulness are mainly revealed throughout the Old Testament they are not exclusive to those under the Old Covenant. God's plan and purpose for His children to be fruitful remains the same for us today! Yet some dispute that Christians can claim these Old Covenant blessings because they believe they are no longer relevant. But why would God not want us to continue to be blessed in the same areas that Abraham and His descendants were?

These blessings are still God's plan because **Genesis 17:7** says that the Covenant that God made with Abraham was for his descendants **and also** for the generations to come. **Genesis 12:3** also says that all peoples on the earth will be blessed through Abraham and **Galatians 3:29** says that *'if you belong to Christ, then you are Abraham's seed, and heirs according to the promise'*. **Galatians 3:6–9** not only repeats this but also states that those who are of faith will be blessed along with Abraham! So it's plain to see that as *'Abraham's seed and heirs according to the promise'*, we are entitled to receive the Old Testament blessings.

Consider also that if God's plan was different for the New Covenant believer, then that would mean that God had changed His mind and will for mankind. But we know that God does not change **(Mal 3:6)**. He is the same today as He was yesterday, and He will remain the same forever **(Heb 13:8)**. We also know that only good gifts come from Him because He is our Father and even earthly fathers know how to give good gifts to their children **(Luke 11:13)**.

As believers in Jesus Christ, not only are we entitled to the promises under the Old Covenant we also have a better Covenant based on better promises than the Old Covenant **(Heb 8:6)**. In fact, Jesus was the fulfilment of all the promises and blessings in the Old Covenant through His death, burial and resurrection. He reversed the curse and paid the price for all sickness and disease including those that affect our fruitfulness. This means that the price **has been paid in full** for infertility and whatever causes it. So, the same blessings of health, provision and fruitfulness in the Old Covenant remain the same truth for us today.

God's Will

In **Hosea 4:6** God says *'my people are destroyed from lack of knowledge'.* This scripture is talking about God's people being destroyed, or suffering through lack of knowledge. If we don't know what God's will is for our life then we won't know what is available to us. But we don't have to be in the dark concerning the will of God for our life. His will and plan for us always remain clear and constant. Why? Because **God's will for our lives is found within His Word!** Any one of us can discover God's plan and purpose for our lives through reading the pages of our Bible.

> *"This is **the confidence we have** in approaching God: that if we ask **anything according to His will**, He hears us. And if we know that He hears us — whatever we ask — **we know that we have** what we asked of Him."* **1 John 5:14–15**

Whatever is in God's Word is His will for your life — and in His Word is provision for healing, prosperity, and fruitfulness. You can always rely on God's Word because it **has already been** established. So God's will for you isn't what the doctors say, what your symptoms say, what your diagnosis is or what the natural circumstances dictate; but rather what His Word says!

There may be times in our lives when our circumstances don't line up with the Word, and we may conclude that what happened was God's will for that situation. But we need to realise that God's Word isn't proved or disproved by our personal experiences. When our circumstances don't line up with what the Word says, we shouldn't judge or assume it is God's will. Instead we should continue to renew our minds with the knowledge that God's Word is the final authority, and when we believe and apply it then God's will can become reality in our lives.

We also need to remember that God will never break His Word — ever! He has sworn by Himself so we can be confident that He will always keep His promises.

When our circumstances speak contrary to what is in God's Word it can be due to any number of reasons. But we can be certain that it was never because it is God's will — as He cannot act contrary to His own Word.

God Watches His Word

> *"The LORD said to me, 'You have seen correctly, for I am watching to see that my word is fulfilled.'"* **Jer 1:12** [**NKJV** says *for I am ready to perform my Word*]

In the Old Testament when God spoke, He saw to it that His Word would be fulfilled. His Words never failed or returned empty, but accomplished what He desired and achieved the purpose for which He sent them **(Is 55:11)**. In fact what God spoke or promised became a contract because God doesn't say one thing and then do another. He cannot lie, change His mind or deceive us **(Heb 6:16–18)**.

> *"This is what the Sovereign LORD says: none of my Words will be delayed any longer; whatever I say will be fulfilled, declares the Sovereign LORD."* **Ezek 12:28**

Much of what God promised in the Old Covenant was pointing to what He would do through Jesus on the Cross. So while the Old Covenant looked forward to what the Cross would accomplish, as New Covenant believers we now look back at what the Cross **has already accomplished!** That means for you and I, God has already performed His Word through Jesus. He is the living Word of God. So when it comes to what is already established in God's Word and what He has **already performed** through His Son, it is no longer a promise **but rather a provision**. This is why ALL of the promises of God are yes and amen (so be it) in Christ **(2 Cor 1:20)**. So, when we discover what God has provided through Christ we don't need to wait for God to perform His Word in our life. Why? Because **He has already** sent forth His Word and healed us, forgiven us, delivered us and set us free from the power of the enemy — *past tense*.

God's Word Is His Seed

In **Matthew 13**, **Luke 8:9–15** and **Mark 4** Jesus shares several parables on how God's Kingdom operates. He compares natural seed with God's Word. In **Mark 4:13** it states that the seed that produces God's Kingdom **is the Word of God**. In talking about seeds, Jesus used something that the people of that day understood. It was a simple yet powerful analogy of how God's Kingdom (His nature, power and ability) comes, grows and outworks in our lives.

In the natural earthly realm, God created plants to reproduce after themselves through the growth and germination of seeds. A seed already has everything created within it to reproduce after its own kind, so when the seed is planted it will come to life, grow and bear fruit. In like manner EVERYTHING has already been programmed into the seed of God's Word so that when it is sown, ALL BY ITSELF it will come to life, grow and bear fruit in your life!

> *"This is what the kingdom of God is like. A man scatters seed on the ground. Night and day, whether he sleeps or gets up, the seed sprouts and grows, though he does not know how..."*
> **Mark 4:26–27**

I recently watched a documentary on Egypt. It showed how wheat seed was found in the pyramids. The seeds were dated to approximately 2500 BC. Incredibly, when the seeds were planted in fertile soil the 4500-year-old seeds grew! In like manner, God's Word does not lose potency over time but continues to powerfully reproduce God's Kingdom in the lives of those who have sown it. Therefore, when the truth of God's timeless Word is planted in the fertile soil of our hearts, God's Kingdom power will come to life, and grow.

No Seed Planted Means No Harvest!

No farmer can expect a harvest without first having planted the seed! Have you ever looked at an unplanted seed? A seed appears dead, shriveled and lifeless before being planted, but when sown into fertile soil, all by itself the seed will sprout and grow. If however the seed is not planted into fertile soil then the seed remains dormant and will not come to life and reproduce. Because there is already life in the seed, the process of the seed coming to life is not dependant on God, but on the seed being planted and the condition of the ground it is sown into.

> *"As the rain and the snow come down from heaven, and do not return to it without watering the earth and making it bud and flourish, so that it yields seed for the sower and bread for the eater, so is my Word that goes out from my mouth: It will not return to me empty, but will accomplish what I desire and achieve the purpose for which I sent it."* **Is 55:10–11**

How Does The Word Grow?

God's Word needs to be sown in our hearts!

> ...*"in a humble (gentle, modest) spirit receive and welcome the Word **which implanted and rooted** [in your hearts] contains the power to save your souls."* **James 1:21b (AMP)**

In the scripture above, implanted literally means engrafted — when something foreign becomes a part of whatever it is grafted onto. Strong's Concordance describes engrafted as: to swell up; to germinate or grow (sprout, produce), literally or figuratively, to spring up! Therefore it is important that you spend time in God's Word until it is engrafted in your heart, so that it can spring to life, take root and grow. You do this by transforming your thinking by renewing your mind with the truth of what God's Word says until that truth springs up and becomes more real to you than what the natural circumstances are saying.

Initially, for many of us the natural circumstances may appear more real and powerful than the truth in God's Word, but the natural report doesn't need to be our final report! When we continue to meditate on what God's Word says instead of what the natural is doing then we are giving the Word the chance to transform the way we think and how we see our situation. This process is vital as it enables the seed of God's Word to spring to life, grow, develop and take root. That way, if we are challenged we won't lose sight of the truth of God's Word because once it has been 'engrafted' it has become a part of us.

God's Word Brings Increase!

The condition of the ground plays an important role in the healthy germination of a seed. In the same way, the condition of the 'soil' of our heart is vitally important for the growth of the seed of God's Word. James says that *'in a humble, gentle, modest spirit we are **to receive and welcome the Word'*** (**James 1:21**). If the message of the seed of God's Word hits stony or hard ground, then the Word will not grow. Jesus shares on this in **Matthew 13**, **Mark 4** and **Luke 8** in the 'Parable of the Sower'. In these passages Jesus mentioned four different conditions of the ground and what happens when the seed is sown in those conditions.

> *"And He said to them, 'Do you not understand this parable? How then will you understand all the parables? The sower **sows the word**. And these are the ones by the wayside where the word is sown. When they hear, **Satan comes immediately** and takes away the word that was sown in their hearts. These likewise are the ones sown on **stony ground** who, when they hear the word, immediately receive it with gladness; and they **have no root** in themselves, and so endure only for a time. Afterward, when tribulation or persecution arises **for the word's sake**, immediately they stumble. Now these are the ones **sown among thorns**; they are the ones who hear the word, and the cares of this world, the deceitfulness of riches, and the desires for other things entering in **choke the word**, and it becomes unfruitful. But these are the ones sown on **good ground**, those who **hear the word**, **accept it**, **and bear fruit**: some thirtyfold, some sixty, and some a hundred.'"*
> **Mark 4:13–20 (NKJV)**

1) No understanding — those who hear the Word and don't understand it, giving Satan the opportunity to come immediately and snatch the Word from their heart. **Matt 13:19** says it this way *'When anyone hears the word of the kingdom, **and does not understand it**, then the wicked one comes and snatches away what was sown in his heart'*.

2) Stony ground — those who hear the Word and at first receive it with gladness BUT because they don't allow the Word to develop roots they stumble and let go of the Word when temptation, tribulation and persecution comes.

3) Seed sown among thorns — those who, when the cares of the world, deceitfulness of riches and the desires for other things come in and choke the Word and it becomes unfruitful.

4) Good ground — those who hear the Word, understand what it says, accept and live in its truth — the seed comes to life, takes root, grows and bears fruit in abundance!

This is the process whereby everything within God's Kingdom comes and grows in our life. We have seen that Jesus is the living Word of God. He was the Word that became flesh and dwelt among us. When the message of the Gospel of Jesus is sown in people's hearts and they believe and receive it, it brings LIFE; abundant life, resurrection life and eternal life! The fullness of what Jesus did through the finished work of the Cross comes and grows the same way.

If we want to see God's power released to change our circumstances then we need to understand this simple process of God's Kingdom growing like a seed. We then need to spend the time feeding on the truth of what God's Word says for our life until it springs to life, develops roots, grows and bears fruit.

How To Receive Revelation From God's Word

When we read God's Word, we can't simply pick out a scripture that sounds good and say to ourselves, 'Yes, I'll have that' and leave it there. We begin with that, but in order to have what that scripture says become a reality in our life we need to receive a personal revelation. The truth of what that Word says needs to progress from being simple 'head knowledge', that is an intellectual understanding of God's Word in your mind, and become 'heart knowledge' which is **revelation** of what the Word of God is saying (the message within the Word) to you personally.

Psalm 119:130 (KJV) tells us that *'the entrance of thy words gives light; it gives understanding unto the simple'*. When God's Word enters **and finds its**

place in us, it brings light, life and revelation. So we need to spend time meditating on the Word until **information** becomes **revelation**.

Head Or Heart?

In the New Testament Greek there are two different meanings for God's *Word* depending on which scripture it is used in:

• *Logos* — general information Word.
• *Rhema* — the revealed Word of God.

It makes a considerable difference to understanding the scriptures if you know whether the Word is based on the *logos* or *rhema* meaning.

Logos Word

Logos is the Bible as a whole — the revealed will of God. When we read the *logos* Word, we receive knowledge of who God is, what His will is and what He has provided for us. It is the spoken Word of God complete with all the covenants, promises and blessings. The *logos* Word is for the **mind** and is used for thinking, meditating, reasoning, calculating, and considering.

> *"For the Word (logos) of God is living and active. Sharper than any double-edged sword, it penetrates even to dividing soul and spirit, joints and marrow; it judges the thoughts and attitudes of the heart."* **Heb 4:12**

> *"Sanctify them by the truth; your Word (logos) is truth."* **John 17:17**

> *"Heaven and earth will pass away, but my Words (logos) will never pass away."* **Matt 24:35**

In the gospel of **John**, *logos* is also used as a title of Christ. Jesus is the Word — He became flesh and dwelt among us!

> *"In the beginning was the Word (logos), and the Word was with God, and the Word was God. He was with God in the beginning. Through Him all things were made; without Him nothing was*

made that has been made. The Word (logos) became flesh and made His dwelling among us." **John 1:1–3,14**

"And He was clothed with a vesture dipped in blood: and His name is called The Word (logos) of God." **Rev 19:13**

Rhema Word

Rhema is the revelation of what the *logos* Word is saying. It is the *revealed* Word of God. It is the individual Word revealed to us by the Holy Spirit for a specific situation.

..."the Spirit will take from what is mine and make it known to you." **John 16:15**

"It is the spirit that quickeneth; the flesh profiteth nothing: the Words (rhema) that I speak unto you, they are spirit, and they are life." **John 6:63 (KJV)**

"And take up the sword of the spirit which is the Word (rhema) of God." **Eph 6:17**

The *logos* Word is the living, active and powerful Word of God but it needs to become real to us personally if we are facing a particular situation.

Today we live in a 'microwave' society. We don't want to wait for anything; we want it now! But it takes time to overcome fear and doubt and renew our mind with the truth of what God has said in His Word. Sometimes the natural circumstances can overwhelm us, so it can also take time for God's Word to get into our heart and become real, personal and deeply rooted in us. For some, to have the truth in God's Word established in their heart is a simple process, whereas for others it can take time for revelation to be realised. Nevertheless it still takes some effort on our part by meditating on God's truth until the revelation comes.

Now, when I say 'meditate' I am referring to biblical meditation, and not that which is associated with Eastern philosophy or religions. In Hebrew the word *meditate* literally means to immerse your whole self in the truth of what the Word says by picturing, pondering, imagining, studying, and musing it over within your mind and inner man, while also muttering,

uttering and speaking this truth to yourself with the words of your mouth. Joshua was instructed not to let God's Word **depart from his mouth**, but to **meditate on it day and night** so that he could **observe himself doing** all that it said. This was the key to how he would make his way prosperous and have good success **(Josh 1:8 NKJV)**. Meditating on the Word therefore is not meant to be a one-off occurrence, but rather it needs to be continued until you are able to see your circumstances through the eyes of God's Word and not through what you see and know in the natural realm.

Revelation Brings Rest

When revelation and understanding comes and you believe God's Word above all else, it positions you into that place of rest. You will find that any striving, hoping, begging or pleading and desperation will fade and disappear, because you will have come to a place where you **know** that God's Word is His will for you personally. The truth of what the Word says will then not be easily lost when you are challenged in that area. Nor will Satan be able to lie to or deceive you anymore because you will **know** the truth for your situation. God's Word will have become **the substance** of what you are hoping for and **the evidence** of what you do not see yet.

chapter

Faith

Faith is an area where I often see Christians struggle — and I used to be one of them! Because of this I now have a passion to teach the truth of the simplicity of faith and how it works. And let me assure you, faith is not meant to be a struggle!

There is so much teaching available on the subject of faith, some of which is unhelpful, condemning or confusing. However, when I discovered the truth about what faith is and how it worked, my life was radically transformed and I have seen amazing breakthroughs as a result.

What Is Faith?

Faith does not come from the natural realm so it is not based on our natural feelings and emotions. We all exercise human faith every day, but the faith I am talking about is the 'God kind of faith' that can move mountains! Human faith is based on what we relate to with our feelings and natural senses — hearing, sight, smell, taste, or touch. The God kind of faith on the other hand is spiritual and based on what we don't see — the forgiveness of sins, our righteousness in God and everything contained within the spiritual realm of God's Kingdom. To believe in a God that we cannot physically see means we possess faith. And that faith was at work when we accepted Jesus Christ as our Lord and Saviour.

> *"Faith comes from hearing the message, and the message is heard through the Word of Christ."* **Rom 10:17**

The day you became a Christian you heard the Word of God (message of Jesus Christ) and faith came! You then used that faith that was quickened through God's Word to accept Jesus' sacrifice, when you received your salvation. As a result you were born again (or made alive) by the Spirit of God.

Faith therefore is simply believing in who Jesus is and resting in what He has done! Our faith in Jesus is enough because when we believed in Him we received everything we needed to live a victorious and blessed life — one that's worth living!

> *"Praise be to the God and Father of our Lord Jesus Christ, **who has blessed us** in the heavenly realms **with every spiritual blessing** in Christ."* **Eph 1:3**

We **have been given** (past tense) every spiritual blessing in Christ. This is exciting because **the spiritual realm has the power to change the natural realm!** And when you understand how to apply God's Word you can see the manifestation of His power released to transform your life!

We All Have Faith!

When I first faced the impossible natural situation of Shaun's sterility, my first thought was that I lacked the faith I needed for our miracle, and so I found myself in a frenzy trying to muster faith out of thin air. The more attention I gave our natural circumstances, the more that faith appeared to be out of my reach. But as I spent time with God seeking Him for answers, He revealed the good news that faith was not only within my reach, but is also available to every believer. **We all have faith**, we just need to learn how to live and walk by it in our everyday life.

Here are some questions that I believe will demonstrate my point:

- *Are you fully persuaded that you are a Christian and that when you die you will not perish but will have eternal life?*
- *Do you have any doubts about this?*
- *Do you have any fears about this?*

When I asked these questions at one of my meetings, everyone was confidently able to say that they knew beyond any doubt that they have their salvation. Not one of them experienced doubts or fears about this. They were fully persuaded and **knew** that they were already saved. If anyone were to question, ridicule or persecute them, they knew that it would not move them from this belief, and I am sure that most of you who are reading this will have the same assurance.

If I ask similar questions to the ones above but this time about healing or regarding the desire for children, I wonder if I would receive the same answers?

- *Are you fully persuaded that you will have children of your own?*
- *Are you fully persuaded that by Jesus' stripes you are healed?*
- *Do you have any doubts about this?*
- *Do you have any fears about this?*

Many Christians do not realise that they **already** have faith and that they live and walk by faith every day of their lives. All they need to do is to have the same assurance for other areas of their lives as they do for their salvation. And this assurance comes when you know what Jesus has purchased through the finished work of the Cross and what you have already inherited as a believer.

Romans 12:3 tells us that we **all** have '*a measure of faith*' [the **KJV** says '***the*** *measure*']. This isn't saying that we all have different measures, but rather it is talking about 'the measure' of faith it takes to receive salvation. It's the same measure, meaning for New Covenant believers it is no longer about someone having 'big faith', 'little faith', or 'great faith'. Instead we need to use the faith we've already got. While it **appears** that some may have more faith than others, the reality is we all have the same measure! This means that we all have the **same potential** to walk in the fullness of what Jesus died to give us, and also the **same ability** to act on what we believe to see God's power released to change our life and our natural circumstances.

Let me explain it this way. It is not 'by your faith' you receive what you need but '**because of faith**' in Jesus **you have already received!** When you heard the message of Christ, you didn't have to build your faith to receive forgiveness of your sins, a relationship with God, or eternal life, did you? No! When you believed in Jesus **you received** forgiveness, relationship and eternal life! This is the same with everything that Jesus has purchased for us! For example we don't need to build our faith to receive healing. Why? **Because of your faith in Jesus** you **have** healing! Your faith in Jesus gives you the legal rights of an heir, which is received upon salvation. Through your faith in Jesus **you have already obtained everything** you need in life. You simply need to renew your mind until you **know this truth** and then act on it by taking possession of what belongs to you. So stop doing or trying to get what is already yours, and start believing and applying this to your life by knowing this truth and by acting on the truth that you already have it!

Under the Old Covenant the Israelites approached God differently to the way we approach Him under the New Covenant today. They didn't have His indwelling Spirit like we do. They put their human faith and trust in God and in His promises. Through our New Covenant, however, we are born again by putting our faith in Jesus! When this takes place we receive within ourselves the fullness of who Jesus is **(Col 2:8–9)**. This means that everything that belongs to Jesus is now ours.

- We become joint heirs with Christ (we have the same inheritance).
- We have the same Father and spiritual DNA.
- We have the same Spirit of power (see **Acts 1:8** and **Rom 8:11**).
- We are seated with Christ in Heavenly Places (see **Eph 1:20** and **Eph 2:6**).
- We have the same position in the Kingdom including His dominion, power and authority (see Position in Christ chapter).
- As Jesus is, so are we in this world **(1 John 4:17)**.

Do you realise what this means? We are no longer limited to our natural human abilities, because we have the same Holy Spirit, the same faith, authority and power that Jesus used to heal the sick, raise the dead, cast out devils, calm storms, and set the captives free!

We Already Have What We Need!

I have had many people ask me to pray for them to receive more faith. I too, in the past, have had times when I felt that I needed more faith to overcome a particular situation. As we have just discovered, however, the reality is that we don't need more faith; we simply need to exercise the faith we already have!

You may also be encouraged to know that we don't need to 'build our faith' to receive what Jesus purchased for us, because as I previously mentioned, through our faith in Jesus — **we have already received**. We need to stop looking at ourselves and at 'our faith' and start looking at Jesus and what He **has done!** If we know what we already have, then we don't need to work to earn what is already ours! The work Jesus did was a complete work and is freely available to all who believe in Him. We **already have the inheritance**; it is our possession so we might as well walk in it!

> *"The apostles said to the Lord, **'Increase our faith!'** He replied, 'If you have faith as small as a mustard seed, you can say to this mulberry tree, "Be uprooted and planted in the sea," and it will obey you'."* **Luke 17:5–6**

The apostles asked Jesus for more faith but look at His reply. He said *'If you have faith as small as a mustard seed you can say…'*. On the surface this may seem like Jesus didn't answer their question but the opposite is true. Jesus showed them how they didn't need to increase their faith but instead they were to start using the faith they had! In the same way we also need to look at using the faith we've already got.

There may be many of you who feel that you are struggling with faith. But be encouraged that it isn't a lack of faith that is the issue but rather a lack of knowledge. However, this is easily resolved because God's Word gives you both the information and knowledge you need for every area of life!

*"His divine power **has given us everything we need** for life and godliness **through our knowledge of him** who called us by his own glory and goodness. Through these **he has given us** his very **great and precious promises**, so that **through them** you may participate in the divine nature and escape the corruption in the world caused by evil desires."* **2 Pet 1:3–4**

Remember, if you are a believer in Jesus then faith is already present. For this reason we don't meditate on God's Word to **get more** faith but rather to receive knowledge, gain understanding and to obtain revelation of **what we already have!**

Saved By Grace Through Faith

In order to live in the fullness of our inheritance we need to know what Jesus purchased for us through the finished work of the Cross so we can then start applying what we have already inherited to our daily lives.

*"For it is by **grace** you have been **saved, through faith** — and this not from yourselves, it is **the gift of God** — not by works, so that no one can boast."* **Eph 2:8–9**

We are **saved** by **grace** through **faith**!

Saved: The word *saved* in the scripture above is the Greek word *sozo* and means: to save, keep safe and sound, to rescue from danger or destruction from injury or peril, to save a suffering one from perishing, (that is, one suffering from disease, to make well, heal, restore to health) and to preserve one who is in danger of destruction. So with this explanation we see that in context the word *saved* has a much broader meaning to the more commonly understood biblical term of *born again*.

We are saved (forgiven, rescued, healed, delivered, protected, and preserved from danger) through what Jesus purchased on the Cross, and as you spend more time in God's Word you will discover that there is a whole lot more that Jesus purchased for us! And by God's grace all of this became your inheritance upon salvation.

By Grace: Grace is God's unmerited favour toward us. Because of our fallen nature we don't deserve His goodness, love and mercy but God has chosen to bless us because of His great love for us. 'By grace' means that we don't need to do anything to gain God's love and acceptance or to receive from Him. Jesus fulfilled all the conditions of the law, which means it isn't about what we can do, but all about what Jesus has ALREADY done.

Through Faith: Unfortunately more emphasis is put on '**our faith**' rather than on '**God's grace**' when it comes to walking in God's provision for our lives. However, when you understand the extent of God's grace you will realise it is not what you 'can do' or about building your faith for what you need. Why? Because it has nothing to do with your own ability or efforts! It is entirely dependant on **what Jesus has done** by God's grace! It's a FREE gift from God so that none of us can boast.

If you are 'trying your best' to do the Word then you have the wrong focus. Faith isn't about what you can or cannot do — or what you have or have not done. Faith doesn't earn salvation and the fullness of what Jesus did on the Cross. But through faith in Jesus **you have** salvation along with everything else that He has purchased for you.

When we focus on the need to build our faith so we can receive healing, we bypass Jesus and God's grace. The focus becomes all about 'our faith' and about what we can do, and we begin to approach God on our own merits. I experienced this when I began to have more of a relationship with the literal Word of God instead of a relationship with the Healer — **the living Word of God, the author and perfecter of my faith**. I was constantly confessing, declaring and trying to get my breakthrough. Consequently, healing didn't manifest because not only was I trying to lay hold of what was already mine, I was also operating in dead works. I was doing everything 'I knew' trying to get what I needed. I didn't understand at the time that because I was already saved, I had **already** received healing. I didn't need to apply a formula, I simply had to apply the truth of what was already mine! Since coming to this revelation, whenever I am challenged, I simply continue to walk by this truth by applying what it says and victory comes!

Can Our Past Hinder Our Breakthrough?

One area that I haven't yet specifically covered is to do with our past. Remember, we are **already** saved — by grace — through faith! This means that what you did in your past will not prevent you from receiving your inheritance. It might, however, prevent you from walking in it — **if you allow it to**. But your past cannot block you from receiving. Why? Because of your faith in Jesus **you have already received** everything you need for both this life and for the one to come!

I have ministered to many women who haven't felt worthy to receive from God because of what they have done in their past. Unworthiness, guilt and shame are lies that prevent you from having confidence in your relationship with God and from feeling worthy to walk in God's blessings. One area where I see this in operation is with women who have had an abortion or who were sexually active in their past. Remember always that what Jesus purchased on the Cross for us was a **FREE gift**. It therefore doesn't matter what you have done in the past. **You have been forgiven** and God **remembers your sin no more!** In fact, God has told us that He has cast the sins of our past into a 'sea of forgetfulness'. And there is no longer any need for you to remember them either, because as far as God is concerned they no longer exist!

How To Walk By Faith

"We walk by faith, not by sight." **2 Cor 5:7** [**AMP** says *not by sight or appearance*].

While we live in the world, as believers we are no longer of the world so we should not live our lives based on the world's standards or on what we see, feel or hear. We are called to live focusing on God's faithfulness and walking by faith, not by sight, feelings or appearances because not only can these change, they are also are unreliable!

"So we fix our eyes not on what is seen, but on what is unseen. For what is seen is temporary, but what is unseen is eternal."
2 Cor 4:18

To live and walk by faith is to simply live and walk by what Jesus accomplished on the Cross, and not by what the natural circumstances are dictating. This doesn't mean that we deny the facts of our situation, or what our senses say to us, just that we do not focus on them and allow them to be greater than what the truth of what God's Word says.

Once we have discovered in God's Word the fullness of what Jesus purchased for us, it is our responsibility to then meditate on that truth until revelation and understanding comes. In other words, we need to believe it! Believing, however, is not based on our natural thinking and understanding because it is not mere mental assent, 'agreeing with' God's Word from a purely intellectual standpoint. Instead, believing comes from knowing what the Word is saying to us personally. This will enable us to live and walk by the truth of what God's Word says, and not by what the natural realm is dictating. On the other hand, if we don't believe God's Word, and we are challenged with an adverse or opposing situation then all we have to go on is what our natural circumstances are doing.

What Walking By Faith Is Not!

If you have a desire to see the power of God released in your life to change your natural circumstances then you will need to know how to walk by faith (by the finished work of the Cross) and not by sight, feelings or appearances. But before I can describe to you the simplicity of what walking by faith is, I believe it is necessary to first highlight what walking by faith is not:

- **Not walking by what the natural realm or senses are dictating** (by good or bad feelings or emotions, what we see, the absence or presence of adverse symptoms, or by a doctor's diagnosis).

God's power isn't based upon natural feelings and emotions, either positive or negative. And walking by faith is not based on what we can or cannot see or feel, or what the natural circumstances are dictating, or upon what you can or cannot do by your own natural ability!

I have ministered to women who have felt positive about their pregnancy but when the doubts or adverse symptoms began they lost sight of the truth of God's Word and were overcome by the natural circumstances. I have also met women who have placed their confidence in what their natural circumstances were doing. If you have pregnancy symptoms, this doesn't mean that everything is going well or that you won't be challenged, as a pregnancy isn't sustained by symptoms or good circumstances. Feelings, symptoms and natural circumstances come and go and can change. They aren't necessarily wrong, however, my point is that they are just natural feelings, symptoms or circumstances.

We need to walk by what we **know** to be the truth in God's Word and not by feelings, symptoms or natural circumstances. We need to train our natural man (mind, will, emotions, feelings and physical body) to line up with what the Word says is fact through the finished work of the Cross. It is imperative that we let our spirit man and not the natural man determine what we believe, how we will behave and how we will live out our day.

If we focus on our natural feelings and circumstances, we can build an account in our minds of why the Word cannot work in our lives. This is especially true when we allow our natural circumstances, diagnosis, symptoms or fears to appear greater or more powerful than what we know God's Word says. When this happens we allow the natural circumstances to undermine the integrity of God's Word and we may not be able to act on the truth when we are challenged. It is therefore important that we don't allow the natural circumstances to blind us, and cause us to lose sight of God's Word and His nature, character, goodness and power.

- **Not walking by presumption, hope or wishful thinking.**

- **Not walking by mental assent** (to 'agree with' what God says in His Word from an intellectual or mental standpoint only).

- **Not walking by works or performance** (what you can or cannot do, or what you have or have not done).

- **Not walking by following rules, steps or a formula** (from both personal experience and from observation following a formula without revelation is not only powerless but also leads to frustration).

- **Not walking by a 'name it and claim it' formula** (as if by simply saying something that it will automatically come to pass).

The confession of our mouth is the out-working of faith, but declaring, confessing, or speaking God's Word is not something we do to make the

Word work or to make God do something for us. Instead we confess, declare and speak out of our mouth what has already been done! We confess what **we have received** because of what Jesus has already established through the finished work of the Cross.

- ## Not walking by prophecies, dreams or fleeces.

There are many Christians who seek a word from a prophet, dreams or signs from God in place of the Word of God. When someone tries to test God's will by looking for a sign this is often described as 'laying out a fleece'. Gideon tested God by throwing out a sheepskin (fleece) asking for a sign because he was not confident in what God had said (see **Judges 6**). Many Christians today seek this type of sign by 'laying out a fleece' to hear from God using Gideon as their example as a legitimate way to get guidance from God.

The truth is, however, a New Covenant believer doesn't need to seek out a word from a prophet, a fleece, or other signs from God. **Hebrews 1:1–2** tells us that in the Old Testament, God used signs and prophets to speak to His people, but under the New Covenant He speaks through Jesus — the living Word of God. We already have God's will for our life outlined in His Word. What more do we need? If we live our lives based upon a word from a prophet, a sign or a dream and something adverse occurs then hope can easily be lost because there was no solid foundation for that word, sign or dream to be built upon. These things are meant as an encouragement for the believer to confirm what has already been established in His Word, and accordingly we should not base our confidence or trust in these things alone. While the Holy Spirit may lead a prophet or give you a dream, the Word still exhorts us to test these things by weighing them up with the Word!

- ## Not walking by a blind leap or step into the unknown.

Are we called to blindly take a step of faith out of our situation? Is 'stepping out in faith' biblical? There is much teaching that suggests that faith is simply making the decision to step out of our comfort zones by taking a giant leap or step into the unknown. And if we blindly step out somehow God will catch us or bring a better outcome to the situation. Many truly believe they are stepping out in faith, when in fact they are only stepping out in their own human strength. Faith isn't a hope in the unknown; instead it is resting in who Jesus is and in what He has done.

When I began to study what the Bible said about faith I found nothing to truly support this erroneous teaching of stepping out or taking a blind leap of faith. There is one passage in scripture, however, that many Christians incorrectly consider to be a biblical example of the 'stepping out in faith' teaching, and that is the account of Jesus' disciple Peter stepping out of the boat and walking on water.

> *"And Peter answered Him and said, 'Lord, if it is you, command me to come to you on the water.' So He said, 'Come.' And when Peter had come down out of the boat, he walked on the water to go to Jesus."* **Matt 14:28–29**

Many misinterpret this passage of scripture by surmising that they just need to step out 'of the boat' in order to overcome their situation. But if you look at this passage closely you will see that Jesus said to Peter **'Come'**, not 'Step out in faith'! Peter was not stepping out in blind faith based on something he **felt**. Rather he stepped out on Jesus' Word that was **revealed** and spoken to Him personally. Peter's trust and focus was in who Jesus was in His revealed Word and this enabled him to walk in the supernatural. But when he looked at the natural circumstances doubt and fear set in; he lost focus and began to sink! We simply cannot do what Peter did by just picking out this scripture and then stepping out and attempting to walk on water. We would need to have something from God that has been personally revealed to us.

What Walking By Faith Is!

Now that we have seen that walking by faith isn't about walking in the natural realm or by our own natural efforts and abilities it is time to discover the powerful simplicity of what walking by faith is.

- **Walking by faith has vision**

Even though faith connects us to what we cannot see, faith is not meant to be blind. Faith has vision, for it knows the end result and sees you with the answer rather than without it. This isn't a case of mind over matter but rather it is about having knowledge, understanding and revelation of the Word of God. We first get the picture for the answers we need in life through reading the Word. We then need to spend time meditating on it until understanding and revelation comes and our thinking changes so we see ourselves 'pregnant' with what the Word is saying. We can then apply that truth to our life by walking by what it says in spite of what the natural circumstances are doing.

I am so thankful the Holy Spirit has shown me the simplicity of what walking by faith is and isn't. During the early stages of my journey I found myself at times viewing my situation through natural eyes and understanding because my situation was medically and naturally impossible. During these times I would often get a picture in my mind of Sydney Harbour. Where the Sydney Harbour Bridge should have been there was a huge void — the bridge had gone! Every time I thought of my hopeless situation I would see this picture and myself standing on one side of the harbour and my longed-for baby over on the other side seemingly miles away. Then one day while I was seeing this image in my mind's eye I cried out to God for a solution. With this image still in my mind I suddenly saw something strong and solid come and bridge the two sides of the Harbour. The substance looked like a brand new bridge that appeared stronger and firmer than what was there before, and I then heard the Lord say to me, **'Faith is not walking blind because My Word has substance and it bridges the gaps!'**

When we face certain situations in life it may feel like we are standing on the edge of a cliff, staring into a vast chasm with no possible way to get to the other side. But that does not mean that we have to muster up some faith to blindly take a giant leap to get to the other side, or step out in the hope that God will catch us. We simply need to gain a revelation of what God's Word says regarding our situation, because His Word is what bridges the gap! It is what links us from our natural situation to the desired supernatural outcome! His Word shows us what we have already received through our faith in Jesus. And when we walk by this truth it becomes a firm foundation allowing us to cross over to the other side. We simply put one foot in front of the other taking one step at a time walking out the truth of what the Word says, keeping our trust and focus on God. Isn't that simple?

At first we will need to be vigilant in the renewal of our minds, and resist all fear and doubts. Fear and doubt positions us back on the edge of the cliff looking through natural eyes and understanding. Looking through the eyes of God's Word, however, positions us on the other side! We therefore need to be careful that we are not walking in fear, doubt or discouragement, but instead continue to walk by faith, knowing that we have already received everything we need through the finished work of the Cross.

- **Walking by faith is a firm foundation.**

While walking by faith goes beyond what we can see, feel or know according to our natural senses, there is actually a strong foundation that has been laid because we are walking by what God has already established in His Word. The Amplified Bible describes faith in **Hebrews 11:1** as the *'…assurance (the confirmation, the title deed) of the things we hope for, being the proof of things we do not see and the conviction of their reality and **faith perceiving as real fact what is not revealed to the senses**'.* Faith perceives as **REAL FACT** what is not yet seen, or revealed to our five natural senses! What Jesus has purchased for you is real and factual, even though you cannot see it. The **KJV** of this scripture says… *'Now faith is the **substance** of things hoped for, the **evidence** of things not seen'.* The dictionary defines *substance* as meaning: that which has actual existence, confidence, firm trust, assurance, and a foundation, and *evidence* as: proof, conviction, title deed, or receipt. God's Word says that we are not barren, that we will not miscarry, that we are fruitful and that by Jesus' stripes we are healed! These scriptures are therefore the substance (the actual existence, assurance and reality) and the evidence (receipt, title deed and proof) of what we are expecting, even though we don't see it in the natural realm — yet!

When you purchase something you are given a receipt of your payment. That receipt is your proof of ownership. And when you understand the finished work of the Cross, the reality is that all the provisions outlined in God's Word were paid for in full by the blood of Jesus. How do we know what was purchased? Through knowledge of God's Word! Therefore what is outlined in the Word shows what is our reality, and the evidence, receipt and proof of what **we have received** through what Jesus purchased for us!

Human hope says 'I might receive' whereas when you walk by faith — by what God's Word says, then you will know that 'you have received!' It's time then to start applying this truth to your life! So start believing and acting on the truth that you have already received the breakthrough, because the reality of God's Word is your evidence, title deed, receipt and the proof of what you have inherited!

- **Walking by faith is a rest!**

*"But because of His great love for us, God, who is rich in
mercy, made us alive with Christ even when we were dead in
transgressions—it is by grace you have been saved. And God **raised
us up with Christ and seated us with Him in the heavenly
realms** in Christ Jesus, in order that in the coming ages He
might show the incomparable riches of His grace, expressed in His
kindness to us in Christ Jesus."* **Eph 2:4–7**

We are seated with Christ in heavenly realms. When Jesus ascended into
heaven — HE SAT DOWN! His work is finished so He is now seated
at the right hand of the Father. When we believe (have faith) in Jesus
we receive our salvation and we enter into that seated position of rest.
We begin our Christian walk in a seated position, which means it doesn't
begin with 'do, do, do' but rather 'done, done, done'!

Remember, receiving from God is not dependent on works or about
following rules, or steps to receive something. It is not about doing or
saying the right thing to try to get God's Word to work, or to get God to
do something for us. We have already seen that what Jesus purchased is
freely available to all who believe in Him. We therefore must make sure we
are careful that we are not looking to **our** faith, or the number of times we
have prayed or spoken the Word to receive from God. Relying on what we
can do is works. If we could earn from God by works — by what we do,
then faith would be void (**Rom 4:14–16**) and Jesus' sacrifice would be in
vain. Remember that faith doesn't earn us anything, it merely positions us
to receive what has already been done!

In order to come to a place of rest in our hearts we also need to have a
revelation and understanding of God's grace. Grace is God's free gift of
provision that we cannot earn to receive, because through Jesus everything
has already been provided.

*..."he who has once entered [God's] rest also has ceased from [the
weariness and pain] of human labors, just as God rested from those
labors peculiarly His own. Let us therefore be zealous and exert
ourselves and strive diligently to enter that rest [of God, to know
and experience it for ourselves], that no one may fall or perish by
the same kind of unbelief and disobedience [into which those in the
wilderness fell]."* **Heb 4:10–11 (AMP)**

The only striving or labouring we need to do is to labour to enter into rest. We are not called to labour or strive for anything else. When we look to the natural circumstances it is easy to lose sight of the truth and become overwhelmed and default to striving (doing, trying, struggling) to get the breakthrough. For this reason in times like these we need to continue to labour to remain in a place of rest. **We rest in what Jesus has purchased for us, through the finished work of the Cross.**

- **Walking by faith is acting on what you believe!**

> *"Jesus said to him, 'If you can believe, **all things are possible** to him who believes.'"* **Mark 9:23**

No matter how impossible our situation appears in the natural realm, we need to remind ourselves that an impossible situation for us is an opportunity for God's healing power! All things are possible to those who believe!

> *"For **with God** nothing is ever impossible and no word from God shall be without power or impossible of fulfillment."* **Luke 1:37 (AMP)**

> *"Jesus looked at them and said, 'With man this is impossible, but not with God; **all things are possible with God.**'"* **Mark 10:27**

Note that these two scriptures say that all things are possible **with God** — not for God! We co-operate with God by agreeing with what His Word says (on what we have received) and also acting on what we believe by applying that truth to our daily life.

> *"**Do not merely listen to the Word**, and so deceive yourselves. **Do what it says**. Anyone who listens to the Word but does not do what it says is like a man who looks at his face in a mirror and, after looking at himself, goes away and immediately forgets what he looks like. But the man who looks intently into the perfect law that gives freedom (the Gospel of Jesus), and continues to do this, **not forgetting what he has heard**, but **doing it** — he will be blessed in what he does."* **James 1:22–25**

Once we have gained the knowledge of what God's Word says we need to then act on what we believe we have received. **James 2:17–21 (AMP)** tells us that faith without actions is inoperative, lifeless and void of power. **James 1:22** also tells us that we are to be doers of the Word and not just hearers. In the context of these scriptures, the 'actions' or 'works' (as some translations state) are corresponding actions that are based on the truth of the Word rather than on the natural facts of the situation. And one way we can do this is by believing what God says in His Word and acting on it by exercising authority over the natural circumstances.

If our actions don't correspond with what we believe then we may not see God's power released in our life. If you say one day 'I am more than a conqueror' then the next day say 'woe is me, you don't know what I am going through' then you will be defeated, because there is no corresponding action to what you believe. If you want to see God's power released to change your natural circumstances then when you say 'I am more than a conqueror' you also need to **act like a conqueror** and resist the temptation to submit to how you feel or to what you see, because faith acts on what you believe! And this applies for healing, fruitfulness, or for any area of life.

> "*Therefore **whoever hears these sayings** of Mine, and **does them**, I will liken him to a wise man who built his house on the rock: and the rain descended, the floods came, and the winds blew and beat on that house; and it did not fall, for it was founded on the rock. "But **everyone who hears these sayings** of Mine, and **does not do them,** will be like a foolish man who built his house on the sand: and the rain descended, the floods came, and the winds blew and beat on that house; and it fell. And great was its fall."* **Matt 7:24–27 (NKJV)**

Note that the storm came to both the man who built his house upon the rock and the man who built his house upon the sand. The difference was however, that the man who had built his house on the rock, who listened to God's Word and put it into practice, was the one whose house was still standing after the storm had passed.

I have listed below some ways to help you to put God's Word 'into practice' and act on what you believe, especially if you are challenged with an adverse situation. It is not my intention to present them as a formula for you to follow to attain your desired result. To use them this way would be 'dead works' that is using them to earn something or get God to do something (not to be confused with 'works' [corresponding actions] as mentioned in the passages in James we looked at earlier). Rather, they are to help remind you of the truth so you can see God's power released in your life to change your natural circumstances!

So, what can you do to enable you to put God's Word into practice?

- **Make the decision** in your heart that His Word is true and act on that in everything you say and do.
- **Walk by faith** — by what you have received through the finished work of the Cross, not by sight or appearances, meaning to overcome doubt, unbelief, natural sight and senses, feelings, emotions, symptoms, your diagnosis and natural circumstances!
- **Meditate on the truth**, remembering that you already have everything you need to walk in victory — it is finished; you already have the inheritance.
- **Fight the good fight of faith**, meaning to fight or labour to stay in a place of rest.
- **Exercise your authority** over the natural facts (symptoms, diagnosis and circumstances).

There will be times when we will be challenged to let go of what God's Word says because our natural circumstances appear too overwhelming, or the fears, doubts or disappointments can seem to get the better of us. It is in these times where we need to put actions to our faith by continuing to stand on God's Word, being determined not to let go of what it says. While these are usually the times when we don't feel like doing anything, we are to resist the fears, doubts and disappointments, and take authority over any symptoms or circumstances that oppose what we are expecting to come to pass. So, if you want to see the breakthrough then you need to stop living by what you see and feel, and continue to 'do the Word' by acting on what you believe you have received according to what Jesus purchased through the finished work of the Cross.

Walking By Faith Is All About Relationship

Over the last few pages I have detailed what walking by faith is, and is not. However above and beyond all these principles, faith is ultimately about having a **relationship** with our Heavenly Father. Faith in Jesus connects us to the Father so we can experience His love and come to know and experience that love practically, personally, and expressly through His blessings **(Eph 3 AMP)**.

The core message of the entire Bible is God's great love for us. He loves us so much that He sent His only Son to die for us so that we can spend eternity with Him. I personally believe making your main focus a stronger relationship with the Father will be the answer to your breakthrough. When you know who God is, trusting Him will not be an issue.

The Amplified Bible translates the word 'faith' in scriptures such as **2 Corinthians 1:20**, **Hebrews 10:22–23**, and **2 Timothy 3:15** as *'leaning of the entire human personality on God in absolute trust and confidence in His power, wisdom, and goodness'*. In other words, faith is committing your entire self to believing and knowing that God is good. This trust, reliance and confidence comes through relationship because generally we cannot place our trust in someone we don't know.

Before I became acquainted with who God is, fellowship with Him seemed like a monologue; I was the one doing all the talking! But when I learned to be still and to be led by His Spirit I realised that God had been communicating with me all along, I just hadn't learned how to discern His still small voice. When I learned how to hear from Him, reading His Word went from being a chore to a delight and every word on the page suddenly came alive and spoke to me personally. Scriptures that had seemed purely informational suddenly transformed into living words of revelation and power. Spending time with the Lord also changed from something that felt ritualistic to being exciting and rewarding, as I learned to experience His love and goodness. I learnt how to overcome fear, anxiety and depression because in His presence is fullness of joy. I also learnt how to overcome times of boredom or loneliness because He is with me wherever I go and He will never leave me or forsake me. I also have discovered how to lean on Him in times of trouble and how to be led by Him to apply His Word to overcome those challenges. I can truly say that there is nothing that anyone could give me that would add to my life. This is because I have all I need in my relationship with my Heavenly Father.

I can testify and teach what God's Word says and I can share how I walked that out and saw it manifest in my life. However, when it comes to a personal relationship with Him this is something you need to learn to experience for yourself. God ultimately created us for relationship! He is not an impersonal energy or force but rather an all-powerful, all-knowing, ever-present loving Father that longs to pour His love in your heart so that you can come to know and experience that love that will forgive your sins, set you free, prosper your soul, heal your body and make you fruitful in every area of your life!

chapter

4

Overcoming Doubt and Unbelief

*"Do not be afraid; **only believe"*...*
Mark 5:36 (NKJV)

We all face doubt and unbelief from time to time. But it is what we do with that doubt and unbelief that matters. We have already seen that as believers in Jesus we already have faith and everything we need to rule and reign in life and over the natural realm. And if we want to experience that victory we need to live our lives walking by faith, not by sight, feelings, appearances or by what the natural realm is dictating to us.

If we do walk by the natural realm and we focus on the natural circumstances instead of the truth in God's Word, then doubt and unbelief can come in, take root, grow and bear fruit in our life. Doubt and unbelief should not be entertained because when left unchecked they will rob you of God's blessings. Therefore, if we want the breakthrough then we need to make sure that we don't allow doubt to come in and affect what we believe.

Doubt And Unbelief Rob You Of God's Provision!

Doubt and unbelief will rob you of God's provision by preventing you from possessing what God has provided for you. This very thing happened to the children of Israel. God had said to Moses *'Send men to spy out the land of Canaan, which I am giving to the children of Israel'* (**Num 13:2**). Moses was chosen by God to lead the children of Israel into the Promised Land. God was giving them the entire land and victory over all its inhabitants. When they reached the borders of the land Moses sent 12 spies ahead to check it out. But instead of returning with a positive report and a strategy to take the land, 10 of the 12 spies came back with a negative report (**Num 13:27–28, 30–33**). And because the people didn't mix the Word with faith, but instead believed the spies' report over God's Word, the Israelites spent 40 years wandering in the wilderness. They missed out on the promise of God and on possessing their Promised Land due to their doubt and unbelief.

It is necessary therefore that we oppose doubt and unbelief at the onset and guard what we believe and what we allow in our heart, because ultimately our heart is the place where we decide which report we are going to believe.

> *"If any of you lacks wisdom; he should ask God, who gives generously to all without finding fault, and it will be given to him. But when he asks,* ***he must believe and not doubt****, because he who doubts is like a wave of the sea, blown and tossed by the wind. That man should not think he will receive anything from the Lord; he is a double-minded man, unstable in all he does."* **James 1:5–8**

Doubt will always come when we take our focus off God and His Word, when we don't know His Word and will for our lives or when we are more focused on what the natural circumstances are doing. We therefore need to continually focus on the truth in God's Word because the **truth that is believed and acted upon** is what will set us free!

The dictionary defines *doubt* as: a feeling of uncertainty or lack of conviction, to disbelieve a person or their word, or to fear or be afraid of something. *Strong's Concordance* defines *doubt* to mean not convinced or fully persuaded. *Unbelief* in the dictionary is defined as an absence of faith, and *Strong's Concordance* explains *unbelief* as faithlessness, disbelief, hardness of heart, or destitution of (spiritual) perception! So by these definitions we can clearly see that doubt stops us believing God's Word, and unbelief is a lack of faith or trust in God, His Word and in His power and ability. They place the facts, symptoms or circumstances over the truth of who God is and what He has said in His Word.

Trust And Believe That God Is Good!

Trust, belief and faith (which basically mean the same thing) are essential for living a victorious Christian life. They come and grow through relationship with God and in knowing Him through His Word. If we don't believe that we can trust God then we need to work on building and strengthening our relationship with Him. We need to continually remind ourselves that He is only good, that His plans are always to bless and prosper us and that He is a rewarder of those who earnestly seek Him (see **James 1:17, Jer 29:11** and **Heb 11:6**). Once we **know** this truth, we will then be able to *'lean our entire human personality on God in absolute trust and confidence in His power, wisdom, and goodness'* (see **2 Cor 1:20, Heb 10:22–23**, and **2 Tim 3:15**).

Our faith needs to be built on who God is (His nature, character and ability). If we don't know who God is and what He has done through His Son then it will be easy to lose sight of the truth in His Word. But when we do know the One who has promised and provided, then believing will be simple. Abraham and Sarah knew who God was and this enabled them to be fully persuaded that He would do what He had promised them.

> … *"not being weak in faith, he did not consider his own body, already dead (since he was about a hundred years old), and the deadness of Sarah's womb. **He did not waver at the promise of God** through unbelief, but was strengthened in faith, giving glory to God, and **being fully convinced** that what He had promised He was also able to perform."* **Rom 4:19–21 (NKJV)**

> *"By faith Sarah herself also **received strength to conceive seed**, and she bore a child when she was past the age, because **she judged Him faithful** who had promised."* **Heb 11:11 (NKJV)**

Abraham and Sarah received strength (God's miracle working power), which enabled them to conceive in spite of their natural circumstances. I believe their key was that they **considered** or **judged God faithful**. When they 'considered' God it meant that they were not considering their natural facts. We know that they weren't in denial because they **had** faced the natural facts that their bodies were as good as dead. BUT they weren't focused on the natural — they were fully convinced that God was able to perform what He had promised.

Overcome Natural Thinking

For many who are wanting to see God's Word come to pass in their life, their greatest obstacle or challenge will not be their diagnosis or natural circumstances but rather their thinking and understanding — **how they see their situation**. This is because for most of us our natural thinking and understanding will always default to looking at and focusing on the natural realm. If we place more emphasis on our natural circumstances, then they will become larger and more powerful in our thinking and this causes us to lose sight of the truth in God's Word. We therefore need to change how we see our natural situation by overcoming our doubts and fears, and guarding what we believe in our heart so we can see, think, feel and act according to what the Word says, and not by what the natural circumstances are doing or saying.

God's Kingdom Is A Supernatural Spiritual Kingdom!

To understand how God's Kingdom works we first need to know that His Kingdom is spiritual, not natural, and that this spiritual Kingdom is more real than the natural realm. In fact the **unseen** realm created this **seen** natural realm!

> *"By faith we understand that the worlds were framed by the Word of God, so that the things **which are seen** were not made of things **which are visible."* **Heb 11:3 (NKJV)**

The unseen created the seen! We are also told that everything in the universe is being upheld, maintained and sustained by God's mighty Word of power **(Heb 1:3)**.

The Spiritual Realm Changes The Natural Realm

I know what it is like to be in a desperate situation with no hope and all seems lost. But we need to learn to keep our focus and thinking out of the natural circumstances and limitations of the natural world and instead learn to understand God's power, which is supernatural and can change what's happening in the natural world. Then we will begin to see God's Kingdom become more real to us than what we are experiencing in this natural realm.

*"But the natural man does not receive the things of the Spirit of God, for they are foolishness to him; nor can he know them, because they are **spiritually discerned**."* **1 Cor 2:14**

We are called to live as strangers in this world (see **1 Pet 1:1**, and **1 Pet 2:11**). Unfortunately many of God's children are strangers not to this world but to His Kingdom and how it works. We therefore need to learn how to be spiritually minded so we can see God's power released in our life.

See Beyond The Natural

We interact in this natural realm with our five natural senses. But did you know we have spiritual senses too? The natural senses keep us operating in the natural realm while the spiritual senses can keep us operating in the spiritual realm of God's Kingdom. When we change the way we think and how we see things, and stop looking at our life through our natural eyes and start looking through the eyes of our spirit (through the eyes of faith, by what God's Word says) then the spiritual realm will become much more real to us than the natural realm.

When we first discover the truth of what we have received through the finished work of the Cross, our natural circumstances may seem worlds apart from that truth. Everything in the natural can seem to be against us. We can be in debt, be broke, have no education, have a rotten past, be infertile, have an incurable disease, or be constantly sick and hurting. But nothing in the natural can disqualify you from walking in your inheritance — unless you allow it to. Get before God and in His Word until your perspective changes and you see yourself with what He has provided for you. Look past the natural hindrances that are preventing your breakthrough and look only to the solution; see your situation through the eyes of faith (through what the Word says you have through the finished work of the Cross) and stop looking at your circumstances with a natural mindset!

When Joshua and Caleb spied out the land they were able to look past the natural circumstances. They looked through the eyes of God's promise; they saw that the giants in the land could easily be defeated. However, the other 10 spies along with the children of Israel focused on the natural hindrances over God's promise and provision. Their fear of the giants and the natural circumstances caused them to doubt God's supernatural power and ability, and the credibility of His Word. As a result their perspective changed to the point where, instead of seeing themselves with the victory, they felt and saw themselves like *'grasshoppers in their own sight'* (**Num 13:33**). They were defeated in their own sight because they couldn't see how God was going to get them into the Promised Land past the giants. They looked at all the 'mountains of impossibility' they faced in the natural realm, so they forgot the promise of God. We too can fall into the same trap when we look at our own 'mountains of impossibility' such as debt, sickness or disease, or our adverse symptoms, diagnosis or circumstances. We need to be like Joshua and Caleb and look at our natural circumstances through the eyes of God's Word, so we are also able to see through the eyes of victory rather than through our natural eyes of defeat!

Believe And Do Not Doubt In Your Heart!

*"Have faith in God,' Jesus answered. I tell you the truth, if anyone says to this mountain, 'Go, throw yourself into the sea,' and **does not doubt in his heart but believes** that what he says will happen, it will be done for him."* **Mark 11:22–23**

Did you know that the heart is the place where we decide which report we are going to believe? When the Bible says to 'believe and do not doubt in your heart' it isn't talking about the physical blood pump but the spiritual centre, substance, and essence of who we are, what we think and feel and the centre of what we believe.

When the truth in God's Word is established in our heart, then out of our heart can *'flow the wellsprings of life'* (**Prov 2:20–23**). We therefore need to spend time meditating on the truth of God's Word until it becomes real and alive to us personally and we believe and do not doubt in our heart what it says.

Romans 10:17 tells us that faith comes by hearing the message of Christ and this message is found in the Word of God. In the same way that you heard the good news of Jesus and accepted Him as your Saviour, meditate on His Word to see the fullness of what your salvation contains. Continue in this until this truth goes from information and becomes revelation.

Throughout this ministry I have seen many believers let go of the truth in God's Word through discouragement or through not seeing any immediate changes to their circumstances. They expected instant results, and while this can happen, generally the process of information becoming revelation, and then seeing the manifestation of that takes time and sometimes effort. If we want to see the breakthrough then we need to spend time meditating on the truth in God's Word until the revelation comes. The definition of *meditate* immersing your whole self in the truth of the Word by picturing, pondering, imagining, studying, and musing it over within your mind and inner man, while also muttering, uttering and speaking forth this truth to yourself with the words of your mouth, implies a period of time.

We have also learnt that God's Word is His seed on this earth and this is how His Kingdom comes and grows in our lives. By comparing His Word with a seed, we see that there is a process of time between when a seed has been planted, before we see the fruit. Meditating on God's Word therefore is not meant to be a one-off occurrence but rather it needs to be continued until revelation comes, and you see your circumstances through the eyes of what it says and not through what you see and know in the natural realm.

Go Take The Land!

God had given the Israelites the command to go TAKE THE LAND. God had **already** given them the land, they just had to possess it. God had given the responsibility to possess the land to them! It was their land BUT through their eyes of doubt and unbelief they rejected God's Word and promise to them.

If you want to possess what God has provided through Jesus in your life then you too need to GO and **possess** the land! Did you know that the word possess means to seize, to get, or to grasp? That means that **you do something!** It's an attitude where you are so determined to see the breakthrough that you don't let go of the promise. You keep trusting, believing and pressing through past the natural hindrances until you see it manifest in your life! This isn't about working or earning your breakthrough, but is all about an unwavering attitude that is determined to possess what already belongs to you. Begin to see it, feel it and embrace it. Go possess your Promised Land right now!

What To Do With Doubt And Unbelief

One of the best ways you can overcome doubt and unbelief is by continuing to feed on the truth of what God's Word says regarding your situation. Don't just skim over the surface of the Word. Instead spend time meditating on it until you believe it. Also keep focused on who God is and not on what the natural facts are saying or doing.

Below are some ways to help in this process:

- **Make a decision** that God's Word is true and act on that in everything you think, say and do.
- Make the decision to **continue to renew your mind** and guard your heart and not let go of the truth of what God has said in His Word.
- **Remind yourself** that God is always good and that He is for you not against you!
- **Fix your eyes on Jesus** the author and perfecter of your faith. You do this by focusing on the finished work of the Cross and remembering that you already have everything you need to walk in victory. It is finished; you already have the inheritance!
- **Fight the good fight of faith**. This means to fight against doubt, unbelief, natural sight and senses, feelings, emotions, symptoms, your diagnosis and natural circumstances and to rest in what God says instead.
- **Worship and thank God for who He is**! We don't worship God to move Him, but to move ourselves to a position where we can believe His goodness and trustworthiness and receive what He has provided. When we look beyond the natural doubt and discouragement and press into God for who He is, the discouragement will soon leave and you will be more aware of His presence! His peace and joy can begin to strengthen and flow from your life. You will also be in a better position to hear His voice and to be led by His Spirit into your victory. We don't praise and worship God to try and get victory, we praise, thank and worship Him because He has already given us the victory!

- Be like Abraham and Sarah — **Judge God faithful** and **don't waver** through unbelief, but be strengthened in faith, give glory to God, and **be fully convinced** that what He has provided and performed in Jesus **already belongs to you!**

Remember always that nothing is impossible for those who believe, so don't waver in doubt and unbelief but be strengthened in faith, and give glory to God for your victory! Don't let go, instead keep trusting and believing and pressing through past the natural hindrances until you see it manifest! Begin to see it, feel it and lay hold of it. Go possess your Promised Land right now!

chapter

5

Overcoming Fear

Isn't it so often true that while we may be hoping for the best, in reality we are actually fearing the worst? The more attention we give to our fears, the more power they have to control our lives. I have had many instances in my life where I have been consumed by a disabling fear. In fact, I used to be a slave to fear. It ruled my life. I now live a life in victory over fear, but it wasn't until I learned to overcome that I realised how much fear had bound me.

Fear will never be your friend! Fear is like a cancer that eats away at our faith and causes us to lose sight of who we are in Christ and what we already have inherited as a believer. When this happens we are deceived into believing that we are weak and powerless. So while faith **enables** us to trust in God (His nature, character and power), fear **disables** that ability.

Fear will always try to exalt itself in our minds to be greater than the power of God and His Word. If we don't know how to gain victory over fear we won't be in the place we need to be to exercise authority over the situation and walk in our breakthrough. We therefore need to learn how to **recognise, face** and **replace fear**, because fear left unchecked can torment and even paralyse you (**1 John 4:18 NKJV**).

*"For God did not give us a spirit of timidity — of cowardice, of craven and cringing and fawning fear — **but He has given us a spirit of power** and of love and of calm and well-balanced mind and discipline and self-control."* **2 Tim 1:7 (AMP)**

God has not given us a spirit of timidity or fear! He has given us His **Spirit of power** and authority over all the works and power of the enemy **(Luke 10:19). And this includes fear!** Therefore, know and act on this truth instead of allowing fear to torment you any longer.

"Submit yourselves, then, to God. Resist the devil, and he will flee from you." **James 4:7**

The word 'resist' in the scripture above means to oppose, to strive against and to withstand — **not** to sit back and be passive. We don't need to fight the devil because he has **already** been disarmed and defeated but we do need to oppose his attempts to keep us from attaining victory over our thought life and natural circumstances.

*"Be well balanced (temperate, sober of mind), be vigilant and cautious at all times; for that enemy of yours, the devil, roams around **like a lion** roaring in fierce hunger, seeking someone to seize upon and devour. **Withstand him**; be firm in faith **against his onset** — rooted, established, strong, immovable, and determined"...* **1 Pet 5:8–9 (AMP)**

Did you notice that the scripture above doesn't say that the devil is a roaring lion, but rather he is **like** a roaring lion? We know that through the finished work of the Cross Jesus disarmed and deprived the devil of his power; He removed his teeth and claws. And what else does this scripture say? **Verse 9** says *'**Withstand him;** be firm in faith **against his onset** — rooted, established, strong, immovable, and determined...'.* We are to resist the lies and deceits of the devil **at the onset!** There are many fears that can arise during our childbearing years. In order for us to avoid being overcome by fear, we must make the conscious decision at the onset not to allow worry to take root, or entertain any thoughts or impressions of fear in our life. That means **the very second** we begin to become fearful we are to use our authority in Jesus, and resist fear immediately.

If we don't oppose these fears when they first enter they will only grow stronger. If you have any concerns, don't ignore them; rather replace them with the truth found in the Word of God. Then exercise authority over the fear, resisting it until it is overcome!

Be Anxious For Nothing!

Everyone experiences fear in differing degrees. Some may simply have niggling concerns that don't seem to go away, whereas for others fear can be a controlling force in their lives. While fear can often manifest as a result of a sudden fright, shock or a traumatic situation, more often than not fear develops when we begin to worry or become anxious. The Bible exhorts us however, not to worry or be anxious about anything **(Phil 4:6)**. Worry or anxiety left unchecked will grow like a weed and choke the life from the Word of God, preventing it from growing and bearing fruit in our life. Instead, as the scripture in **1 Peter 5:9** exhorts us, resist, oppose, withstand and strive against it and it will flee from us!

Watch Your Vision!

As we discovered previously in the 'Faith' chapter of this book, faith has vision because it both sees and knows the end result. Faith enables you to see the things you desire before you receive them. As we know, I'm not talking here about looking through your natural eyes but through the eyes of faith. That means to look through the eyes of God's Word. His Word 'paints the picture' of what we want to receive.

It is important to note that fear has vision too! While faith pictures us with the answer, fear pictures us without it!

Fear Vs Faith

Fear has vision:	Faith has vision:
Fear has a language (speaks)	Faith has a language (speaks)
Fear sees you without the answer	Faith sees you with the answer
Fear sees the worst result	Faith sees the desired result
Fear links you to the natural	Faith links you to the supernatural

Learn to recognise when you are looking at your circumstances through the eyes of fear so you can stop yourself, change focus, overcome your fears and walk by faith instead!

Fight The Good Fight Of Faith – Fight Fear With The Word!

When we are challenged with an adverse or opposing situation, fear is usually the first thing to surface. While the experience of fear is not wrong in itself, it is how we respond to fear that matters. It is important to note that to walk by faith doesn't mean there is an absence of fear because there will be times when we need to continue walk by the truth in spite of fear. But if we continue to entertain or submit to our fears we can lose sight of the truth of God's Word and fear can easily overwhelm us. When this occurs and we react only to the natural circumstances, we may not experience the breakthrough we need. We therefore need to learn how to recognise and overcome fear so that we don't lose sight of the truth or give up hope, but rather continue to act on who we are in Christ and on what we are believing for.

When it comes to facing and overcoming fear we need to know the POWER of God's love toward us!

> *"There is no fear in love; but **perfect love casts out fear**, because fear involves torment. But he who fears has not been made perfect in love. [**NIV** says fear has to do with punishment]."*
> **1 John 4:18 (NKJV)**

> *"For as many as are led by the Spirit of God, these are sons of God. For **you did not receive the spirit of bondage again to fear**, but you received the Spirit of adoption by whom we cry out, 'Abba, Father'."* **Rom 8:14–16**

> *"For I am persuaded that neither death nor life, nor angels nor principalities nor powers, nor things present nor things to come, nor height nor depth, nor any other created thing, shall be able **to separate us from the love of God** which is in Christ Jesus our Lord."* **Rom 8:38–39**

To have lasting victory over fear we need to replace our fears by meditating on the truth of what God's Word says. If we don't, then fear will deceive us into believing in and giving in to the strength of the natural situation. We need to trust what God has already established for us in His Word because when we believe the truth, the devil has no more ammunition. Even God trusts His Word. He has exalted His Word above His name (**Ps 138:2**). But don't simply quote scripture — the **power** of God is released when you **believe** His Word, **act** on it by declaring that truth, and **know** you have His power and authority and then exercise it over the situation!

I encourage you to meditate on the following scriptures, which deal with the subject of fear, along with those that describe who you are in Christ. Continue to renew your mind with them and make them personal to you by speaking them out as a confession over your life.

> ...*"but whoever listens to me will live in safety and be at ease, without fear of harm."* **Prov 1:33**

> *"In righteousness you will be established: tyranny will be far from you; you will have nothing to fear. Terror will be far removed; it will not come near you."* **Is 54:14**

> *"So do not fear, for I am with you; do not be dismayed, for I am your God. I will strengthen you and help you; I will uphold you with my righteous right hand."* **Is 41:10**

> *"Be strong and of good courage, fear not nor be afraid; for the Lord your God is with you wherever you go. He will not leave you nor forsake you."* **Deut 31:6–8; Josh 1:9**

> *"God is our refuge and strength, an ever-present help in trouble. Therefore we will not fear, though the earth give way and the mountains fall into the heart of the sea"*... **Ps 46:1–2**

> *"There is no fear in love. But* **perfect love drives out fear**, *because fear has to do with punishment. The one who fears is not made perfect in love."* **1 John 4:18**

chapter

Renewing Your Mind

The area of the mind and the thought life is one where many of us struggle, whether it's from fear, anxiety, worry, memories of our past or from other torments of the mind. We may also struggle to maintain our trust in God because our natural circumstances may appear larger than our faith, which invariably causes us to end up doubting, worrying or fearing the worst. But the real battle is not a lack of faith, our past, or our natural circumstances — **the battle is in the mind!** But there is good news! As a believer in Jesus Christ, you don't have to be a slave to your thought life any longer, because you can learn how to obtain victory over how you think and feel, and maintain a peaceful mind!

As well as being the place where we reason, calculate and judge the things of this world, our mind is also where we sow knowledge and gain understanding of the Word of God. But if we don't guard our mind and keep God's Word in the forefront then the Word may never get the chance to spring to life, grow and transform our life. In this case the seed of God's Word may never have the ability to be planted in our hearts, develop roots and grow from **information** to become **revelation.**

Romans 8:6–7 tells us that the mind controlled by the Spirit has life and peace. If you want to have victory over your thought life then it is important that you understand what the mind is, how it functions and how you can actively cooperate with the Spirit of God so He can show you how to change your thinking.

The Mind And Physical Symptoms

As we have already discovered, for many of us the real battle isn't our natural circumstances but rather how we see our situation. While the physical realm and natural circumstances are real, they can be changed by the power of God's Kingdom. But in order for this to take place, we need to learn to be Kingdom-minded and not natural-minded so that we can both see and walk in the victory we need.

When it comes to healing, for example, we need to be careful that we don't allow any condition, symptom or diagnosis to appear to be greater to us than God's healing power. If we think or believe that what we are facing is greater, then we will be unable to believe that God wants us well, and as a consequence, we may fail to benefit from the healing that God has already provided.

While we don't deny our natural symptoms, we do have the **choice** to decide whether we are going to receive what comes upon our bodies and into our minds (positive or negative). God has given us all a free will that enables us to make our own choices. Most of us blame Satan for our condition but Satan can't legally touch our lives without our permission. The only access he has is the access we allow him to have!

If we allow our natural circumstances, persecution, afflictions, symptoms or the cares of this world to distract us, then these can grow like weeds and choke the life and power of the Word from flowing in our lives (**Mark 4:19**). This is why it is important that we don't focus on our situation but rather remain focused on who God is and on what He has already done through His Son, through the finished work of the Cross. We can't believe both at the same time, so we need to make the decision not be tossed to and fro in our thinking. We are not to be double-minded but instead single-minded on what we are going to believe. Our mind is the controlling factor. This is where the real battle is. Change to our condition or situation, therefore, begins in our mind!

The connection between the mind and the body is extremely powerful. I have known women who have been able to prevent their menstrual cycle from commencing because in their mind they falsely believed that they were pregnant. Some were so convinced of their 'pregnancy' that their bodies were falsely manifesting symptoms such as nausea, tiredness and even milk from their breasts! Other women have found that even when everything was going well and they began to think or become anxious about a particular adverse symptom such as cramping and pain in menstruation, the threat of miscarriage or pain in childbirth, this has actually produced the symptoms. Their **thoughts** brought on the manifestation of the symptoms in their bodies. If these types of manifestations occur in our body through what we focus on, imagine what would happen if we operated through a Kingdom mindset instead!

Wrong Thinking Leads To Strongholds!

An uncontrolled mind doesn't develop overnight but progresses over time through our attitudes, emotions, thought patterns, or mindsets that we have meditated upon. And these, if left un-challenged, will become strongholds in our lives. A stronghold is a belief or thought pattern of defeat where we see no way out and causes us to accept something as unchangeable. Just as a natural stronghold is a fortification that protects and defends what it holds inside, a stronghold in the mind protects and defends the beliefs it holds — beliefs that are contrary to the Word of God.

Fear or anxiety are just two examples of what can lead to strongholds forming in our lives. In fact, any thought pattern that prevents us from believing or seeing something as changeable can become a stronghold because we become captive to how we see that situation. Strongholds will consequently alter the way we see and think, and therefore, how we behave in certain situations. So it stands to reason that if we never challenge those strongholds, we can remain captive and bound not only in our thinking but also to our natural circumstances.

How To Gain Victory Over The Thought Life

"For though we walk in the flesh, we are not carrying on our warfare according to the flesh and using mere human weapons.

> *For the weapons of our warfare are not physical weapons of flesh and blood, but they are mighty before God for the **overthrow and destruction of strongholds**. Inasmuch as **we refute arguments** and **theories** and **reasonings** and every proud and lofty thing that sets itself up against the true knowledge of God; and **we lead every thought and purpose away captive** into the obedience of Christ the Messiah the anointed one."* **2 Cor 10:3–5 (AMP)**

I used to believe that when someone had a stronghold, was overcome with fear or depression or were struggling in their thought life, they had to be delivered from it through the laying on of hands and through prayer. However, the scripture above shows us that we don't need to seek someone to pray for us where our mind is concerned because we can make the decision to guard our thoughts, renew our mind and change the way we think.

> *"Casting down **imaginations**, and every high thing that exalteth itself against the knowledge of God, and bringing into captivity **every thought** to the obedience of Christ."* **2 Cor 10:5 (KJV)**

We obtain victory over our thought life by casting down any imagination, argument, thought, theory, reasoning, feeling, emotion, symptom or diagnosis that doesn't line up with the truth within the Word of God. That means that we are to refuse to entertain any thoughts that are contrary to the Word **at the time they come to mind**. We are to bring all those thoughts captive (rather than being a captive to them) to what God says. We cannot fight the lies of the enemy by simply trying to think happy or positive thoughts. Freedom comes when we renew our minds with God's thoughts and by refusing to accept any wrong thinking. Remember that Satan's strength and power is in deception and lies whereas our strength and power is in the truth! So, next time you are tempted or challenged, stop and ask yourself *'What does God's Word say about my situation?'* Then exercise your authority over the deceptions and lies and replace them with the truth in God's Word.

Proverbs 23:7 says that *'as a man thinks in his heart, so is he'*. The word *thinks* here in the Hebrew is literally translated to mean to act as a gatekeeper! Just like a gatekeeper is vigilant in exercising his authority by choosing who he allows to pass, we need to be just as vigilant about what we allow into our minds. When we don't guard what we think upon we allow strongholds to take root, so we need to be careful about what comes in! If we pay too much attention to our natural situation such as our symptoms or diagnosis, or even how we feel then it can cause us to worry, fear or doubt. The negatives of the situation begin to be amplified and we can lose sight of the power of God and the truth in His Word. Knowing this, why allow the negatives to be magnified?

> *"Do not conform any longer to the pattern of this world, **but be transformed** by the **renewing of your mind**. Then you will be able to test and approve what God's will is — His good, pleasing and perfect will."* **Rom 12:2**

The dictionary defines the word 'transform' as used in the scripture above as meaning: to make a thorough or dramatic change in the form, appearance, or character. Make the decision then to focus on God, not on the negatives, renewing your mind so that He is magnified instead! We need to starve the natural thoughts, understanding, reasoning and analyzing, and start feeding the inner man on God's Word. It can take some time to transform our thinking, and the battle may seem constant at first, but it is well worth the effort.

A Renewed Mind Is A Victorious Mind

We **can** lead a victorious thought life and overcome any evil suggestion. Nowhere in the Bible has God declared that we would not be tempted. Even Jesus was tempted. So when we are tempted with old thought patterns, we can refuse to allow ourselves to dwell on them, or on any evil thing for that matter. The Bible speaks very clearly about the thoughts that we need to possess:

> *"Brethren, whatever is true, whatever is worthy of reverence and is honourable and seemly, whatever is just, whatever is pure, whatever is lovely and lovable, whatever is kind and winsome and gracious, if there is any virtue and excellence, if there is anything worthy of praise, think on and weigh and take account of these things [fix your minds on them]."* **Phil 4:8 (AMP)**

Think only of things that are going to build you up — not tear you down! If thoughts come in that are not of God then don't allow yourself to dwell on them for one second.

"Cast your burden on the Lord [releasing the weight of it] and He will sustain you; He will never allow the [consistently] righteous to be moved (made to slip, fall, or fail)." **Ps 55:22 (AMP)**

Remember that God is not going to renew our mind for us. We are totally responsible for what we allow ourselves to think about. It is in our power to renew our minds. God has given us discipline and self-control and a free will so that we can choose what we are going to do or think.

… "be clear minded and self-controlled so that you can pray."
1 Pet 4:7

I know first hand what it is like to be subject to your feelings, emotions and to be a slave to your thought life. I lived a life that was constantly harassed by thoughts of condemnation from my past and other evil suggestions. But when I discovered through God's Word that I could refute and cast down these thoughts by taking authority over them, order soon came to my mind and I have maintained that victory ever since. My mind became renewed to the truth about who I am in Christ and what the Word says about my situation. I was also able to deal with other areas in my life that had been a struggle. For the first time in my life I experienced peace in my mind rather than being constantly bombarded by a barrage of different thoughts. I learnt how to be still and hear God's voice and this enabled me to be led by Him in many other areas of life. I have since been able to minister to many women who have had similar struggles. The majority of these women found these problems were exacerbated when they were in a vulnerable position. Many of these women learnt to exercise authority over their thought life and they too are now experiencing lasting victory, not only in this area but in many other areas of life as well.

When we are emotionally or physically exhausted, we can drop our guard and not be as quick to recognise what is happening. Our bodies are constantly going through hormonal and chemical changes and if something is out of balance or if we are sleep-deprived, our emotions can be affected. So it is important that we learn to recognise when we are vulnerable and at these times be on guard. As well, during childbearing there are many concerns in the natural that can cause you to worry or fear. I encourage you therefore **not to** entertain these thoughts at all. Instead meditate on and renew your mind with the truth in God's Word until you know the truth about your victory. There is power in the Word and as Jesus said *'when you know the truth, the truth will set you free'* (**John 8:32,36**).

Once you learn to guard your mind and keep God's Word in the forefront, the Word will soon have preeminence in your thought life and will transform your perspective until you see your natural circumstances in a different light. The supernatural (God's Kingdom and His Word) will become more real to you and you will begin to see the fullness of God's Kingdom outworking in your life!

The Power of Prayer

"The prayer of a righteous man is powerful and effective."
James 5:16

P rayer changes lives! It is a channel by which God's power can be released here on this earth. When you know how to pray effectively, you will begin to see answers not only in your own life but also in the lives of those you pray for. Sadly, however, many Christians struggle in the area of prayer so they don't devote much time to it. They consider prayer as something they are obligated to fulfil and perceive it as a burden or chore that takes time, effort and work. When this perception is in place, prayer becomes something we 'have' to do rather than something we 'want' to do. The truth is however that we don't 'have' to pray, because prayer isn't a requirement of our salvation. But without prayer our Christian walk may become lifeless, powerless and ineffective.

When it comes to prayer it is important to note that this is not something we do in order to get God to do something for us. On the contrary, prayer is all about spending time with God, and building our relationship with Him. When we truly know God through personal relationship and His nature and character, then believing what He said in His Word and trusting Him comes easily. This enables us to believe what He says is true so we can then confidently apply it to our daily life. I believe it is essential then for us to spend time getting to know God and allowing Him to **reveal Himself** to us **personally** as our Saviour, Healer, Deliverer, Provider, Strengthener and Protector!

I encourage you to take time out of the busyness of life and make a time and a place to pray, otherwise you will probably never start. Begin to grow in prayer and you will also be more likely to keep the appointment. Time spent alone with God is necessary to build your relationship, however you don't just have to pray this way alone. You can also fellowship and chat with Him when you can throughout your day. The more I learn about prayer, the more I realise that I don't have to pray for hours to have an effective prayer life. Quality is more important than quantity. A five minute heartfelt prayer based on the Word of God is more effective than praying for hours using methods or principles. Prayer isn't about following a set of rules and regulations. If you pray using a method or formula that you have learned or memorised, it can become legalistic and ineffective. Simply speak to God from your heart.

God doesn't want us to approach Him in prayer like it's a chore or ritual. Fellowship with God is a blessing. The book of Psalms tells us that He is present in our praises and that in His presence is fullness of joy! (see **Ps 22:3** and **Ps 16:11**). When I learnt how to declare what God said in His Word, prayer for most situations went from taking hours to minutes! I was then free to spend time with God for who He was and not for what I needed. I now spend more time in worship and fellowship than I do praying 'for' things.

I have also discovered that **there are some things we don't need to pray for**. For instance, when it comes to what Jesus purchased through the finished work of the Cross, we don't need to pray or ask God to do **what He has already done**. We are heirs, so we don't have to ask for what already belongs to us, we simply need to learn to embrace and enjoy it by taking what we have inherited and applying it to our daily life.

There are also times where we don't pray but rather use our authority in Christ. For example, when we are faced with fears, doubts, or an adverse situation, then we need to actively **exercise authority** over the circumstances. We don't ask God to do it for us because God has **already given** us **His power and authority** here on this earth. It is now up to us to exercise it! We have God's very Spirit (His resurrection power) dwelling within us, and when we follow His leading He will show us how to use our authority, walk by faith and obtain the victory.

Pray The Word

Sometimes we may not know what to pray, so we might pray or ask for 'God's will' to be done. As previously mentioned, God's will for every area of life has been made clear and known to us through His Word. For this reason, in order for prayer to be effective, we need to learn how to pray scripturally. Don't focus on the problem or give it more attention than necessary, but start with the solution by learning to pray with your Bible open.

In **John 15:7** Jesus said *'If you remain in me and my Words remain in you, ask whatever you wish, and it will be given you.'* When you know who you are in Christ and how to release God's power through prayer, you will develop a confidence and boldness when you pray.

> *"This is **the confidence we have** in approaching God: that if we ask **anything according to His will**, He hears us. And if we know that He hears us — whatever we ask — **we know that we have** what we asked of Him."* **1 John 5:14–15 (NIV)**

Remember always that God's will isn't what the doctors say, what your symptoms say, or what your circumstances are, but what His Word says. So when we declare what God says in His Word we then have the answers on our lips because we are praying in agreement with the truth in His Word. **John 1:1–2,14** and **Revelation 19:18** both tell us that another name for Jesus is the Word of God. So, when we say what God's Word says then we are declaring the life, power and reality of Jesus into that situation.

> *"'Is not my Word like fire,' declares the LORD, 'and like a hammer that breaks a rock in pieces?'"* **Jer 23:29**

Early on in this ministry, the Lord taught me the importance of exercising my authority in Christ by declaring the truth of what God said in His Word. Both Julie (my prayer partner) and I had spent months praying for the ministry but were experiencing limited breakthrough. I asked the

Lord to reveal to us why it was taking so long. The Lord gave me a vision. I saw a huge masonry wall standing in our way. I saw that every time we prayed we were chipping away at the wall. The Lord then showed me how His power was released when I spoke what His Word said out of my mouth. When I spoke the Word huge chunks were coming out of the wall and it smashed into pieces. From that moment on we began to say what God said and to this day we continue to see an increase in breakthroughs!

Pray Believing!

All things are possible for those who believe!

> *"And Jesus answering said unto them, 'Have faith in God. For verily I say unto you, that whosoever shall say to this mountain, be thou removed, and be thou cast into the sea; and **shall not doubt in his heart**, **but shall believe** that those things which he said shall come to pass; he shall have whatsoever he saith. **Therefore, I say unto you, what things soever ye desire, when ye pray, believe that ye receive them, and ye shall have them'.**"*
> **Mark 11:22–24 (KJV)**

This scripture shows us the keys to receiving what we pray or say. It says that **if you have faith** in God, **believe** and do **not doubt** and **speak to** the mountains, (which is the natural situation or what you are facing), then you will have whatever you say! Jesus did not say you would get something that resembles what you said. He said **whatever** you say, that is what you will get. He also didn't say **see, understand** or **feel** like you have received — He said **believe** that **you have received!**

If we don't see immediate answers to prayer, we can often make the mistake of giving in to reasoning. Reasoning is a mental reaction, which will rob us of God's provision every time. God's Kingdom is spiritually discerned, not naturally understood, therefore walking by faith goes beyond what we see, feel or know by our natural senses.

Hebrews 11:1 describes faith as the **substance** of what we hope for and the **evidence** of what we don't see in the natural — yet. God's Word is His will and shows the fullness of the finished work of the Cross and what is contained within our inheritance. We therefore need to walk by faith, which means we believe and act according to what God's Word says and not by what we can see, feel, hear or perceive by the natural sense realm. That means that when the Word says that we are not barren, that we will not miscarry, that we are fruitful and that by Jesus' stripes we are healed, then that is our evidence and proof! When we walk by faith — by God's Word, we know that we **'have received'!** So when the fears and doubts come or your natural circumstances press against you, declare the truth of what Jesus has done!

Jesus said *'according to your faith will it be done unto you'* **(Matt 9:29)**. Remember we **already** have faith! And because of what Jesus did on the Cross, we also **already** have our victory in the Spirit. It's time to start walking this out! If we understand this truth then this will enable us to believe and act as if we have already received the breakthrough in the natural because we have the substance (the reality) and evidence (title deed, proof, receipt) of it through God's Word!

Be Confident In Your Relationship

"In Him and through faith in Him we may approach God with freedom and confidence." **Eph 3:12**

When we come into a relationship with God through Jesus we become the righteousness of God **(2 Cor 5:21)**. All our sins are removed and we are washed, cleansed, sanctified and justified in the name of Jesus and by the Spirit of God **(1 Cor 6:11)**.

When we approach God we are not coming by our own righteousness or by what we have or have not done. We don't come before Him as slaves or servants that need to grovel, plead or beg. No! We come with Jesus' righteousness imputed to us as children before our Heavenly Father.

*"For we do not have a high priest who is unable to sympathize with our weaknesses, but we have one who has been tempted in every way, just as we are—yet was without sin. Let us **then approach the throne of grace** with confidence, **so that we may receive mercy and find grace to help us in our time of need."*** Heb 4:15–16

We can therefore be confident when we approach God. Remember that you have God's very Spirit living on the inside of you, so be secure in the fact that you can fellowship with Him wherever you are!

Be Led By The Holy Spirit

"Now to Him Who, by (in consequence of) the [action of His] **power that is at work within us***, is able to [carry out His purpose and] do superabundantly, far over and above all that we [dare] ask or think [infinitely beyond our highest prayers, desires, thoughts, hopes, or dreams]."* **Eph 3:20 (AMP)**

This scripture doesn't say according to **God**, but according to the **power** that is **at work within us**! So while God is able to do superabundantly, far over and above what we are expecting, He can be limited if we don't allow that power to flow. Therefore we need to learn how to be led by His Spirit so that His power can be released both in and through our life to transform us.

When you made Jesus Christ the Lord of your life you received an inheritance. That inheritance is everything that is contained within the Kingdom of God. That means you also received the Holy Spirit!

"In Him you also trusted, after you heard the word of truth, the gospel of your salvation; in whom also, having believed, **you were sealed with the Holy Spirit of promise***, who is the guarantee of our inheritance until the redemption of the purchased possession, to the praise of His glory."* **Eph 1:13–14 (NKJV)**

The Holy Spirit is the very same resurrection power that raised Jesus from the dead and He **dwells in you (Rom 8:11)**. You are empowered with His power and ability to do what Jesus did while here on the earth and to carry out the will of God for your life and in the lives of others.

"But you will receive power when the Holy Spirit comes on you; and you will be my witnesses in Jerusalem, and in all Judea and Samaria, and to the ends of the earth." **Acts 1:8**

The Holy Spirit is the power of God and also the Helper in your prayer life. The Apostle Paul exhorted us to walk by the Spirit, be led by the Spirit and to live by the Spirit (see **Rom 8:6,9, 13–14, 1 Cor 2:13, Gal 5:5,16,18,25**). But how can we walk by, be led by or live by the Spirit if we don't know who He is?

> … *"when the **Spirit of truth**, comes, **He will guide you into all truth**. He will not speak on His own; He will speak only what He hears, and He will tell you what is yet to come. He will bring glory to me by **taking from what is mine and making it known to you.** All that belongs to the Father is mine. That is why I said the Spirit will take from what is mine and make it known to you. ..**Vs 26** But the Counsellor, the Holy Spirit, whom the Father will send in my name, will **teach you all things** and **will remind you of everything I have said** to you."* **John 16:13–15,26**

If you want to know how to walk in victory and the steps to take to get there, then spend the time to get to know the Holy Spirit and how to be led by Him.

Pray In The Spirit

> *"For if I pray in an unknown tongue, my spirit (by the Holy Spirit within me) prays."* **1 Cor 14:14 (AMP)**

Praying in the spirit (praying in tongues) is not just something we do whenever we pray. It is also for those times when we don't know what to pray or how to express our feelings in words to God. When we pray in tongues, the Holy Spirit works with our spirit and puts into spiritual words exactly what needs to be said or expressed.

> … *"the Spirit helps us in our weakness. We do not know what we ought to pray for, but the Spirit himself intercedes for us with groans that words cannot express. And He who searches our hearts knows the mind of the Spirit, because the Spirit intercedes for the saints in accordance with God's will."* **Rom 8:26–27**

When we pray in tongues we also build up our faith and strengthen our inner man.

> *"But you, dear friends, **build yourselves up** in your most holy faith and pray in the Holy Spirit."* **Jude 1:20**

The more time we spend in communion with the Holy Spirit the more we develop our spiritual senses. When we spend time with Him we learn how to be sensitive to the Holy Spirit's voice so that we know when He is giving us the unction to do something or the utterance to speak. He guides us in the ways of God, teaches us about Jesus and leads us into victory! When we know how to hear His voice then we can act on what He has led us to do.

Practical Help To Get You Started

When praying for your conception, pregnancy, birth, recovery and postnatal period, it is important that you spend time renewing your mind with the truth of what God's Word says regarding what you want to receive. Remember, when it comes to receiving what Jesus did on the Cross, it's not about praying or asking God to do what He has already done. Prayer is more about fellowship with God and spending time learning how to be led by His Spirit. The Holy Spirit will warn you of things to come, guide you into all truth and lead you into victory, as well as help you to overcome any fears or doubts. If you do have any fears or doubts, **don't ignore them**. Instead spend time meditating on the truth of God's Word and transforming the way you think about that situation. You do this by continuing to put God's Word in your heart and mind until you **believe** what God's Word says and see it as being our final authority.

Remember that faith comes and grows by hearing, and fear comes and grows by hearing too. Therefore, continue to renew your mind with what God's Word says and on the finished work of the Cross until fear goes, and you **know** that you have the substance of what you are hoping for, and the evidence of what you don't see yet.

Get A Vision

Remember that faith has vision because it both sees and knows the end result. Faith enables you to see the things you desire before you receive them, not through your natural eyes but through the eyes of faith. That means to look through the eyes of God's Word. His Word 'paints the picture' of what we want to receive.

When we walk by faith (by what we have received through the finished work of the Cross) it is important that we have a goal to work towards. **Habakkuk 2:2** says to write down the vision (or your goals) and make it plain so that you can run with it! You can begin by writing down what God says in His Word as well as any specifics you want to believe for to help you when you pray. Do you want to experience a pregnancy free from morning sickness, or nausea? Do you want a birth that is free from complications, pain, or trauma? Make a decision on what you want (and don't want for that matter) and then write it down!

Many women have said to me that they haven't prayed for specifics or made a decision for what they desire because they are 'leaving everything in God's Hands'. The thing is that God is not going to do this for you. He has **already made provision** for you through Jesus and this is outlined in His Word.

If you need a breakthrough in any area of childbearing, know that you don't have to accept everything that happens to you as 'your lot in life'. Instead of leaving things to chance, act on what you believe and take authority over the natural circumstances.

Now It Is Up To You!

Grab some blank pieces of paper and jot down your prayer points, or alternatively use the 'Prayer Points' pages at the end of my other book, **God's Plan for Pregnancy — Pocket Companion.** Anything you desire, even if it seems trivial, or any fears you have, I encourage you to write them down. You may also want to write down any scriptures that are personal to you, or some declarations in your own words. Remember that this is not about getting God to do something for you or to make the Word work, but rather is all about helping you to:

- Transform your natural thinking and understanding until you see your situation through the eyes of faith (the truth of what God's Word says).
- Walk by faith (by what we have received through the finished work of the Cross) and not by sight, the natural realm and senses.
- Overcome doubt, unbelief, natural sight and senses, feelings, emotions, symptoms, your diagnosis and natural circumstances and to rest in what God says instead.
- Act on what you believe by taking authority over your natural circumstances.

- Call those things that are not as though they are **(Rom 4:17)**.

If you are challenged, or you know you need a breakthrough in certain areas then you will be able to act on what you believe. Above all, don't give up hope, but rest in who Jesus is and what He has done for you and the rest will be history!

chapter

Healing

The conception of our children was not meant to be a battle but rather a natural process that comes as a blessing from the union of a husband and wife. When everything in your body is functioning as God designed, then sooner or later conception should naturally occur. In spite of this, many believe their lack of fertility is part of God's will or is a situation brought about so He can teach them something. God's Word tells us that we were created to be fruitful so if God was withholding children from us this would mean He was preventing us from doing what He had created us to do, and this simply does not make sense.

More often than not the reason why couples struggle with infertility or miscarriage is as a result of physical complications in their bodies due to an abnormality, unbalanced hormones, or sickness or disease. But, **praise God, through Jesus there is good news!** When you know who you are in Christ, your position in Him and what you have inherited as a believer (all through the finished work of the Cross) you will realise that you no longer have to be subject to your body and what state it is in. You can exercise your authority and walk in the healing and fruitfulness that Jesus has purchased for you.

In the beginning God created all things to be good **(Gen 1:31)**! Sickness, disease, pain and death did not exist because God did not create them. So when God created Adam and Eve in the Garden of Eden they were perfect — fearfully and wonderfully made. God had created them with everything they needed to conceive and bring forth children. Children were His plan and purpose for mankind. He blessed them and said to them '*Go forth and multiply*' (see **Gen 1:26–28**).

What Happened?

If God created all things to be good and for mankind to go forth and to multiply, then what happened? Why is there sickness, disease, infertility and miscarriage in this world?

> "*And the LORD God planted a garden eastward in Eden; and there he put the man whom he had formed. And out of the ground made the LORD God to grow every tree that is pleasant to the sight, and good for food; the tree of life also in the midst of the garden, and the tree of **knowledge of good and evil**.*"
> **Gen 2:8–9 (KJV)**

> "*And the LORD God took the man, and put him into the garden of Eden to dress it and to keep it. And the LORD God commanded the man, saying, Of every tree of the garden thou mayest freely eat: But of the tree of the **knowledge** of good and evil, thou shalt not eat of it: for in the day that thou eatest thereof thou shalt surely die.*" **Gen 2:15–17 (KJV)**

Adam was to keep the garden. However, in **Genesis 3:6**, he stands by while his wife eats of the forbidden tree and then he takes and eats it also. Many think that God was withholding something from them by telling them not to eat the fruit of the tree of the 'knowledge' of good and evil. The truth is, however, God actually wanted to protect Adam and Eve!

In Hebrew, the word *knowledge* in **Genesis 2:17** means: to know by observing and reflecting (thinking about) and to know by experiencing. The day Adam and Eve ate of the fruit of the tree of the knowledge of good and evil, they **experienced** evil. It became a part of them. The word 'evil' in Hebrew means: calamity, adversity, affliction, curses, bad, distress, displeasure, grief, harm, heavy, to hurt, mischief, misery, sadness, sorrow, trouble, vexed, wicked, and wretchedness. Up until that point they had only known and experienced good. But when they disobeyed God by taking the fruit and eating it, their 'eyes were opened' and consequently they now not only knew evil, they **experienced** it. So, God had not been withholding anything good from them but had actually been protecting them from knowing and experiencing evil!

Notice **verse 17** says *'In the day that you eat from it you shall surely die'*. However, Adam and Eve did not die **that** day, did they? They did not die **physically** at the moment they ate from the tree, but they did die **spiritually. Spiritual death** was the consequence of Adam's sin and spiritual death brought with itself eventual physical death. And as we know there are many forms of sickness and disease that can also lead to physical death. God never intended His children to suffer from sickness, disease and death. He only ever wanted them to experience His blessings. But sickness, disease and death entered the world through Adam's sin. Physical death is an **effect** or **consequence** of his sin. Adam's spiritual death affected the entire physical or natural world.

Adam and Eve had been given dominion and authority over all the earth **(Gen 1:26)**. And because God had given Adam a free will, He had to stand by and watch while Adam disobeyed His command and unwittingly handed over his God-given authority to Satan. Through Adam's disobedience sin entered and he made Satan god of this world. The effect of sin in the world meant that the world was now in a fallen state. Since then, every person is born in the likeness of Adam (with a sinful nature) and into a sinful and fallen world **(Rom 5:12)**.

God said to Adam in **Genesis 3:17–19** that the ground was now cursed because of what Adam had done. This came into effect the moment Adam sinned. But God's plan wasn't to leave mankind suffering in this fallen state, so through His goodness and mercy, He set a plan in action to redeem and reconcile us back to Himself. He established Covenants for His children so they would be protected and blessed. And over the course of time God sent His Son into the fallen world as Saviour to redeem mankind from sin and to reverse their fallen state.

The Finished (Or Complete) Work Of The Cross

As we have already discovered, God has already made the provision for everything we need in this life through the work Jesus did on the Cross, and that includes healing of every sickness and disease. The work Jesus did on that Cross was a complete work. In fact, His last words before He drew His final breath were *'It is finished'*. But what does the 'finished work of the Cross' actually mean? It means that we don't have to wait for a miracle, or wait for God to heal us. We can possess our healing right now.

> *"Surely He hath borne our griefs, and carried our sorrows: yet we did esteem Him stricken, smitten of God, and afflicted. But He was wounded for our transgressions; He was bruised for our iniquities: the chastisement of our peace was upon Him; and with His stripes we are healed."* **Is 53:4–5 (KJV)**

The word ***griefs***, or *choli* in the Hebrew, is translated as: malady, anxiety, calamity, disease, grief, or sickness, while the word ***sorrows*** in the Hebrew, *makob*, means: anguish, grief, pain (physical), sorrow (emotional), pain (mental). Our English versions of the Bible have all been translated from the original Hebrew in the Old Testament and predominantly from Greek in the New Testament. However, many versions of these English language Bibles do not often correctly translate the words *choli* and *makob* as written in **Isaiah 53:4**, and mistakenly translate them as 'griefs' and 'sorrows'. Elsewhere in scripture, however, these exact same words are translated as 'infirmities' and 'diseases' in verses such as this one in Matthew:

> **"***When evening came, many who were demon-possessed were brought to him, and he drove out the spirits with a word and healed all the sick. This was to fulfil what was spoken through the prophet Isaiah: '**He took up our infirmities and carried our diseases.***' [KJV says '...and bore our **sicknesses**']."*
> **Matt 8:16–17**

Therefore, **Isaiah 53:4–5** should rightly read that Jesus took up **all our sicknesses, diseases and griefs** and **carried all our sorrows and pains away!** He took **all** forms of sickness, disease, grief, sorrow, distress and pain upon the **Cross in our place!** We don't have to **cope** with them, instead we can **overcome** them through the work of the Cross. Therefore, symptoms of any form of sickness and disease are a lying vanity (i.e. empty). They are a lie because Jesus took them away! Therefore if a symptom of sickness or pain surfaces, make the decision to resist it. Take authority over it and declare the truth and say, '**No**, by Jesus' stripes I am healed.'

The Type Of The Brazen Serpent

To further explain the complete work that Jesus did on the Cross, I want to show you a 'type' of Jesus under the Old Covenant. A type is an Old Testament picture of a New Testament truth. It was a picture of what Jesus would accomplish on the Cross. The type that I would like to spend some time looking at is that of the Brazen Serpent seen in the book of **Numbers**.

> "*And the people spake against God, and against Moses, Wherefore have ye brought us up out of Egypt to die in the wilderness? For there is no bread, neither is there any water; and our soul loatheth this light bread. And the LORD sent fiery serpents among the people, and they bit the people; and much people of Israel died. Therefore the people came to Moses, and said, We have sinned, for we have spoken against the LORD, and against thee; pray unto the LORD, that he take away the serpents from us. And Moses prayed for the people. And the LORD said unto Moses, Make thee a fiery serpent, and set it upon a pole: and it shall come to pass, that every one that is bitten, when he looketh upon it, shall live. And Moses made a serpent of brass, and put it upon a pole, and it came to pass, that if a serpent had bitten any man, when he beheld the serpent of brass, he lived.*" **Num 21:5–9 (KJV)**

The children of Israel had been walking in the wilderness and they had begun to mumble, moan and complain, claiming that it would have been better for them if they'd stayed in Egypt. In **Numbers 21:4** we read that God 'sent' many 'fiery serpents' among the people and they had begun to attack and kill the people of Israel. **Deuteronomy 8:15** tells us that fiery serpents were already in the land and that God had wanted '*to lead them through*' that place! The snakes were there the whole time that the Israelites were in the wilderness. Up until this point they had not been harmed as they had been miraculously protected for 38 years. God never intended for them to be bitten. However on this occasion they were being struck down and overwhelmed by them.

The word *sent* in **Numbers 21:4** has often been used as an example of the incorrect theology that God sends sickness and disease and that He kills people who disobey Him. But when we look at the original Hebrew word, *shâlach*, one of the meanings is to leave or let depart. As a part of His Covenant to His children, God had set up protection for the people. But as a result of the curse of the law of sin and death, every time they complained or sinned they removed themselves from this protection and were left wide open to experience the effects of the fallen world. God had clearly outlined this in **Deuteronomy 30:15–20** — they were told to obey and **choose life** so that they and their children would be blessed and would live.

Let's continue with the story.

> *"Therefore the people came to Moses, and said, 'We have sinned, for we have spoken against the LORD and against you; pray to the LORD that **He take away** the serpents from us.'"* **Num 21:7**

So here we see the people turning to God for a solution to their problem. And **immediately God gave them a solution.**

> *"So Moses prayed for the people. Then the LORD said to Moses, 'Make a fiery serpent, and set it on a pole; and it shall be that **everyone who is bitten, when he looks** at it, **shall live'**."* **Num 21:8**

The Lord gave Moses instructions to make a serpent of bronze and set it on a pole so that everyone could look upon it. Those who looked at the bronze serpent lived. The people had asked God to take away the serpents BUT God told Moses to make one out of bronze and stick it on a pole! God didn't take the serpents away — He deprived them of power! They couldn't hurt the Israelites anymore! The VERY SOURCE of their pain, poison and death was nailed on a pole and DISARMED!

The 'fiery serpents' spoken of in this passage were therefore a type of Satan and his power, and the bronze serpent on the pole was a type of Jesus on the Cross!

> *"as Moses lifted up the serpent in the wilderness, even so must the Son of Man be lifted up, that whoever believes in Him should not*

perish but have eternal life." **John 3:14–15**

When Jesus took our sin to the Cross, He also took Satan and his power over us to the Cross **(Heb 2:14 AMP)**. Jesus has nailed the devil to the Cross for us! He became sin and took our sin in our place!

> "*And you, being dead in your trespasses and the uncircumcision of your flesh, He has made alive together with Him, having forgiven you all trespasses, having wiped out the handwriting of requirements that was against us, which was contrary to us. And He has taken it out of the way, having nailed it to the cross. Having disarmed principalities and powers, He made a public spectacle of them, triumphing over them in it.*" **Col 2:13–15**

> ... "*that by (going through death) He might bring to nought and make of no effect him who **had** the power of death — that is the devil.*" **Heb 2:14 (AMP)**

The very reason why Jesus came to live and die was to release us from Satan's grip (to set us free from sin and the consequences of sin).

> "*And the Lord has laid on Him the iniquity of us all.*" **Is 53:6**

> "*For He made Him who knew no sin to be sin for us, that we might become the righteousness of God in Him.*" **2 Cor 5:21**

Jesus became the curse for us. Man's sin and its consequences (i.e. the curse, including sickness, pain and death — all the result of spiritual death in Adam) were laid upon Jesus. Spiritual death came into His spirit and corrupted and marred His spirit and His body. **Isaiah 52:14** says Jesus' appearance was more marred (disfigured) than any other man. **Isaiah 53:4–5** shows the punishment Jesus bore. He bore our griefs (sickness and disease) and carried our sorrows (pains) and was wounded and bruised.

> "*Jesus took away sin and guilt (and the consequences) from many and that He made intercession for the rebellious.*" **Is 53:11b (AMP)**

Jesus Took Sin And The Root Of Sin

Do you see the picture here? Spiritually speaking, Jesus took the poison for us, and became marred and 'corrupted to look upon' in His spirit.

In order for the Israelites to live, they must be…

- Healed of their bites.
- Delivered of the fiery serpents (the poison, pain and death was rendered powerless)!

> *"So Moses made a bronze serpent, and put it on a pole; and so it was, if a serpent had bitten **anyone**, when he **looked** at the bronze serpent, he lived. [**KJV** says beheld].*" **Num 21:9**

Any person who *'looked at'* or *'beheld'* the serpent of bronze lived. For the people to be looking at the serpent on the pole meant that they were not looking at the serpents on the ground or to their injuries. The **Amplified Bible** says that those who looked *'attentively, expectantly, with a steady and absorbing gaze, lived'*. So it was not a quick glance. The word beheld (or looked) is the Hebrew word *nabat*, and means to scan, i.e. *look intently at* by implying to **regard** with pleasure, favour or **care**; behold, consider, look, regard, have respect, **see**. When we look intently to what Jesus has done for us we will receive our healing! And when we **look intently** at God's Word it shows us what Jesus has done!

Let's have a look at a scripture in the New Testament that shows us this:

> *"But be doers of the word, and not hearers only, deceiving yourselves. For if anyone is a hearer of the word and not a doer, he is like a man observing his natural face in a mirror; for he observes himself, goes away, and immediately forgets what kind of man he was. But he who looks into **the perfect law of liberty** and continues in it, and is not a forgetful hearer but a doer of the work, this one will be blessed in what he does."* **James 1:22–25**

> *"But he who looks carefully into the faultless law, the [law] of liberty, and is faithful to it and perseveres in looking into it, being not a heedless listener who forgets but an active doer [who obeys], he shall be blessed in his doing (his life of obedience)."*
> **James 1:25 (AMP)**

The perfect (or faultless) law of liberty is the Gospel of Jesus! If Old Covenant people could **receive healing through faith in a type of Christ** on the Cross, how much more should we be able to receive healing through faith in Jesus Himself! The people under the Old Covenant believed in a type (symbol). Under the New Covenant we have the real thing!

As **we look** attentively, expectantly, with a steady and absorbing gaze at Jesus on the Cross, let us perceive ALL of what He has done for us.

He has taken: Our sin and nailed it to the Cross.
Our sickness and disease and nailed it to the Cross.
Satan and his power over us and nailed it to the Cross (picture the devil nailed to the Cross!).

He has provided us with: Eternal life.
Deliverance.
Healing.

Jesus became a curse for us. Man's sin and its consequences (the curse, including sickness, pain and death — all the result of spiritual death in Adam) were laid upon Jesus (**Gal 3:13**). By Jesus' stripes we are healed and made whole.

The Israelites saw the source of their pain and sickness on the pole disarmed and deprived of power, and they were healed and lived. I therefore encourage you to see your condition on Jesus' body on the Cross also deprived and disarmed of any power to harm you! See infertility, miscarriage, morning sickness, pain in childbirth and postnatal depression on Jesus' body on the Cross, deprived and disarmed. Stop looking at the source and start looking at the solution! Do not look at or behold your natural sickness, disease or pain any longer but instead FIX your eyes on Jesus — the author and perfecter of your faith!

The Curse Of The Law

Deuteronomy 28 lists the blessings and curses under the law. **Verses 1–14** list all the blessings that came through obedience to the law and **verses 15–65** lists the curses that came as a result from disobedience to the law.

The Blessings

"If you will listen diligently to the voice of the Lord your God,
being watchful to do all His commandments which I command
you this day, the Lord your God will set you high above all the
nations of the earth. And all these blessings shall come upon you
and overtake you *if you heed the voice of the Lord your God."*
Deut 28:1–2 (AMP)

As you read through **verses 1–14** you will find a list of God's blessings of
fruitfulness, prosperity, health and protection in every area of life. We have
just discovered that God only created mankind to be blessed, prosperous
and fruitful and that sickness and disease of every kind came as a result of
sin being introduced because of the fall of Adam and Eve in the Garden
of Eden. God's plan for mankind did not change; He continued to reveal
His true nature and character as Healer, Deliverer, Provider, and Protector
and we discover this throughout the Old Covenant.

Through Abraham God set up Covenant with Himself to bless mankind
and so that man would receive forgiveness of sins and to receive His
protection from the fallen state of the world. However, under the law the
blessings were conditional on the people's obedience. If the people obeyed
the Lord then every aspect of their life would be blessed. However just as
obedience brought blessings, disobedience would leave them unprotected
and open to experience the curses.

The Curses

"But if you will not obey the voice of the Lord your God, being
watchful to do all His commandments and His statutes which I
command you this day, then all these curses shall come upon you
and overtake you:" **Deut 28:15 (AMP)**

As **Deuteronomy 28** continues, it shows an extensive list of curses,
beginning at **verse 15**, and they speak of destruction in every area of life.
These curses meant that the people would suffer from sickness, barrenness
and poverty in the fruit of their womb, and in everything they put their
hand to. They would also have no rest from their enemies and all of this
would eventually bring total devastation to every area of their lives. The
curses are a complete opposite to the blessings and they showed no way of

deliverance or way out from under them. There was no hope for those who were not in relationship with God or who had forsaken His Covenant.

The curses were to warn the Israelites and help turn them from disobedience. God did not create the curses; they were already operating in the fallen world and were introduced through sin. Before the law God's children were made righteous, protected, blessed and prospered through faith. However, under the law the blessings came through works and obedience to the law. Everything was dependent on them keeping the law. Whenever the children of God failed to keep the law they broke fellowship with God and left themselves open to experience the curses. It wasn't God cursing them, but rather through their own disobedience they walked out from God's protection and would experience the curses that were in operation as the result of living in a fallen world.

> "See, I set before you today life and prosperity, death and destruction. For I command you today to love the LORD your God, to walk in his ways, and to keep his commands, decrees and laws; then you will live and increase, and the LORD your God will bless you in the land you are entering to possess. But if your heart turns away and you are not obedient, and if you are drawn away to bow down to other gods and worship them, I declare to you this day that you will certainly be destroyed. You will not live long in the land you are crossing the Jordan to enter and possess. This day I call heaven and earth as witnesses against you that I have set before you life and death, blessings and curses. **Now choose life**, so that you and your children may live and that you may love the LORD your God, listen to his voice, and hold fast to him. For the LORD is your life, and he will give you many years in the land he swore to give to your fathers, Abraham, Isaac and Jacob." **Deut 30:15–20 (NIV)**

The Children of God ALWAYS had a choice! God only ever wanted His children to be blessed. His Covenant with them was for them to be blessed, prosperous, healthy and fruitful. But through their disobedience, by their own free will and their doubt and unbelief they refused to trust God. We see many accounts where they doubted God's Word and goodness to them and they mumbled, moaned and complained. This attitude was what left them stranded in the wilderness for 40 years unable to possess the Promised Land that God had wanted to give them. This was not God's decision or perfect will for them but instead was the consequence of their own disobedience.

Redeemed From The Curse Of The Law

Praise the Lord, we are no longer under the law but are under a New Covenant of Grace! Jesus went to the Cross to deliver us from that curse of the law. He was our substitute. He died in our very place under the curse and was cursed for us. Jesus has redeemed mankind from the curse of the law.

> *"Christ has **redeemed** us from the curse of the law by becoming a curse for us; for it is written, Cursed is everyone who is hung on a tree ...."* **Gal 3:1**

The word *redeemed* in Greek means payment of a price to recover from the power of another, to ransom, buy off. Christ **has redeemed** — totally removed and released us from all the curse of the law. He was made a curse for us. Therefore, no curse of the law has any right, legal or illegal, over our lives any longer. This includes everything in the extensive list of curses in **Deuteronomy 28:15–65**. We are redeemed from **every** part of this list.

We have already seen that God never intended His children to be cursed. He only ever wanted them to experience His blessings. This is why in the New Covenant there are no curses, only blessings! For the New Covenant believer no longer is **Deuteronomy 28:15–65** a list of curses but rather a redemptive list of all the sickness, diseases, plagues and disasters that we are redeemed from!

Deuteronomy 28:18, 60–61 shows some of what we are redeemed from under this extensive list of curses:

- We are redeemed from sickness or disease on the fruit of the womb.
- We are redeemed from an endless list of diseases that were brought upon the Egyptians.
- We are redeemed from **EVERY** sickness, and every plague, disease, and disaster that is not recorded in the Word of God.

- We are redeemed from **EVERY** sickness and disease that can be named!
- We are redeemed from **EVERY** sickness and disease that is not named! That means that we have been redeemed from every sickness that has not yet been discovered or named!

Christ has redeemed you from all forms of sickness, disease, and plague, including the ones the doctors haven't discovered yet! It does not matter what name it has been given. You have been made free from all of it. And did you know that infertility and miscarriage are simply different forms of sickness? Because you are redeemed from the law, this means you are also redeemed from all forms of sickness and disease, including those that occur in your reproductive organs! So, in the context of childbearing, we have been redeemed from:

- **Barrenness and infertility** and whatever causes it in either the husband or the wife.
- **Miscarriage and whatever causes it** — antibodies, low hormone levels, blood disorders etc.
- Emotional pain and **prolonged periods of grief** and sorrow after the loss of a child.
- Shortened life span.
- **Pregnancy complications** — morning sickness, nausea, blood pressure, blood sugar problems, even anything wrong with the growth, development of your unborn baby.
- **Childbirth complications** — any sickness or disease or complication during the labour or delivery or the postnatal period.
- **Physical pain** and complications in childbirth.
- **Emotional and mental pain** so that we don't have to be oppressed or depressed or suffer with the baby blues or postnatal depression.

You are redeemed from the curse of barrenness and are free to be fertile. You are blessed and free to conceive, carry and give birth to healthy children!

Jesus paid the price for **all** forms of sickness and disease! The size or severity of the sickness or disease is only evaluated or graded by our minds and how we see the condition. I encourage you, therefore, to continue to meditate on this truth until you know that, no matter whether you are experiencing a simple cold, a sore throat, a headache, infertility, miscarriage, stomach ulcers or even cancer, **ALL** have been disarmed through the complete work of the Cross.

Continue to meditate on the truth until you see your sickness as God sees it — disarmed and powerless. Don't allow any sickness or disease to have an exalted position in your life anymore. We need to stop being spiritual beggars — going for the crumbs under the table! We are not slaves or servants, we are children! Stop looking at yourself and what you can or can't do, look to what Jesus HAS DONE! Healing is a free gift that we received upon our salvation. We were saved by grace through faith (**Eph 2:8–9**). God will NOT withhold what He has already provided! **Healing is your inheritance** so simply receive what Jesus has done!

Physical Healing Is Incorporated In Our Salvation!

*"Everyone who calls on the name of the Lord will be **saved**."*
Acts 2:21

*"Believe in the Lord Jesus, and you will be **saved**—you and your household."* **Acts 16:31**

The word *saved* above is the Greek word *sozo* and means: to save, keep safe and sound, to rescue from danger or destruction from injury or peril, to save a suffering one from perishing, (that is, one suffering from disease, to make well, heal, restore to health) and to preserve one who is in danger of destruction. So with this explanation we see that in context the word *saved* has a much broader meaning to the more commonly understood *born again* sense of the word *salvation*. And in the same way that we can be saved from any adverse situation, we are also saved (rescued, healed, delivered, protected, and preserved from danger) during childbearing.

Let us look at some more examples of this word *sozo* in the Gospels.

Matt 9:18–22 recounts the story of the woman with the flow of blood (a physical problem) being healed. In **verse 22** Jesus says to her, *'Be of good cheer, daughter; your faith has made you **well** (sozo)'.*

"Wherever He (Jesus) entered, into villages, cities, or the country,

*they laid the **sick** in the market places, and begged Him that they might just touch the hem of His garment. And as many as touched Him were made **well** (sozo)."* **Mark 6:56**

Again in **Mark 10:46–52,** from the account of Bartimaeus receiving his sight in **verse 52:** *'Then Jesus said to him, 'Go your way; your faith has made you **well** (sozo)'. And immediately he received his sight and followed Jesus on the road.'*

In **Luke 17:12–19** we have the account of ten lepers being healed of leprosy. One returned to thank Jesus. *'And He (Jesus) said to him, 'Arise, go your way; your faith has made you **well** (sozo)'.*

Notice in every one of these scriptures, it is a physical sickness that is being healed. Our English definition of the word *salvation* does not do God's meaning of the word salvation (*sozo*) justice. Salvation in the mind of God covers or provides for every part of our being or every part of our lives (not just for our spirit).

> *"And the very God of peace sanctify you **wholly**; and I pray God your whole spirit and soul and body be preserved blameless unto the coming of our Lord Jesus Christ."* **1 Thess 5:23 (KJV)**

We are spirit, soul and body. Only the Word of God can separate or distinguish between each part.

> *"For the Word of God … piercing even to the division of soul and spirit, and of joints and marrow (body)…"* **Heb 4:12**

When we received salvation, God provided something for our entire being. Let's take a look at the 'benefits' of our salvation.

> *"Praise the LORD, O my soul, **and forget not all His benefits** — who forgives all your sins and heals **ALL** your diseases, who redeems your life from the pit and crowns you with love and compassion, who satisfies your desires with good things so that your youth is renewed like the eagle's. [**verse 5 AMP** says: Who satisfies your mouth (your necessity and **desire at your personal age and situation**) with good so that your youth, renewed, is like the eagle's (strong, overcoming, soaring)]."* **Ps 103:2–5**

God has healed all sickness and disease! God's will is for all to be healed in the same way that it is God's will for all to receive salvation. However, just like how salvation is not always received, it is the same with healing. If you need healing in your body, then know that Jesus has already borne your sickness and carried your diseases at the same time and in the same manner that He bore your sins. If you are 'saved' by having received Jesus as Lord and Saviour then you are healed also! Healing is your inheritance upon salvation through the finished work of the Cross!

Frequently Asked Questions

Q: Does Sickness, Disease Or Pain Come From God?

*"Every **good and perfect** gift is from above, coming down from the Father of the heavenly lights, **who does not change** like shifting shadows."* **James 1:17 (NIV)**

As we have already discovered throughout the beginning of this book, God is good — all the time! Sickness, disease or pain of any kind are not good gifts! The nature and character of God is always to heal, deliver, set free, rescue and to protect. When you understand His true nature and character you will understand that:

- Healing is not something that God does — Healing is who He is. (Jehovah Rapha)
- Deliverance is not something that God does — Deliverance is who He is. (Jehovah Nissi)
- Provision is not something that God does — Provision is who He is. (Jehovah Jireh)
- Protection is not something God does — Protection is who He is!
- Salvation is not something God does — Salvation is who He is!

To be confident in who God is you need only to look at His Son Jesus. Jesus came as God in the flesh. He revealed that the nature and character of God is only ever good. He showed that good cannot come out of evil, and evil cannot come out of good.

"Out of the same mouth come praise and cursing. My brothers, this should not be. Can both fresh water and salt water flow from the same spring? My brothers, can a fig tree bear olives, or a

grapevine bear figs? Neither can a salt spring produce fresh water."
James 3:10–12

*"every good tree bears good fruit, but a bad tree bears bad fruit. **A good tree cannot bear bad fruit**, nor can a bad tree bear good fruit."* **Matt 7:17–19**

If God is the one who has redeemed you from sickness and disease then He **cannot** be the one that put it there in the first place, can He? No! Because:

- Good cannot come off the same tree as evil.
- Sickness cannot come off the same tree as healing!
- Barrenness cannot come off the same tree as fruitfulness!
- Lack, debt, and poverty cannot come off the same tree as prosperity and abundance!

If God is the one setting you free, He cannot also be the one that bound you in the first place. He cannot do both because He cannot work against Himself! A kingdom that is divided against itself will not stand!

*"Then was brought unto him one possessed with a devil, blind, and dumb: and he healed him, insomuch that the blind and dumb both spake and saw. And all the people were amazed, and said, Is not this the son of David? But when the Pharisees heard it, they said, This fellow doth not cast out devils, but by Beelzebub the prince of the devils. And Jesus knew their thoughts, and said unto them, **Every kingdom divided against itself** is brought to desolation; and every city or house divided against **itself shall not stand**: And **if Satan cast out Satan, he is divided against himself**; how shall then his kingdom stand? And if I by Beelzebub cast out devils, by whom do your children cast them out? Therefore they shall be your judges. But if I cast out devils by the Spirit of God, then the kingdom of God is come unto you."*
Matt 12:22–28 (KJV)

Note that **verse 26** says that if Satan drives out Satan, he is divided against himself. In other words, Jesus was saying that the sickness came from Satan and if Jesus was working under Satan's power then he would be working against Himself. If God is putting sickness on people and Jesus (sent from the Father) is then healing the sickness then they would both be working against each other. A house divided cannot stand! Many Christians actually believe that God is the one who puts sickness on people. But as you look at the above scripture this is not so! God is not the author of sickness. He is not into afflicting people with sickness or disease. He is light, and in Him is no darkness at all **(1 John 1:5).**

As I mentioned earlier, to see God at work, we need only to look at Jesus **(John 14:7).** Jesus was God on the earth. He was the exact image and representation of the Father **(Heb 1:3).** Jesus clearly showed us that the works He did were the works of the Father. He sent Jesus to do good on this earth. In fact, **Acts 10:38** tells us that *Jesus went about doing good and* ***healing ALL who were oppressed by the devil*** *because God was with Him'.* Jesus never gave someone a sickness or disease. He touched people, healed them and removed their diseases.

Often, when people get sick, miscarry or can't conceive, God ends up getting the blame. But God created all things to be good.

> *"The thief does not come except to steal, and to kill, and to destroy. I have come that they may have life, and that they may have it more abundantly."* **John 10:10 (NKJV)**

In the Old Testament God's people didn't know that they had an adversary. They wrongly believed that everything good came from God, and everything bad came from God. Unfortunately, many Christians today also believe the same thing. However, Jesus revealed the truth that God is the Healer and that Satan was the one behind all the sickness, disease and death.

> *"So Satan went forth and smote Job with sore boils."* **Job 2:7**

> *"Satan had bound her and she had a spirit of infirmity."* **Luke 13:11–16**

The whole purpose of Jesus coming to earth was to destroy the works of the devil, not to enforce or use them. Jesus became sin for us and through the work He did on the Cross He disarmed and defeated Satan and all his works **(Col 2:14–15).** Jesus gave us back our authority over the earth and over the devil that was taken from Adam during the fall in the Garden of

Eden.

> *"Behold, I give you the authority to trample on serpents and scorpions, and over all the power of the enemy, and nothing shall by any means hurt you."* **Luke 10:19 (NKJV)**

> *"The reason the Son of God appeared was to destroy the devil's work."* **1 John 3:8**

God doesn't want His children to suffer from any form of Satan's oppression. He wants us to walk in our authority and position in Christ and walk in victory over the devil and all his works. So, we don't have to be captive to Satan's works any longer. We can resist them and watch them flee from our lives.

The devil is the source **BUT God has the answer! He sent Jesus!** He sent forth His Word and healed you **(Ps 107)**. STOP looking at your diagnosis, symptoms or past experiences and **GO TO THE SOLUTION!** Fix your eyes on Jesus the author and perfecter of your faith.

Q: Does God Use Sickness To Test Us?

One of the most distressing things I can ever hear a person who is going through trials or sickness say is that they believe God is making them sick to teach them something, or to force them to come closer to Him. If you believe God is using sickness or disease to teach you something or use it in some way, then you will not be able to accept that God wants you well or that He has provided a way for you to be healed.

God does not put sickness or disease on people. He is the one who **has redeemed** you from it. If you act as if God put it there, you will remain under that condition for a long time. It is time therefore to react against sickness. It is under the curse of the law, and Christ has totally redeemed you from every part of this curse. To say that God is the one testing people today with sickness is the same as saying that He is also the one tempting them with sin and this is not truth.

Firstly, God is never tempted with evil, nor will He enforce evil. It is simply not in His nature.

> *"When tempted, no one should say, 'God is tempting me.' For God*

cannot be tempted by evil, nor does he tempt anyone." **James 1:13**

Only good and perfect things come from God. That which is not good and not perfect is not from God. So when people are sick, it is not because God is testing them with that sickness.

In order to begin to see your healing manifest you must know that it is God's will for you to be healed. God says in **Hosea 4:6** that *'my people perish through lack of knowledge'*. Many Christians are suffering because they simply lack knowledge of what God has provided for them. This knowledge is found within His Word because that is where God has provided His written will for our lives. Therefore, His will for your situation isn't what the doctors say, what your circumstances say, what your past history is but what His Word says! So get to know what the Word says is available to you and then begin to walk by faith by applying that truth to your life!

Q: Does God Delay Healing For Our Spiritual Growth?

Absolutely not! God will **never** withhold healing! If we say God wants us to wait for healing for some reason then what we are actually saying is that God is withholding the healing blood of Jesus from us! See how absurd that sounds? We have already seen that healing and salvation were provided at the same time and in the same manner. So, in the same way that God would not withhold salvation He will also not withhold healing. In fact, He cannot withhold what He has already given to us!

Unfortunately, many don't know this truth. They wrongly believe that God wants them to wait in order to do a work in them. They use scriptures about trials and tests out of context, and removed from their original meaning to try and rationalise their situation by saying that God is using it to make them grow or to teach them something.

> ... *"now for a little while you may be distressed by trials and suffer temptations, so that [the genuineness] of your faith may be tested, [your faith] which is infinitely more precious than the perishable gold which is tested and purified by fire. [This proving of your faith is intended] to redound to [your] praise and glory and honour when Jesus Christ (the Messiah, the Anointed One) is revealed."*
> **1 Pet 1:6(b)–7 (AMP)**

Jesus said that we will face trials and distresses of many kinds in this world.

> *"In the world you have tribulation and trials and distress and*
> *frustration; but be of good cheer take courage; be confident, certain,*
> *undaunted! For **I have overcome the world. I have deprived it***
> ***of power to harm you and have conquered it for you.***"
> **John 16:33 (AMP)**

But look at what else He said, '*be of good cheer for I have **overcome** the*
*world **for you!*** The tests and trials that the disciples and believers faced
in the Bible were caused by persecution for spreading the Gospel **not**
sickness or disease. It was their faith in Christ that was tested.

All forms of sickness and disease including infertility and miscarriage are
the corruption of Satan! Jesus has **already** purchased your healing, so why
would God withhold it from you? Knowing this then, don't allow Satan to
enforce something in your body that Jesus died to free you from any longer.

Often when many reach a desperate situation they decide to call upon
God to respond to their needs or to help them cope. God's nature is to
work good from things that Satan intended for harm. That is why many
people find God through suffering. But they could have grown and been
touched just as powerfully without being in a desperate situation.

We need to keep to the New Covenant and get to KNOW what Jesus
did on the Cross. He paid the price for all sickness and disease. When
you asked Him to be Lord of your life you were born again by the Spirit
of God. Your inheritance is NOW from Him. You are joint-heirs with
Christ. Does He have any sickness or disease? No! Therefore allow Jesus'
life, blood, healing and resurrection power to flow in your body!

> *"I am crucified with Christ: nevertheless I live; yet not I, but*
> *Christ liveth in me: and the life which I now live in the flesh I live*
> *by the faith of the Son of God, who loved me, and gave himself for*
> *me."* **Gal 2:20 (KJV)**

Jesus has redeemed us; He has reversed the curse! It has already been
done! It is by faith in Jesus Christ that we receive the fullness of what He
purchased for us through the work of the Cross. We need to remember
that upon salvation all the inheritance of the flesh, and the fruit of sin was

put to death (or put to the Cross)! We therefore need to stop living by the flesh and live by the Spirit of life and the truth of who we are in Christ, and what we have inherited as believers. We are redeemed from the fruit and outworking of sin, which includes all sickness and disease. So, why allow what Jesus died to set you free from stay on your body any longer?

Take God's Medicine — Healing Scriptures

If you are challenged with any form of sickness or disease, remind yourself of the finished work of the Cross. Jesus hung on the Cross, He was made a curse for you. He took your place and every curse was laid upon Him, and you are now free. You need to put more faith in what God says than in what your symptoms, diagnosis or doctors say.

If your doctor says you can't have children and you believe it, then you will begin to plan your life based on the doctor's report. But that is just a doctor's report — in short, the word of a man. But what does God say? The Bible says you shall know the truth and the truth shall make you free. The Word of God is the truth that will make you free. Believe God's truth in spite of the doctor's report and act accordingly. Begin to meditate on the truth and take God's Word as medicine into your heart so you can see the outworking of what Jesus has purchased for you become reality in your life!

> *"My son, **attend to my Words**; consent and submit to my sayings* [**KJV** says *incline your ear to My sayings*]. *Let them not depart from your sight; keep them in the centre of your heart. For they are life to those who find them, healing and **health** to all their flesh. **Keep your heart with all vigilance** and above all that you guard, for out of it flow the springs of life.* [**NIV** says… *Guard your heart, for it is the well-spring of life*]." **Prov 4:20–23 (AMP)**

If we want to have the 'springs of life' flowing out of our heart, affecting our body, mind and outward circumstances, then we need to keep God's Word before our eyes and ears by reading it, meditating upon it, hearing it preached, and hearing our own voice speaking it. Whatever we think about and focus our mind on will penetrate into our spirit man. God's Word is alive and full of power **(Heb 4:12)**. Think about it — when you keep meditating on something that's alive and full of power in your spirit, it has to bring **healing and health** to your flesh!

The word *health* in **Proverbs 4:21** means *cure* or *remedy*. God's Word is the cure, remedy, or the **medicine** we take to receive healing in both our physical bodies and our outward circumstances! If you went to a doctor and he prescribed medication for you to take three times a day, would you take it? Of course you would. You would take it in faith expecting it to cure you. Since God's power is greater than any worldly medicine, it will not only cure the symptoms, but can also bring healing to what was causing the condition in the first place. **Now that is good news!**

Meditate on the following truths in God's Word allowing time for them to penetrate into your heart so that they will bring life to your outward circumstances and healing and health to your flesh.

> *"For I am the LORD, who heals you."* **Ex 15:26**

> *"Worship the LORD your God, and His blessing will be on your food and water. **I will take away sickness from among you**, and none will miscarry or be barren in your land. I will give you a full life span."* **Ex 23:25–26**

> *"Then your light will break forth like the dawn, and your healing will quickly appear; then your righteousness will go before you, and the glory of the LORD will be your rear guard."* **Is 58:8**

> **"***But for you who revere my name, the sun of righteousness will rise with healing in its wings. And you will go out and leap like calves released from the stall."* **Mal 4:2**

> *"'Nevertheless, I will bring health and healing to it; I will heal my people and will let them enjoy abundant peace and security.'"*
> **Jer 33:6**

> *"But I will restore you to health and heal your wounds,' declares the LORD..."* **Jer 30:17**

> *"But those who suffer He delivers in their suffering; He speaks to them in their affliction."* **Job 36:15**

*"And the prayer offered in faith will make the sick person well;
the Lord will raise him up. If he has sinned, he will be forgiven."*
James 5:15

If the prayer offered in faith can make the sick person well, then that same faith can heal the barren couple!

Healling Prayer & Declaration

*I bind Satan's power over my body and I resist ALL sickness,
disease, pain and complications and I command you to leave! Jesus
bore my sickness, disease and pain in my place so I can be set free.*

*I am redeemed from the curse of the law. I am redeemed from
miscarriage and from anything that causes it. I am redeemed from
barrenness and from anything that causes it. Therefore I command
my body in Jesus' name to come in line with the Word of God
and to behave healed.*

*Body, you are to function the way God created you to: perfectly and
efficiently because you are fearfully and wonderfully made. You are
to function in perfect working order.*

*I walk in victory over sickness and disease and I declare in Jesus
name that I AM healed and made whole!*

AMEN!

chapter 9

Your Position in Christ

"And God said, 'let us make man in our image, after our likeness: and let them have **dominion** *over the fish of the sea, and over the fowl of the air, and over the cattle, and over* **all the earth***, and over every creeping thing that creepeth upon the earth. So God created man in His own image, in the image of God created He him; male and female created He them. And God* **blessed them***, and God said unto them, be* **fruitful***, and* **multiply***, and* **replenish** *the earth, and* **subdue it***: and have* **dominion** *over the fish of the sea, and over the fowl of the air, and over every living thing that moveth upon the earth."* **Genesis 1:26–28 (KJV)**

God created man to have dominion and to rule and reign on the earth as well as to be blessed, fruitful, and to multiply. But while God's original plan was for mankind to rule, reign and have dominion in this world, Adam forfeited this right and handed it to Satan through his sin in the Garden of Eden. That means that God is not ruling the earth right now — but He will one day! He cannot legally and justly move in and take away dominion from the devil. Satan has a legal right because Adam handed it over to him **(Luke 4:6)**. **1 John 5:19 (AMP)** tells us that *'...the whole world [around us] is under the power of the evil one'*.

Paul, in Ephesians 2:2, calls him the prince of the power of the air who works in the sons of disobedience (those who are unsaved) and in **2 Corinthians 4:4** he tells us that Satan is the god of this world.

But praise God, Jesus paid the price for Adam's sin and redeemed everything that belongs to us through the work He did on the Cross. He DISARMED the world, the flesh and the devil. And He gave us His dominion, power and authority.

While God wants us to freely receive what He has already provided through Jesus, we still experience life with all of its ups and downs. This is particularly so in the area of childbearing. We live in a fallen world and just because we are Christians does not mean we will never be challenged. The reality is we will experience distress and face trials of many kinds. But through Jesus, God has made provision for us to exercise authority over what we face so we can overcome and walk in victory.

> *"In the world you have tribulation and trials and distress and frustration;* ***but be of good cheer*** *[take courage; be confident, certain, undaunted]! For* ***I have overcome the world****. [I have deprived it of power to harm you and* ***have conquered it for you****.]"* **John 16:33 (AMP)**

God has provided for every area of our lives and He sealed it through the work Jesus did on the Cross.

> *"For whatever is* ***born of God is victorious over the world****; and this is the victory that conquers the world,* ***even our faith****. Who is it that is victorious over [that conquers] the world but he who believes that Jesus is the Son of God [who adheres to, trusts in, and relies on that fact]?"* **1 John 5:4–5 (AMP)**

You don't have to live life the world's way, with its natural limitations; rather you can experience the abundant life that Jesus purchased for you.

> *"Now thanks be to God* ***who always leads us in triumph in Christ****, and through us diffuses the fragrance of His knowledge in every place."* **2 Cor 2:14 (NKJV)**

"But thanks be to God! **He gives us the victory through our Lord Jesus Christ.** *Therefore, my dear brothers, stand firm. Let nothing move you."* **1 Cor 15:57**

Knowing you can triumph and have victory in Christ does not mean that you will never be challenged. How can you walk in triumph if there was never anything to overcome or triumph over? This needs to be spelt out, because I have seen many fall into fear and disbelief when they have been challenged about something they were specifically praying about. Sadly, when this happens, many let go of the Word. However, if we know who we are in Christ then we can exercise our authority to triumph over the circumstances and see that victory manifest.

In order for us to learn how to walk in victory and how to exercise our authority, we first need to know and understand the fullness of our authority in Christ, and our position in His Kingdom.

Know Your Position In Christ

Did you know that through our belief in Jesus and being joint-heirs with Him, we have the same power and authority on the earth as He had? Unfortunately, many of us don't understand this truth so we find ourselves waiting and wondering why God isn't doing anything to help us. But the truth is that we **have already been given** what we need for the victory. All along **we have had the power and authority to overcome** what we face. So we have been 'putting up with' the things in our lives that instead we should have been 'putting a stop to!'

*"And Jesus came and spoke to them saying, '**all power is given unto me** in heaven and in earth,* **go ye therefore** *and teach all nations, baptising them in the name of the Father and of the Son, and of the Holy Ghost; teaching them to observe all things whatsoever I have commanded you; and lo, I am with you always, even unto the end of the world. Amen'."* **Matt 28:18–20 (KJV)**

God gave Jesus all His power and authority. And that same power and authority is then transferred to the one who believes in Jesus! When you were 'born again' the same Spirit of God that raised Jesus Christ from the dead came to dwell in you. That means that as post-Cross New Covenant believers, we have the very Spirit of Jesus living on the inside of us, meaning that wherever we go we don't go just in His name, rather we go in His person!

> *"But if the Spirit of Him that raised up Jesus from the dead **dwells in you**, He that raised up Christ from the dead shall also make alive your mortal bodies by His Spirit that **dwells** in you."*
> **Rom 8:11**

> *"Little children, you are of God [you belong to Him] and have [already] defeated and overcome them [the agents of the antichrist], because **He Who lives in you** is greater (mightier) than he who is in the world."* **1 John 4:4 (AMP)**

> *"For in Christ all the fullness of the Deity lives in bodily form, and **you have been given fullness in Christ**, who is the head over every power and authority."* **Col 2:9–10**

We have been given Jesus' power, which is far above any power of the devil. All things are under our feet so that we might be the fullness of Jesus here on earth to continue His work.

Know Your Authority

> *"Behold, **I give unto you** power to tread on serpents and scorpions **and over all the power of the enemy** and nothing shall by any means hurt you."* **Luke 10:19 (NKJV)**

If God said it, He meant it! You have power over **all** Satan's power. When Jesus said this Satan was still fully armed! Jesus had not yet disarmed him on the Cross. Yet, the disciples were still able to go out in the authority of Jesus and cast out devils and heal the sick!

How To Exercise Our Authority

When you know who you are in Christ, where you are seated and what belongs to you as a believer then you will understand that: *'As Christ is, so are we in this world'* **(1 John 4:17)**. All creation is waiting expectantly, even groaning for the sons of God (that is us) to be revealed **(Rom 8:19)**. It is therefore time for us to stand up in our position in Christ as believers and begin to exercise and move in our authority.

Remember Satan Has Already Been Defeated!

We must never forget that the battle has **already** been won and Satan has already been defeated. Stop living under the circumstances or under the diagnosis and start living above them. No matter what you are facing, exercise your authority in Jesus and place the situation **under** your feet.

> *"When you were dead in your sins and in the uncircumcision of your sinful nature, God made you alive with Christ. He forgave us all our sins, having cancelled the written code, with its regulations, that was against us and that stood opposed to us; He took it away, nailing it to the cross. And **having disarmed the powers and authorities, He made a public spectacle of them, triumphing over them by the cross."*** **Col 2:13–15**

Satan has been disarmed! Therefore, the only power Satan has in your life is what you allow him to have.

> *"For this purpose the Son of God was manifested, that he might destroy the works of the devil."* **1 John 3:8**

> *"The Father **has delivered and drawn us** to Himself **out of the control and the dominion of darkness** and **has transferred** us into the kingdom of the Son of His love, in Whom we have our redemption through His blood, [which means] the forgiveness of our sins."* **Col 1:13–14 (AMP)**

When you understand who you are in Christ, you will realise that you no longer need to struggle with any spiritual attack, because Satan's power and hold over you **has already been broken.**

Resist The Devil And He Will Flee!

> *"Be well balanced (temperate, sober of mind), be vigilant and cautious **at all times**; for that enemy of yours, the devil, roams around like a lion roaring in fierce hunger, seeking someone to seize upon and devour. **Withstand him**; be firm in faith **against his onset** — rooted, established, strong, immovable, and determined…"* **1 Pet 5:8–9 (AMP)**

As we have discovered previously, this scripture doesn't say that the devil is a roaring lion, but rather **he is like** a roaring lion! Jesus has disarmed and deprived him of power; He has removed Satan's 'teeth and claws'. We have also discovered that it is important that we resist the lies and deceits of the devil at the onset. **The very second** we begin to feel challenged we are to use our authority in Jesus, and resist the situation immediately. We are to resist any sickness, disease, pain, fear, complication or first sign of a symptom when they occur. When we resist (oppose, withstand and strive) against these things they will flee!

> *"Submit yourselves, then, to God. **Resist** the devil, and he will flee from you."* **James 4:7**

Remember, the word resist in the scripture above means to oppose, to strive against and to withstand — **not** to sit back and be passive. Satan has already been disarmed and defeated but we still must oppose His attempts to keep us from attaining victory over our circumstances.

Stand Your Ground!

As we have seen previously, we are not called to 'fight' the devil because he has already been defeated. All we are called to fight is *'...the good fight of faith'* **(1 Tim 6:12)**. Faith comes and grows by hearing about the finished work of the Cross — found within God's Word. **Ephesians 6:17** calls God's Word the Sword of the Spirit. We have one absolute truth for eternity and that is *'heaven and earth shall pass away: but my words shall not pass away'* **(Mark 13:31)**. Therefore, stand on what God says and not what your situation dictates to you!

God tells us through the apostle Paul to *'...put on the full armour of God, so that when the day of evil comes, you may be able to stand your ground'* **(Eph 6:13)**. He says that when we have done all that we can, we are to continue to stand! The word stand in this scripture means to endure, to adhere to, to persist, to insist, to hold a course of direction, to continue in force, to sustain, or to withstand. We need to continue to stand on what God's Word says by being determined to not let go of what it says so we can continue to walk by faith by the finished work of the Cross, and not be moved by what the natural realm is dictating!

Binding And Loosing

While Jesus has given you power and authority here on this earth, if you want to walk in that power and authority then you will need to start using it!

> *"I tell you the truth, whatever **you bind** on earth will be bound in heaven, and whatever **you loose** on earth will be loosed in heaven."* **Matt 18:18**

Jesus said 'I tell you the truth', and this is one of the truths that will set you free! Whatever **you bind** will be **bound** and whatever **you loose** will be **loosed**! How? By using your authority in Jesus! You **have** the authority to bind Satan's power and loose sickness and disease, death and miscarriage, barrenness and infertility off your life so that you can experience the healing that belongs to you as a believer.

Use Your Authority In Jesus!

> *"And this is His command: to believe in the name of His Son, Jesus Christ, and to love one another as He commanded us."* **1 John 3:23**

The first step to becoming a victorious Christian is to believe in the name of Jesus Christ. He came not just so we could be set free from the power of sin and death and enter into heaven, but also so that we could live a life of victory and peace, not discouragement and defeat. Through Jesus we have dominion in this world. But that's not all! Through Him we also have the power of God's Word behind us because Jesus and the Word are one (see **Rev 19:13** and **John 1:2,14**). We have the whole corporate structure of the universe backing us up when we exercise our authority in Jesus.

> *"I tell you the truth, anyone who has faith in me will do what I have been doing. He will do even greater things than these, because I am going to the Father. And I will do whatever you ask **in my name**, so that the Son may bring glory to the Father. You may ask me for anything **in my name**, and I will do it."* **John 14:12–14**

> *"And these signs will accompany those who believe: **in my name** they will drive out demons; they will speak in new tongues; they*

> *will pick up snakes with their hands; and when they drink deadly poison, it will not hurt them at all; they will place their hands on sick people, and they will get well."* **Mark 16:17–18**

> *"Lord, even the demons are subject to us in Your name."* **Luke 10:17**

The definition of the word *name* in the original Greek in the scriptures above is *authority*. That means as believers in Jesus when we do something in His name we are doing it in His power, authority and person!

> *"And being found in appearance as a man, He humbled Himself and became obedient to death — even death on a cross! Therefore God exalted Him to the highest place and gave Him **the name that is above every name**, that **at the name of Jesus** every knee should bow, in heaven and on earth and under the earth, and every tongue confess that Jesus Christ is Lord, to the glory of God the Father."* **Phil 2:8–11**

What are you facing right now in your life? Does it have a name? Exercise authority over it in the authority of Jesus and it has to bow down and obey. If you tell it to be removed, it will be removed. If you tell it to die at the root it will die at the root. If you resist it, then it must flee!

So what are you waiting for? You **HAVE the authority** to bind and loose sickness, disease, infertility, miscarriage, and barrenness from your life. We are not **trying** to get power and authority, because we **already have power and authority** because of our position in Christ. We are seated with Christ in heavenly places far above all rule and authority, power and dominion, and every title that can be given, not only in the present age but also in the one to come (see **Eph 1:21** and **Eph 2:6**). Therefore, stop living under the circumstances, instead put a stop to them and exercise authority over them and command any sickness in your body to leave!

Mirror God's Word — Do And Say What God Says!

Another important way to exercise our authority is to look at who we are in Christ through the mirroring of God's Word.

"Do not merely listen to the Word, and so deceive yourselves. Do what it says. Anyone who listens to the Word but does not do what it says is like a man who looks at his face in a mirror and, after looking at himself, goes away and immediately forgets what he looks like. But the man who looks intently into the perfect law that gives freedom, and continues to do this, not forgetting what he has heard, but doing it-he will be blessed in what he does."
James 1:22–25

When we begin to look at ourselves in the mirror of God's Word, (found in the New Testament), we will first see our own reflection. But we need to look beyond ourselves and see **who we are in Jesus.** Regardless of how we feel about ourselves we need to believe what God says and put it in our hearts and in our mouths and mirror God's Word.

Below I have personalised a number of very powerful scriptures that reveal our position and authority in Christ. I encourage you to meditate on them and mirror them by speaking them out aloud into your life. Continue in this until their truth is established in your heart and you believe what they say. Then simply apply this truth to your life by exercising authority over the circumstances when the need arises.

Who I Am In Christ!

- God always causes me to triumph in Christ. **2 Cor 2:14**
- God always causes me to have victory in Christ therefore I stand firm and let nothing move me. **1 Cor 15:57**
- I resist the devil and he flees from me. **James 4:7**
- I can do all things in Christ who strengthens me. **Phil 4:13**
- I am more than a conqueror. **Rom 8:37**
- I am an overcomer in all things! **John 16:33**
- Because I am born of God I overcome the world by faith. **1 John 5:4, John 16:33**
- I have power to tread and trample on snakes and scorpions and over all the power of the enemy and nothing by any means shall harm me. **Luke 10:19**
- Whatever I bind on earth will be bound in heaven; whatever I loose on earth will be loosed in heaven. **Matt 18:18**
- Greater is He who is in me that he who is in the world. **1 John 4:4**

- If God is for me then who can be against me? **Rom 8:31**
- No weapon formed against me shall prosper. **Is 54:17**
- I don't have a spirit of fear but a spirit of power, a sound mind and self-control. **2 Tim 1:7**
- I am redeemed from the curse of the law. **Gal 3:13**
- The joy of the Lord is my strength. **Ps 28:7**
- I have been forgiven. **Heb 8:12, 1 John 1:9**
- I am fearfully and wonderfully made. **Ps 139:14**
- I am blessed. **Deut 2:7, Matt 5:3–10, Matt 13:16**
- I was a captive but now I am free and I am free indeed! **Is 42:7, Is 61:6, John 8:36**
- I HAVE BEEN DELIVERED, HEALED, SET FREE AND MADE WHOLE. **Is 53:5, Matt 8:16–17**

I encourage you from now on to make the decision to say **only what God says** about you! I know that it is easy to lose sight of who you are in Christ and what belongs to you as a believer but regardless of how you feel, remember that you have **the same authority here on this earth as Jesus had**. Therefore, when you **feel** yourself begin to lose sight of this truth, stop and remind yourself of your true heritage.

chapter 10

The Power of Your Words

Once we know our authority, and our position in Christ and what belongs to us as believers, we then need to apply this to our daily lives. We discovered in the previous chapter that the way we exercise authority over any situation we face is by our words and what we say. Now let us look more closely at the power of our words.

> *"The tongue has the power of life and death, and those who love it will eat its fruit."* **Proverbs 18:21**

There is power in our words! Our words can either create or destroy. If a child is raised hearing words like *'you are no good'* or *'you are clumsy'* or *'you are stupid'* these words can affect their self-esteem. Words bring either life or death and over time children spoken to in this way will become programmed to see themselves that way and will behave accordingly. On the other hand, when you speak positive words of affirmation to children such as how loved and special they are, you sow words of life into their spirits and they will act and behave on that level. When we speak words of life, we eat the fruit of those life-filled words, and when we speak words of death, we eat the fruit of those words as well.

Commanding God?

There is a distinct difference between ordering God around and simply declaring the truth in His Word. Many misunderstand this powerful principle and think that by speaking to their situation they are being irreverent and demanding things of God. When this thinking is in place a reluctance to exercise authority can develop because it appears insolent or disrespectful.

The truth is that God **wants** you to walk in what He has **already** provided for you. Why else would He have given you His power and authority? His power penetrates every realm: the physical, spiritual and emotional, and can bring life, health and restoration to your cells, organs and tissues. If you want to see that same power of God released in your life then you need to act on what you believe. And we put actions to our faith by exercising our authority over our natural circumstances and putting what God has said in His Word in our mouth.

It is important to note that declaring, confessing or speaking God's Word isn't about trying to get God to do something for us, or to make the Word work. We confess what God says because of **what has already happened!** The work has already been done so command it to come into manifestation according to **what Jesus has done** through the finished work of the Cross!

This is all about enabling you to:

- Transform your natural thinking and understanding until you see your situation through the eyes of faith (what God's Word says).
- Walk by faith (by faith in the finished work of the Cross), not by sight or appearance.
- Replace any fears and doubts you have with the truth in God's Word that sets you free.
- Act on what you believe by taking authority over your natural circumstances.
- Call those things that are not as though they were (see **Rom 4:17**).

Putting Your Words Into Action

*"Have faith in God. For assuredly I say to you, **whoever says** to this mountain, 'Be removed and be cast into the sea', and **does not doubt in his heart**, but **believes** that those things **he says** will be done, he **will have whatever he says**." Mark 11:22–23 (NKJV)*

Note that **Mark 11:22–23** mentions the word says three times.

- whoever **says** to this mountain
- believes those things he **says** will be done
- he will have whatever he **says**

So, what are **you saying**? Remember, we act on what we believe by taking authority over the natural symptoms, circumstances, fears and doubts by **speaking to them**. The natural symptoms and circumstances will 'speak' to you so you need to exercise authority over them and speak to them instead!

*"[Jesus] replied, 'If you have faith as small as a mustard seed, **you can say** to this mulberry tree, "Be uprooted and planted in the sea," and it will obey you'." Luke 17:6*

*"He replied, '...I tell you the truth, if you have faith as small as a mustard seed, **you can say** to this mountain, "Move from here to there" and it will move. Nothing will be impossible for you'." Matt 17:20*

Don't speak to God **about** your mountain but speak to your mountain about God! Stop speaking about the mountains, situations or circumstances in your life and begin to speak **to** them. In other words, speaking **about** your circumstances will change nothing, but speaking **to** them with your God-given authority will. Put simply: say what God's Word says. If you believe God's Word is true then do what it says, and if something opposing comes, then act on what you believe and exercise your authority over the situation. Declare the truth of what God has done and command the reality of that truth to manifest.

*"no weapon formed against you shall prosper, and every tongue which rises against you in judgement **you shall condemn**. This is*

the heritage of the servants of the Lord, and their righteousness is from Me, says the Lord." **Is 54:17 (NKJV)**

It is clear in the scripture above that **we** are to condemn or refute the tongues (and situations) that rise up in judgement against us. God is not going to exercise His authority for us because **it is our responsibility!** As we have already seen, we have been given all authority through Jesus, so we can exercise authority over what we face in life to see the breakthrough.

Believe What You Say!

*"For assuredly, I say to you, whoever says to this mountain, 'be removed and be cast into the sea,' **and does not doubt in his heart**, but believes that those things he says will be done, he will have whatever he says. Therefore I say to you, whatever things you ask when you pray, **believe** that you receive them, and you will have them."* **Mark 11:23–24 (NKJV)**

When it comes to saying what God says in His Word, we can't just simply speak out something and expect a result; we need to believe it and not doubt it in our heart. Additionally we can't believe one thing and then confess something else because our heart and confession need to work together in agreement.

"It is written: 'I believed; therefore I have spoken.' With that same spirit of faith we also believe and therefore speak." **2 Cor 4:13**

When you have a revelation of the truth of God's Word in your heart you will automatically speak out what you believe. If you have to keep reminding yourself of your confession and what you believe then continue to meditate on the Word until revelation comes. Once you believe God's Word you won't have to keep reminding yourself to speak it out because from the overflow of your heart your mouth will speak.

*"For **out of the overflow of the heart the mouth speaks.** The good man brings good things out of the good stored up in him, and the evil man brings evil things out of the evil stored up in him."* **Matt 12:34–35**

When you keep God's Word pertaining to your situation in your heart in abundance, the overflow of your words will line up with what you believe in your heart. And once the Word of God releases that faith within, and you declare it out of your mouth, then your mountains will be removed!

Positive Words Create Change

I recently read a pamphlet on how to manage depression. It spoke about a program where people with different kinds of depression were taught to 'play act' and pretend they were well. They were told to speak only positive words when describing their condition or how they were feeling. The pamphlet concluded by stating that when patients followed this advice, they were not only able to manage their depression and reduce their medication, but many of the patients no longer needed medication at all! This included people who had suffered long term and severe types of depression.

This is a great example of the incredible authority we have over our own lives and how that authority is released through the words that we speak. Remember, this pamphlet was using examples of people in the world who had no idea of the power of their words, yet they had unwittingly tapped into this powerful God-designed principle. It is such a shame that many people in the world understand and use this principle and reap the results moreso than many of God's own children!

Dr David (Paul) Yonggi Cho states in his book *The Fourth Dimension, The Creative Power of the Spoken Word* [1],

> One morning I was eating breakfast with one of Korea's leading micro-surgeons, who was telling me about various medical findings on the operation of the brain. He asked, "Dr Cho, did you know that the speech centre in the brain rules over all the nerves? You ministers really have power, because according to our recent findings in neurology, the speech centre in the brain has total dominion over all the other nerves." (p. 67)

If you say or think something like… *'I am tired'* or *'I feel sick'* then your body will respond and react accordingly. If on the other hand you say, *'I feel great today'*, or *'I have strength for all things through Christ who strengthens me'* then your body will respond to that instead!

"We all stumble in many ways. If anyone is never at fault in what he says, he is a perfect man, able to keep his whole body in check. When we put bits into the mouths of horses to make them obey us, we can turn the whole animal. Or take ships as an example. Although they are so large and are driven by strong winds, they are steered by a very small rudder wherever the pilot wants to go. Likewise the tongue is a small part of the body, but it makes great boasts. Consider what a great forest is set on fire by a small spark. The tongue also is a fire, a world of evil among the parts of the body. It corrupts the whole person, sets the whole course of his life on fire, and is itself set on fire by hell. All kinds of animals, birds, reptiles and creatures of the sea are being tamed and have been tamed by man, but no man can tame the tongue. It is a restless evil, full of deadly poison. With the tongue we praise our Lord and Father, and with it we curse men, who have been made in God's likeness. Out of the same mouth come praise and cursing. My brothers, this should not be." **James 3:2–10**

James shows us that the tongue plays a huge role in our lives. In the same way that huge ships have their direction determined by a small rudder, so too our lives have their direction set by our words. James also says that a 'perfect man' is a man that has full control of his tongue. Every one of us must therefore learn to take authority over our tongue and hold it in check. Just as a horse is held by a bit, we must control our words and be careful what we say.

Sometimes we use silly expressions such as *'I am sick or scared to death', 'you make me sick'*, or *'I nearly died when...'* without even realising it. Nothing usually happens when we say these things because we don't really believe it when we say it. But it is important to know that when you say what you believe things change. This can work both for us and against us.

I don't want you to become fearful or dogmatic when it comes to your confession. That is not my intention in any way. We simply need to be careful what we believe in our heart and what we say out of our mouth. This is particularly so in regards to our health.

A friend of mine who had been diagnosed with arthritis would always say *'my arthritis'* when describing her condition. I would constantly pick her up on her words asking whether she really wanted it to **belong** to her. Obviously her answer was no! I was not trying to be facetious in any way but rather I wanted her to understand my point, and instead of submitting to the condition, begin to exercise her authority over the condition. Thankfully, we were close friends and she was mature enough in God to see my point and heed my advice. She then started to 'talk to' her condition rather than always 'talking about' it, exercising her authority over the diagnosis and symptoms, and healing soon took place in her body.

As you can see, if we are giving something a legal right to afflict us through letting it run its course unchallenged, or by calling it our own by saying 'my sickness' then it has the right to be there, its existence is reinforced by what we believe and by what we are saying. So stop living under the diagnosis and talking **about** the symptoms and condition, and instead master your tongue, just like a bit masters a horse, and begin to speak **to** it! Take authority over barrenness, endometriosis, polycystic ovaries, miscarriage, pain, depression, cancer, or heart disease, and tell them to be removed. Don't submit to them or own them; instead rebuke them!

I want to make it clear that I am not talking about **denying** the existence of your physical pain, sickness, or condition but rather encouraging you to exercise your God-given authority over your life and possess the healing that God has already provided for you. When you resist the symptoms or circumstances and declare to them what God has done, through your words you are releasing the power to change your situation!

God's Words Have Creative Power!

"Through faith we understand that the worlds were framed by the Word of God, so that things which are seen were not made of things which do appear." **Heb 11:3 (KJV)**

We know from the first chapter of **Genesis** that God spoke and the world was created. God's power was released through His Words. When He spoke His Words were full of creative power, and framed and fashioned what He directed. **And God has not diminished in power!** He is so powerful that the whole universe is still being upheld and suspended in space by His Words.

... *"**upholding** and maintaining and guiding and propelling the universe **by His mighty Word of power.**"* **Heb 1:3 (AMP)**

131

*"For **the Word that God speaks** is **alive** and **full of power** [making it active, operative, energising, and effective]; it is sharper than any two-edged sword, penetrating to the dividing line of the breath of life (soul) and [the immortal] spirit, and of joints and marrow [of the deepest parts of our nature], exposing and sifting and analysing and judging the very thoughts and purposes of the heart."* **Heb 4:12 (AMP)** [**NIV** reads, *for the Word of God is **living** and **active***]

Jesus was God in the flesh and, as we have already seen, He was given all of God's power and authority. He then in turn delegated that same power and authority to all who believe in Him. **Remember, as God's children we have the same authority that Jesus has!** When you know who you are in Christ, where you are seated and understand your power and authority as a believer, you too can see the power of God released in your life through your words! God's power penetrates every realm; the physical, spiritual and emotional and can bring life, health and restoration to your cells, organs and tissues.

When the doctors told Shaun that we would never have children of our own we didn't allow this report to be our final report. God said in **Exodus 23:25–26** that we would not miscarry or be barren. He also told us in **John 17:17** that His Word is truth and in **Hebrews 6:18** that it is impossible for Him to lie. So we made God's Word our final authority! While our circumstances were real, we didn't ignore them but we knew we didn't have to live under them because they could be changed by God's healing power. We continued to declare what God said over our situation knowing that God's Word is true, He does not lie, and that we would not be barren, and the result was four children within four and a half years!

We Can Imitate God

There are two biblical examples that we can follow when it comes to the power of our words. The first example is Jesus and the fig tree.

"Seeing in the distance a fig tree in leaf, He went to find out if it had any fruit. When he reached it, He found nothing but leaves, because it was not the season for figs. Then He said to the tree, 'May no one ever eat fruit from you again.' And His disciples heard him say it"... **Mark 11:13–14**

"In the morning, as they went along, they saw the fig tree withered from the roots. Peter remembered and said to Jesus, 'Rabbi, look! The fig tree you cursed has withered!' So Jesus answered and said to them 'Have faith in God'." **Mark 11:20–22**

Jesus knew and acted on His authority. He spoke to the fig tree and it obeyed him. The life of the tree is in the roots, so even though it looked like nothing happened on the surface, the tree had died instantly at the roots (the life source). It took time for the effect of Jesus' words to spread to the leaves and branches of the tree.

You can expect to walk and operate as Jesus did because that is the authority that He has given to you. So when you speak to a situation, you can expect change and even though you may not see any change on the surface, know that it has died at the root of the situation.

The second example is from **Romans 4:17 (NKJV)** *'God, who gives life to the dead and calls those things which do not exist as though they did'!*

We can also imitate God by speaking His Word and call those things that aren't as though they are. To be confident that what you want to 'call in' is the will of God, stick to what the Word says. You will then be in agreement with God on that issue. Remember that you can have everything God says you can have because His will for your life is in His Word. God's Word is living and active and can give life to a dying body and also put life into your womb! Therefore, if you believe God's Word then rise up and begin to declare it by speaking life to the circumstances you are facing today. And begin to call those things that do not exist as though they did!

1 Dr Paul Yonggi Cho, (1979), *The Fourth Dimension, The Creative Power of the Spoken Word*, Bridge-Logos Publishers, Gainsville, Florida 32614 USA. www.bridgelogos.com

PART II
Infertility to Conception

11

Taking Charge of Your Fertility
— God's Way

In the world there are many books devoted solely to issues of fertility and childbearing. They provide information on how your body works and also how to pinpoint the perfect time for conception. The trouble with these books however, is that they tend to keep you focused on the natural and what the flesh is doing. What's more, those who have physical complications in their bodies due to an abnormality, unbalanced hormones, sickness or disease will not be able to successfully apply this knowledge. But, **praise God, through Jesus there is a better way!** When you know who you are in Christ, your position in Him and what you have inherited as a believer (all through the finished work of the Cross) you will realise that you no longer have to be subject to your body and what state it is in. You can exercise your authority and walk in the healing and fruitfulness that Jesus purchased for you.

Remember Your Authority In Jesus!

In the previous chapters we have seen that we have the same power and authority as Jesus has. We are seated with Christ in heavenly places far above all rule and authority, power and dominion, and every title that can be given, not only in the present age but also in the one to come (see **Eph 1:21** and **Eph 2:6**). So when you face an adverse situation in any area of your life, including childbearing, you can exercise your authority and place the situation under your feet.

I was diagnosed with an underactive thyroid and was told I would be on medication for the rest of my life. However, the first report wasn't my last report! I took authority over my body and commanded my thyroid and metabolism to come into line with the truth in God's Word, which said by Jesus' stripes I was healed. Within a couple of weeks I experienced complete healing and to this day my thyroid continues to function perfectly.

What are you facing in your body right now? Don't put up with it any longer; simply take authority over it! Command your body to get into perfect working order and to function the way God designed it to. Regardless of your condition, you have authority over your own body. Don't allow it to be the other way around! So what are you waiting for?!

You have authority over:

- **Female factor infertility** — command your reproductive system to do what God created it to do without complication. Speak life to your ovaries and command them to do their job and produce healthy, mature follicles and to ovulate.
- **Male factor infertility** — encourage your husband to take authority over his own body and command his reproductive organs to function how God created them to, by producing and releasing healthy, strong and mobile sperm.
- **Irregular cycles** — command your body to do what it needs to do for a perfect and uncomplicated 28-day cycle.
- **Hormones** — command your hormones to get into perfect balance and to function efficiently and perform the way that they were created to function during the conception, pregnancy, and postnatal period. Low hormone levels can cause miscarriage so it is beneficial to have them working at their best.

If you exercise authority and command any form of sickness to be removed, then it must be removed. If you tell it to die at the root then it will die at the root. If you resist it, then it must flee! This means that unbalanced hormones, polycystic ovarian syndrome, endometriosis, infertility, miscarriage, migraines, PMT, and even cancer must flee when you resist them!

The majority of the couples who discover **New Life Ministries** are in a desperate situation. They have usually tried every avenue and like the account of the woman with the issue of blood in the Gospels, instead of getting better they have grown worse. But through the truth of God's Word they discover that they don't have to live with their diagnosis, because they can exercise their authority over any condition in their bodies and experience healing. Consequently there have been many amazing testimonies of couples from all around the world who have received breakthroughs such as:

- Healing of threatened miscarriages.
- Lifeless babies brought back to life in the womb (including blighted ovum and chemical pregnancies).
- Babies moving position in the womb (even from the fallopian tube to the womb).
- Placentas relocating from off the cervix (placenta previa) to the top of the uterus.
- Overcoming pain and/or complications in labour.
- Overcoming many different postnatal issues.
- Miraculous recoveries after both minor and major surgeries (including Caesareans).
- Long, irregular, painful and complicated cycles becoming perfect 28-day painless, complication-free cycles.
- Regular ovulatory cycles after missing cycles for many months.
- Reproductive systems that had shut down beginning to operate perfectly.
- Husbands experiencing difficulties in their reproductive organs or having intimacy issues being healed and able to function normally.
- Husbands diagnosed with low sperm counts or abnormal sperm later tested with normal, healthy levels.
- Husbands diagnosed with no sperm still being able to impregnate their wives.
- Reversal of menopause and its symptoms.
- Unbalanced hormones getting back into balance.
- Ovaries that had shut down and stopped ovulating coming back to life and working efficiently.

- Cysts, fibroids and tumours (such as PCO) disappearing.
- Endometriosis disappearing.
- Underactive and overactive thyroids functioning in perfect balance.
- Unbalanced emotions returning to balance.
- Fear, depression, oppression leaving.
- Lives being restored and many walking in a spirit of victory.

Start Where You Are At Right Now!

When you begin to exercise authority over your body (or your situation) start with what you can believe right now. While absolutely nothing is impossible, sometimes there are mindsets in place that highly regard the size or type of the condition. We live in a world that almost glorifies illness, so sometimes your mind will consider your condition according to what the natural circumstances are, or on the strength of what your diagnosis is. You may also feel that you have to accept certain conditions due to your past, your genetic makeup or your age. Remember that Jesus has already paid the price for ALL forms of sickness and disease! Continue to meditate on this truth until you see your condition through the eyes of the finished work of the Cross, and the natural facts lose their power over you.

In order to begin to learn how to exercise your authority and experience healing, I suggest you focus on your menstrual cycle and on any reproductive imbalance. If there is an imbalance in any part of your reproductive system then that is where the trouble begins because even a slight imbalance can prevent conception. It is beneficial to have your cycles working efficiently because it is the core of your reproductive system. I encourage women to start with their cycles because they are a process that repeats itself every month and this helps you for the next stage — pregnancy.

Remember always that premenstrual syndrome, clotting, pain, irregular cycles and an unbalanced reproductive system are simply different forms of sickness and as we have already discovered in the 'Foundations' section of this book, Jesus has taken **all forms** of sickness in our place! Why then should we allow our bodies to function with an imbalance? Why put up with anything less than perfect order in our cycles?

In my late teens and early twenties I used to suffer with long and painful cycles. I also experienced mood swings, food cravings, bloating around my abdomen and other symptoms. I had tried herbal remedies and painkillers in search of a cure, but nothing seemed to work. It was not uncommon for me to spend a day in bed because the pain during my cycle was so unbearable. I really disliked having cycles and I would have been happy if they never came back. I dreaded the thought of having to one day give birth. If I couldn't cope with the pain of my cycles; how on earth was I going to cope with the pain in childbirth?

However I soon discovered the truth that I did not have to suffer because **Isaiah 53:5** says Jesus took our sickness, pain and sorrow in our place! It doesn't matter what form the sickness or pain comes in: whether it be menstrual cramps, headaches, toothaches, sporting injuries, or childbirth! Once I discovered what Jesus had done I then needed to apply that truth, because it sure wasn't manifesting on knowledge alone! I continued to renew my mind with the truth and I acted on what I believed and took authority over the condition and natural symptoms. I also exercised authority over my own body and told it to have a cycle without pain, clotting or any other complication. I knew that what is considered to be normal is a 28-day cycle so that is what I chose to declare. I wanted my body healthy and to stop being out of balance. It wasn't long before I experienced a breakthrough in my cycles. And once I experienced healing from the pain in my cycles I realised that I could apply the same principles to my moods, cravings, headaches and other PMT symptoms.

The name and authority of Jesus was above the symptoms, so as far as the Word of God was concerned they had to leave — and they did! Since then I have experienced regular cycles without any pain or complication. What a dramatic difference from my long, heavy, and painful cycles!

Throughout this ministry I have seen many other women receive the same result. Some of these women hadn't ovulated or had a menstrual cycle for a long time — some months, some a couple of years. But by taking authority over the situation their bodies soon responded and these women experienced regular menstrual cycles without pain or complications. It is great to see women rejoice when they experience a menstrual cycle the way God created them to be!

Of course, if you're not experiencing complications with your monthly cycle then begin with any other areas that may require healing. Start somewhere and continue to walk by faith (by the finished work of the Cross) not by sight or appearance, and exercise your authority until your breakthrough is realised.

Two Frequently Asked Questions

Q: *How Often Do I Need To Speak To My Body?*

I do not believe there is a right or wrong way when it comes to how many times you should speak to your body. My intention in writing this book is never to present a formula for you to follow to attain your desired result, because it is not about works or doing something to earn your breakthrough. From both personal experience and from observation, following 'steps' without revelation is not only powerless but also leads to frustration. As we have already discovered, you have already received the victory you needed upon your salvation. Healing is **already** your provision. So you don't exercise authority over your body to get God to do what Jesus has already done! Instead you are exercising your God-given authority over your natural circumstances to put a stop to them outworking in your life, and enabling you to walk in your healing and the fruitfulness that already belongs to you.

When I first received the revelation on the power and authority I had in Jesus, I would exercise authority over my cycles every time I had a concern about it or felt a symptom. I found this kept me focused on the truth in God's Word and not on what the natural circumstances were doing. Initially this was a continual process until my mind was renewed and I saw the condition through the eyes of God's Word and not through my natural understanding. I was determined not to let go of what I believed to be the truth. While it initially took time before I saw change in the natural symptoms (even when I applied this to a sore throat or a common cold), I now see more immediate results.

It can take time to renew our mind and truly believe what Jesus has already done. And it also takes time to learn to not walk by what the natural symptoms or circumstances are doing. It is so easy to give in, but when you continue to walk by faith and exercise authority over the natural situation then changes do begin to take place. I therefore want to encourage you not to become disheartened if you don't see instant results. If after a while however, there are no signs of improvement, then I suggest you seek God and go back to His Word for a fresh revelation.

142

Also one question I would ask is, *do you expect your body to respond when you command it to change?* If you simply speak over your body and hope for the best then you will only be deceiving yourself. You need to know and believe in your heart that you have the same power and authority as Jesus. Say, **'NO!** *Body you are to bow down to the name and authority of Jesus'* and then tell it what to do. I would suggest that you keep focused and continue until you do see change.

Q: Isn't Making Confessions Legalistic?

When you become a Christian you don't have to remind yourself to say the right thing and speak about Jesus do you? No! When your heart has been changed you automatically speak it out. The Bible says that out of the abundance of the heart the mouth speaks. Whatever is coming out of your mouth is usually what is in your heart. Faith is not just mere confession but is a knowing in your spirit (it's believing in Jesus). When you know something you can't help but speak it out! Your conversation simply lines up with what you believe. For this reason if you get into fear about your confession or about saying the wrong thing then it can easily become legalistic.

Confession is not about how many times you pray or speak the Word. Repetition and the number of prayers do not bring the Word to pass. Jesus **has already** paid the price for all sickness in your body. You can't earn or work for it because it is a free gift. We simply need to walk in our inheritance by applying this truth to our daily lives. Remember that God released His power by what He said. His Words framed and fashioned what He desired and the natural realm submitted and responded to His power. We need to remember the power of God's Kingdom is dwelling on the inside of us through the Holy Spirit. We also have God's will, plan and purpose already established in His Word through the work Jesus did on the Cross.

If we want to see this truth become a reality in our life then we need to know, believe and act on the truth, by opening our mouth, and exercising God's power and authority over the natural hindrances and circumstances that are preventing God's plan from being fulfilled in our life. This is not trying to get God to do something for us but is instead about laying hold of what He has already done!

Testimonies

From the time I began sharing this teaching through New Life Ministries there have been many healings. I have received testimonies about cycles becoming regular along with various other healings — babies have been conceived, others saved from threatened miscarriage, and women have conquered premature labour to deliver safely at full term. Many are now walking in victory after learning what Jesus has accomplished for them!

Described on the next few pages are just some of the testimonies I have received.

Increase In Sperm!

My husband and I have been trying to conceive for seven months. Past test results came back with low sperm counts between four-six million, low motility at ten percent and very low testosterone. After looking up information on the Internet and finding the **New Life Ministries** website, my husband and I began praying the conception prayer and speaking to our bodies and believing we would conceive. We began looking to God not the doctors. We had a return visit to the Urologist. My husband's sperm count was 71 million with 60 percent motility! His sperm increased despite the fact that his testosterone was still very low. Thank you Jesus! I am giving God the glory!

Jackie B., USA

The Word Works!

I was particularly interested in the messages regarding taking authority over your body in Jesus' name. When it came time for me to ovulate this month — I decided to try it. I was having some definite pressure on my left side and decided that it was probably the optimal time to do some earnest praying. I put my hand on my left side and began to command my body to ovulate in the name of Jesus Christ — to conceive (I even got so bold as to ask for a girl), and for a healthy implantation and pregnancy and lastly, for a baby with no neurological problems. I immediately felt a release in my side. It was definitely not imagined. The last couple of weeks I have been excited to test, but not over-anxious like I was the month before. Well, to make a long story short — I took a pregnancy test and got a positive result! This whole experience has really let me know in no uncertain terms that God is still very involved in my life.

Wendy T., USA

No Pain!

Ever since I can remember I've had to take painkillers for my period pain. In February this year, I joined the NLM support group meetings and have been learning lots about what God says in His Word about my health, healing, walking by faith, speaking out against what's not of God and generally claiming the victory Christ died to give me over all aspects of my life. So next time my period arrived, I was eager to put into practice the things I'd been learning. I wanted this cycle to be pain free and I resolved to get through it without taking any painkillers, but just through prayer, praise and speaking to my body. When I started to feel the first twinge of pain, I commanded my body to submit to the name of Jesus and for the pain to go away — and that's what it did! The pain went, and it tried to come back a couple of times, but each time I just did the same thing; spoke to my body and accepted the healing that Jesus has given me. The pain left again and I didn't need to take a single painkiller! I always thought period pain was normal and it probably is for a lot of people, but now I know that as a child of God under the New Covenant, I don't have to accept it anymore.

Bronwyn C., Sydney, Australia

Healing Of Premature Labour!

After several IVF treatments, one negative, one chemical, and another cancelled, I then finally conceived. I thought I was on Easy Street until I went in for a normal sonogram at 17 weeks. The doctor informed me my cervix was opening and I would have to have an emergency operation called a cerclage where they sew your cervix shut. He gave me many doom and gloom stats, including that the operation may rupture my membranes and if it didn't, I only had a 50 percent chance of this procedure working. The operation was a success with no ruptured membranes, but I still had the 'it only works 50 percent of the time' speech in my head. I now had to put my faith into practice. I had come too far and worked too hard to let the devil get this victory. I knew that I knew that I knew... like I know my own name, that God had placed this child in my womb. I knew it was His will for me to have this baby. So I started speaking to my cervix and telling it in the name of Jesus to close up. I would speak scriptures that were relevant to my cause... the one that really settled my spirit when I would become afraid was *'this is the confidence we have in approaching God, if we ask ANYTHING according to HIS WILL... HE HEARS US... and if HE hears us, then we shall have what we have asked of Him'!* (**I John 5:14**) I knew it was God's will I have this baby, so when I asked for this pregnancy to be full term, I knew I was praying the will of God. I knew God was listening, and the Word says if He hears us...THEN WE SHALL HAVE WHAT WE HAVE ASKED FOR! I never stopped quoting the Word! Never! I knew it was my daughter's literal lifeline. My daughter was born healthy and full term. In fact when they removed my stitches two weeks before my due date, the doctor said I would probably go into labour immediately. 'That is just the way it is when you have an incompetent cervix'. Guess what... it didn't happen! My daughter was born full term and healthy.

Gina F., Florida, USA

I Am Pregnant!

Nerida's teaching on speaking to your body and taking authority over your body has had a big impact on me. In December I decided to tell my body to have perfect 28-day cycles and conceive in Jesus' name. I had a 28-day cycle in December and in January I also started to speak to my body that 'I am a fertile woman'. This really changed the way I was thinking about myself and in January I conceived.

Gwili H., Canberra, Australia

chapter

12

Infertility to Conception

Too many couples take the conception of their children for granted. They **assume** they will conceive when **they** plan to. For some, conception naturally occurs, while for others no amount of love, money, or medical intervention will bring this desired event to pass. There are numerous complications that can occur in either the husband or wife to prevent them from conceiving and therefore leaving them to suffer with infertility. The medical definition of the term 'infertility' is the failure to conceive after a year of unprotected intercourse. Infertility, or secondary infertility, can also occur in a couple that has previously conceived. Sterility is the term given when conception is impossible due to irreversible problems such as genital abnormalities, disease, poor quality, quantity or immobile sperm, poor quality or quantity of ova (eggs), abnormal ovulation, hormonal imbalances or restrictions caused by surgery.

If you are suffering with any form of infertility or have been told you can't have children then I have good news for you!

Children Are A Blessing

"Behold, children are a heritage of the Lord: and the fruit of the womb is His reward." **Ps 127:3 (NKJV)**

Children are our heritage or our inheritance as children of God. They are a gift, a blessing and a reward from Him. In the 'Foundations' section of this book we discovered that God does not withhold the blessing of children from anyone. So while you may have been diagnosed as infertile and told that you can never have children of your own, don't despair because God's plan is to *'maketh the barren woman to keep house, and to be a joyful mother of children'* (**Ps 113:9 KJV**).

Fruitful By Design

You were not created to be barren, infertile or sterile! If there is something missing in your body it **can** be replaced, if something has been damaged it **can** be restored and if there is a sickness or disease it **can** be removed! Jesus came so that you may have life and life more abundantly (**John 10:10**) and this includes conceiving, giving birth and raising godly children.

When God created the first human beings, Adam and Eve, He blessed them by proclaiming, *'be fruitful and increase in number; fill the earth and subdue it'* (**Gen 1:27–28**). Do you think the Lord would command them to do something that they could not do? God, as part of His perfect plan, created every bone, cell, muscle, tissue and organ, including those in your reproductive system. That means that you were created with everything you need within your body to go forth, be fruitful and multiply.

Some say that this scripture in Genesis was speaking only to Adam and Eve. But there is no way that Adam and Eve alone could fill the earth. Furthermore, if this verse was to be interpreted this way, it implies that God did not intend for anyone else to have children. Of course, we know this isn't true. Adam and Eve were the only people on the earth at the time, so of course it was originally spoken just to them, but this was not meant exclusively for them. God also repeated this same blessing and command to Noah and his sons after the flood (**Gen 9:1**).

Fruitfulness is God's blessing and was intended for all of mankind. His plan is all about increasing — not decreasing. Even under the Old Covenant, when His children were in exile, God's plan was still for them to be fruitful. His plans were not to harm them but to bless them and to give them a hope and a future (**Jer 29:11**).

> *"This is what the LORD Almighty, the God of Israel, says to all those I carried into exile from Jerusalem to Babylon: 'build houses and settle down; plant gardens and eat what they produce. Marry and have sons and daughters; find wives for your sons and give your daughters in marriage, so that they too may have sons and daughters.* **Increase in number there; do not decrease'."**
> **Jer 29: 4–5**

And God has not changed! He still delights in His children increasing in number! He is seeking godly offspring (**Mal 2:15**) with plans to raise up a mighty army to bring glory to Him and to reach the lost in these last days.

Barrenness Came With The Fall

God delights in His children increasing in number! He is NOT the one behind barrenness or loss of the fruit of the womb. Satan is the one behind decrease, loss and lack. He is the thief that comes against the seed of a woman. His plan is for God's children to decrease and suffer from lack and loss in the fruit of the womb.

When Adam and Eve sinned in the Garden of Eden, the blessing of fruitfulness was corrupted. The consequence of their sin introduced sickness, disease and complications (the fruit of sin) and Satan was made god of this world. However, God did not plan to leave the human race in this fallen state. He immediately began to introduce Covenants to bring restoration.

Redeemed From The Curse Of The Law!

Barrenness is listed as one of the curses of the Mosaic Law in **Deuteronomy 28:18**. God never intended His children to be cursed; He only ever wanted them to experience the blessings. Mankind was created perfectly healthy. God created all things to be good (**Gen 1:31**). But due to the fall many couples are now experiencing barrenness or other complications during the conception, pregnancy and birth of children. The enemy has corrupted man's nature and God's perfect plan. So God's blessing of:

- *Provision* was corrupted into *lack*.
- *Prosperity and wealth* was corrupted into *debt and poverty.*
- *Health* was corrupted into *sickness and disease.*
- *Fruitfulness* was corrupted into *barrenness.*

But despite the fact that Satan corrupted God's plan we are not left defenseless. Through Jesus, the price has been fully paid. Jesus redeemed you from the curse of the law, so that it has no legal hold over you any longer. When Jesus was crucified, He nailed all sickness and disease to the Cross. And because infertility and miscarriage are simply different forms of sickness, this means that when Jesus redeemed you from sickness He also redeemed you from **every** complication that can occur in your reproductive organs.

> *"Christ redeemed us from the curse of the law by becoming a curse for us, for it is written: 'cursed is everyone who is hung on a tree'."*
> **Gal 3:13**

You are redeemed from the curse of barrenness and are free to be fertile. You are blessed and free to conceive, carry and give birth to healthy children!

The Blessing Of Fruitfulness

> *"Worship the LORD your God, and His blessing will be on your food and water. I will take away sickness from among you, and* **none will miscarry or be barren** *in your land. I will give you a full life span."* **Ex 23:25–26**

This is God's promise to us — that **none** shall miscarry or be barren. He created us to be blessed and prosperous in the fruit of our wombs.

God promised Abraham and Sarah when they were barren that they would have descendants as numerous as the stars in the sky and as the sands on the seashore. He also promised that **all** of Abraham's descendants would be blessed, prosperous and fruitful. In fact, there are several scriptures in the Old Testament showing God's provision of a blessed and a prosperous womb.

> ... *"because of your father's God, who helps you, because of the Almighty, who blesses you with blessings of the heavens above, blessings of the deep that lies below, **blessings of the breast and womb.**"* **Gen 49:25**

> *"All these blessings will come upon you and accompany you if you obey the LORD your God: you will be blessed in the city and blessed in the country. **The fruit of your womb will be blessed**, and the crops of your land and the young of your livestock — the calves of your herds and the lambs of your flocks."* **Deut 28:2–4**

> *"You will be blessed more than any other people; **none of your men or women will be childless,** nor any of your livestock without young The LORD will keep you free from every disease"* **Deut 7:14–15** (see also **Deut 30:9** and **28:11**).

> *"You will eat the fruit of your labour; blessings and prosperity will be yours. Your wife will be like a fruitful vine within your house; your sons will be like olive shoots around your table. Thus is the man blessed who fears the LORD."* **Ps 128:2–4**

If you have been told that you can't have children, then renew your mind with the truth in God's Word until it becomes alive and personal to you, and you know beyond doubt that you **will** conceive, carry and give birth to healthy children.

As I have already revealed in the 'Foundations' section of this book, as a New Covenant believer the Old Testament blessings given to Abraham and to his descendants are still relevant to us today. God promised Abraham that all the peoples of the earth would be blessed through him. We know as a New Covenant believer that *'if you belong to Christ, then you are Abraham's seed, and heirs according to the promise'* therefore we are heirs to the very same blessings (see **Gal 3:6, 9** and **29**).

Consider also that if God's plan was different for the New Covenant believer, then that would mean that God had changed His mind and will for mankind. But we know that God does not change (**Mal 3:6**). He is the same today and He will remain the same forever (**Heb 13:8**). In addition, as believers in Jesus Christ, we have a better Covenant based on better promises than the Old Covenant (**Heb 8:6**). In fact, Jesus fulfilled all the promises and blessings in the Old Covenant, reversed the curse and paid the price for all sickness and disease including those that affect our fruitfulness. The price **has been paid in full**. Therefore, the same blessings of health, wealth and fruitfulness available to those under the Old Covenant remain the same for us today!

Blockages To Fruitfulness

Now you know the provision in God's Word for your children, you will need to meditate on these truths until God's Word becomes your final authority regardless of any negative diagnosis, or physical condition in your body. Know that you don't have to live 'under' any condition or natural symptom! You have been given everything you need in life through Christ so you can exercise authority and walk in your inheritance of healing and fruitfulness.

When I was trying to conceive my first child, the Lord revealed to me that the size or severity of any condition is not an issue because Jesus paid the price for **all** sickness and disease. So it didn't matter if I was facing a sore throat, infertility or something I considered to be more serious, the size of the condition was only in my natural mind and understanding. By judging the possibility of healing based on the severity of Shaun's sterile condition, I was exalting the condition to a place greater than the power of God and His Word. Instead, I needed to bring the condition into **submission** to the truth of the Word, which said that 'by Jesus' stripes Shaun was healed' and that 'I would not miscarry or be barren'.

I needed to renew my mind until this truth in God's Word found place in my heart and I believed I would have my own biological children. And true to His Word, God's healing power brought restoration to Shaun's body and enabled us to have four children within four and a half years.

Your Age Is Not An Issue!

While we are in this world, God says we are not of this world (**2 Cor 6:17**). We need to remember that Jesus has overcome the world for us. He has deprived it of power to harm us (**1 John 5:18 AMP**). Regardless of what your situation is, you do not have to be subject to the same concerns as the women of this world. A great example of this is the concern that a person's age creates in their desire for children. While medical science has found that a woman's age can be a determining factor in whether she can conceive, and that the older a woman is when she conceives the more chance there is of complications in the pregnancy and with the health of the baby, the reality is that age is no barrier when it comes to God's Word and His healing power.

If you are faced with a medical prognosis suggesting conception is greatly reduced due to your age, know that the truth in God's Word is available to **all** who believe in Him. God says you can be kept fresh and green and bear fruit into old age.

> *"The righteous will flourish like a palm tree, they will grow like a cedar of Lebanon; planted in the house of the Lord, they will flourish in the courts of our God. They **will still bear fruit in old age, they will stay fresh and green**, proclaiming, the Lord is upright; He is my Rock, and there is no wickedness in Him."*
> **Ps 92:12–15**

I have a collection of newspaper articles that show women in their 50s and 60s who have conceived and given birth to healthy children. If mature women in the world can conceive then how much more so can God's blood-bought Covenant Children! There are also many examples in the Bible that speak of mature women giving birth. Both Abraham and Sarah were past the age of childbearing but they received strength (God's miracle working power) that enabled them to conceive because they judged God faithful (**Heb 11:11**). Sarah said, *'who would have said to Abraham that Sarah would nurse children? Yet I have borne him a son in his old age'* (**Gen 21:7**). Regardless of their age and natural circumstances Abraham and Sarah were fully persuaded that God would do what He said He would do (**Rom 4:20–21**).

Elizabeth was another case of a woman conceiving in her old age and overcoming barrenness. The Bible says of Elizabeth and Zechariah, *'they had no children, because Elizabeth was barren; and they were both well along in years'* (**Luke 1:7**). But just like Sarah, the life and power of God overcame Elizabeth's natural circumstances and she gave birth to a son!

"Even Elizabeth your relative is going to have a child in her old age, and she who was said to be barren is in her sixth month. For nothing is impossible with God." **Luke 1:37**

If you are concerned about your age affecting your ability to conceive or have healthy children, then spend time meditating on the truth for a personal revelation or until you see your life through the eyes of what is in the Word and not through your natural eyes and understanding. You must come to a point of agreement with what the Word says and not rely on your natural circumstances. Worrying about your age and your physical condition will keep you focused on the natural realm and the facts, but faith keeps you connected to God's healing power and what you have received through the finished work of the Cross.

Absolutely nothing is impossible with God and no Word from God shall be without power! God is not a respecter of persons. This means that no matter what your age or your condition, if you believe in Jesus and the truth in His Word then you already have everything you need in Christ to overcome the natural so you can conceive, carry and give birth to your own healthy biological children!

You Are Not Alone!

"He settles the barren woman in her home as a happy mother of children. Praise the LORD." **Ps 113:9**

No matter what trials you experience in life they are not uncommon to man (**1 Cor 10:13**). That means somewhere in this world someone else has already experienced what you are facing right now. You are therefore not alone in the struggle of infertility. There have been many couples who have gone down this road before. There were many couples in the Bible who were unable to conceive. They didn't have the medical technology that we do today to diagnose or help them in their struggle. As it turned out they didn't need it because they went to God and He intervened. In fact, every godly couple who cried out to God for children received the answer to their prayers. Their children all grew up to be great men and women of God who accomplished great things for His kingdom!

- Abraham and Sarah — parents of Isaac (**Heb 11:11–12, Rom 4:16–24**).

- Isaac and Rebekah — parents of Jacob and Esau
  (**Gen 25:19–26**).
- Jacob, Rachel and Leah — parents of the 12 Tribes of Israel
  (**Gen 29:30–31:1–3, Gen 30:20–25, Gen 30:17,22,
  Gen 35:23–26**).
- Elkanah and Hannah — parents of Samuel (**1 Sam 1:1–28**).
- Zechariah and Elizabeth — parents of John the Baptist
  (**Luke 1:5– 20, 1:36–37**).
- The Shunamite Woman (**2 Kings 4:8–17**).
- Manoah's wife — mother of Samson (**Judges 13**).

God does not change. He always remains the same! The only thing that has changed are the times we live in. God does not show favouritism (**Rom 2:11**), which means the same breakthrough is available for you today! As we have already seen, if you are in Christ then healing and fruitfulness is already your inheritance. You can exercise authority to walk in that health and be delivered from what is preventing conception so you can go forth and multiply!

Through this ministry I hear many testimonies in which couples were told there were no medical options left for them to conceive. Whether it was polycystic ovaries, endometriosis, blocked or damaged tubes, non-ovulatory cycles, unbalanced hormone levels, antibodies or no sperm, none of these conditions were an obstacle for the healing power of God. When these couples put their trust in God and the finished work of the Cross, they experienced their breakthrough and they conceived their children.

Relying On Natural Abilities

When trying to conceive a baby it is very easy to get caught up in trying to pinpoint the perfect time for conception. When I was trying to conceive my first child I was constantly charting temperatures for ovulation, and trying to plan the perfect time to conceive. The Lord revealed to me, however, that my desire for a baby had come before the desire to love and follow Him. I had to let go, lay it down and give my all to Him. It was shortly after I did this that I conceived! I later discovered that I ovulated much later than normal. Therefore, all of my planning and charting had been in vain!

There are many methods and self-help procedures available that are meant to 'assist' with conception such as herbs, lotions, potions, diets, timing of intercourse and charting temperatures, just to name a few. While there is nothing really wrong with planning or charting temperatures, it can become obsessive. God created the female cycle for a reason and to know your cycle and the changes in your body may be helpful. However, if you become obsessed with pinpointing days for conception, then you need to be careful. In doing this you are actually trying to control the situation, thereby placing more faith in your efforts and what you can do than in God and His provision. If this is your current struggle, then you need to take your focus off trying to conceive and instead strive to enter into a place of rest, by trusting in God's provision for your breakthrough.

I encourage you, therefore, not to put all of your focus on the fertile time. A close friend of mine had been trying to conceive for over a year and discovered from plotting temperature charts that she had a non-ovulatory cycle. This was also confirmed by her doctor. She stopped all her charting, timing and planning and placed her trust in the Lord and what His Word said. She knew it was God's will for her to have children so she took authority over her body, commanded healing and for her body to ovulate and for conception to take place. Her healing was made manifest shortly after and she now has a beautiful daughter.

I have lost count of how many women have testified that they finally conceived when they had stopped striving, and rested on the finished work of the Cross. Some even said they had only been intimate maybe once that month and not around their fertile time. God is so much bigger than the 'perfect time' and it is He who gives us the strength to conceive seed. Therefore, *'trust in the Lord with **all** your heart! Lean not on your own understanding. In **all** your ways acknowledge Him and He will make your paths straight'* (**Prov 3:5–6**).

Faith And Pregnancy Tests

Another area where women can become consumed and obsessed is in using off the shelf pregnancy testing kits. These types of tests are not always accurate, so there will be times when you need to go by what is in your spirit and not by the results of a test. If you are **fully persuaded** (based upon a personal revelation, not upon natural hope) that you are pregnant, even when the test says negative, then keep standing on what the Word says and don't allow a natural test to discourage you. You may have conceived at a later date than you realised and it is too early to detect. I experienced this first hand with my second child, Aidan. I just knew beyond doubt in my spirit that I had conceived. However both a urine test administered by my G.P. and a blood test came up negative. I did not let this discourage me, so I continued to walk by what I had in my spirit and not by the results of these tests, and a subsequent blood test revealed what I already knew — a positive result!

If your period is definitely well overdue and you have had a couple of negative test results and you are not sure that you are pregnant then I would suggest you pray for godly wisdom on what is happening. If there is an imbalance in your body and not a pregnancy then you need to exercise authority over your body and 'call' the period in.

There could also be another reason for delay in your menstrual cycle. I have seen women so desperate to be pregnant that they unknowingly submitted to the imbalance in their body because they had convinced themselves that they were pregnant. Some went without a menstrual cycle for up to six months until they realised the truth of the situation. Infertility can be a painful journey and it is so easy to lose yourself and some common sense in the process. I cannot stress enough the importance of developing your personal relationship with the Father, so He can lead you by His Spirit in each situation so you will know what to do to walk in your victory.

I have also ministered to many women who were in fear of taking a pregnancy test due to the amount of negative ones they had experienced in the past. Remember, fear is not faith. It is the opposite of faith and the two never work together. If you want to overcome this fear you need to face it head on. Take the test, overcoming your fear through the Word of God.

Further, do not place your hopes for conception in any symptoms you may experience. Just because a woman may experience symptoms of pregnancy, it doesn't necessarily mean that she is actually pregnant. Pregnancy symptoms for some women can be similar to menstrual cycle symptoms, so if we place all our hope in the symptoms and then have a negative pregnancy test result, we may become discouraged and lose sight of the truth in God's Word.

Generally speaking, pregnancy symptoms don't usually appear until a few weeks into the pregnancy anyway. In fact, some women don't experience any pregnancy symptoms at all, even though they are actually pregnant, so relying on feeling some kind of symptom to 'prove' you are pregnant is not helpful. Even while pregnant with my twins, I didn't feel pregnant until my belly began to grow!

For these reasons we need to be careful not to put our trust in symptoms or on how we feel at the time. We need to stop walking by sight, feelings and appearances, and fix our eyes on Jesus and on what He has done. And if we continue to do what the Word says and be anxious for nothing then God's supernatural peace, which transcends all understanding will guard our hearts and minds in Him (**Phil 4:6–8**)!

Conception With Medical Help?

Let me first state that I have nothing against the medical profession. One of my closest friends who is on our ministry team in **New Life Ministries** is a medical doctor. There have also been many women involved in this ministry who have medical backgrounds. What I do want to point out though is that medical science can't do everything. I have ministered to many men and women who had been told there was nothing medical science could do to help them. But while some things are impossible with man, all things are possible with God!

Some of these people I mentioned had parts of their reproductive systems removed through surgery, or had deformed organs **but** they now have children! Medical science cannot accomplish this, let alone explain it! While they can treat symptoms and sometimes cure sickness, they can't form a new womb or create living tissue from dead tissue. But God's healing power can!

You may have complications or parts missing in your body and you may be finding it hard to believe God's Word for your family. If you believe you need medical intervention, it's important that you are aware that while doctors have the ability to treat your symptoms they can't do everything. In the gospel of **Mark**, we see a perfect example of a woman who had spent all she had on doctors and experienced no lasting help.

*"And a woman was there who had been subject to bleeding for twelve years. **She had suffered a great deal under the care of many doctors and had spent all she had; yet instead of getting better she grew worse.** When she heard about Jesus, she came up behind Him in the crowd and touched His cloak, because she thought, 'if I just touch His clothes, I will be healed.' Immediately her bleeding stopped and she felt in her body that she was freed from her suffering. At once Jesus realised that power had gone out from Him. He turned around in the crowd and asked, 'Who touched my clothes?' 'You see the people crowding against you,' His disciples answered, 'and yet you can ask, Who touched me?' But Jesus kept looking around to see who had done it. Then the woman, knowing what had happened to her, came and fell at His feet and, trembling with fear, told Him the whole truth. He said to her, '**daughter, your faith has healed you. Go in peace and be freed from your suffering'.**"* **Mark 5:25–34**

This woman had placed all her hope in the doctors, and in the end they still couldn't help her. She had already spent all that she had and instead of getting better, she grew worse. In the natural, some sicknesses have no cure, so doctors can only treat the symptoms; they often cannot provide lasting help. When it comes to fertility challenges, some may find themselves losing sight of the power of God and the truth of His Word. It is impossible to focus on what is happening in the natural and focus on the spiritual at the same time. You either look to God and believe His Word or look to your circumstances and believe the diagnosis. So if you want real help, just like the woman with the issue of blood, go to Jesus so you can be free from your suffering and be made whole!

*"This is what the LORD says: 'cursed is the one who trusts in man, who depends on flesh for his strength and whose heart turns away from the LORD. He will be like a bush in the wastelands; he will not see prosperity when it comes. He will dwell in the parched places of the desert, in a salt land where no one lives. **But blessed is the man who trusts in the LORD, whose confidence is in Him**. He will be like a tree planted by the water that sends out its roots by the stream. It does not fear when heat comes; its leaves are always green. It has no worries in a year of drought **and never fails to bear fruit'.**"* **Jer 17:5–8**

Because we have many medical options available to us, it is easy just to go and seek help. However, we need to remember that as believers and followers of Jesus Christ there is another way. We don't have to run to the doctors, seek treatments or use medications every time we are sick. We can learn to experience healing that we have received from Jesus — the living Word of God.

I made this decision a long time ago. I'd had enough of always running to the doctors and spending my money on medications. Equally frustrating was the fact that for many of my ailments there was no known cure or medication available. Having had enough, I began to walk by faith (by what I had received through the finished work of the Cross) in different areas of my health. I began with headaches and allergies and then worked my way through the various complaints and sicknesses, such as an under-active thyroid, anaemia, bronchitis, viral asthma, headaches, and allergies. I am now in a place where I do not accept **any** sickness into my body. At the first sign or symptom, I resist them and the symptoms leave.

You need to be honest with God and with yourself on what you can believe. If you want healing without intervention but can't truly believe for that, then you may not be able to walk it out by applying God's Word to your circumstances, and you will only be wasting your time. Go to the Word for a deeper personal revelation on healing. If your decision not to go to the doctor is based on fear of a diagnosis or fear of medical intervention this may only prolong your situation. Fear is the opposite of faith and you can't walk by faith (by the finished work of the Cross) when fearful.

Because modern medicine does not have all the answers, many go down alternative pathways and seek different counsel, such as alternative and holistic medicines and practices in search of an answer. These can often leave an open door for you to become confused and discouraged.

"You are wearied with your many counsels and plans."
Is 47:13 (AMP)

Infertility can be a long journey of discouragement, which often leaves a couple feeling emotionally, and often financially, drained. However, whatever report you have received concerning the state of your body, it does not have to be your final report. What has been diagnosed may be factual but you can't lose if you go to God, because those who look to

Him will never be put to shame (**Ps 34:5**). Be careful therefore not to put your trust in a diagnosis, report, scan, or test result, because they will keep your focus in the natural realm and can destroy your hope. You need to guard what you allow doctors (or anybody else for that matter) to speak into your life. A diagnosis from a doctor can give a name to what may be affecting your ability to conceive, but you don't have to submit to that report because it isn't the final authority! Instead use this to your advantage and specifically exercise authority over your situation. Allow the truth that is in God's Word to be your final authority! Begin to walk in victory by applying that truth and exercising authority over what is holding you back from conceiving and from going forth and multiplying!

Conception Prayer

I thank You Father that Your Son Jesus Christ bore all my sickness and disease and carried all my pains on the Cross and by His stripes I am healed.

This means I have been healed from infertility and of any sickness or disease that causes it! Therefore, body, I command you in the name of Jesus: conceive and be pregnant! Every part of you is to come in line with the Word of God. You will function efficiently, the way you were created to: because you are fearfully and wonderfully made.

I also pray for good solid attachment of my baby to the uterine wall (not in the fallopian tubes), and for my baby to grow perfectly, be nourished, and protected for the full nine months (40 weeks) and to be kept free from all harm.

Lord, I give You all the glory for my healing and for my baby.

Let it be done to me according to Your Word!

AMEN!

chapter 13

Waiting for the Promise

Throughout the previous chapters we have discovered that God has created us to be fruitful and that He has already provided everything we need through the finished work of the Cross, so we can apply this truth to see our breakthrough. However, for some it can be a process to learn how to walk this truth out in their daily lives. It can take time to overcome wrong thinking, break strongholds of any negative diagnosis or bad report, and renew your mind with the truth in God's Word. In the same way that it takes time for a seed to grow after being planted, to develop roots and grow into a mature fruit-bearing plant, God's Word needs to take root in your heart and go from information to revelation, and become personal to you.

God's Timing?

I have heard many say that God is waiting until they are ready, or until they have grown or have learnt something before He will allow them to have children. Let me tell you, this is definitely not scriptural. A lot of people find God through infertility or miscarriage but that doesn't mean that God caused or used it. In fact, He will work in spite of it. What Satan intended to harm and destroy, the Lord will take and work for good.

Often when faced with a desperate situation, people call upon God as a kind of last resort. But we don't have to wait until we are desperate to seek God. We can find Him anytime. We should seek Him for who He is and for a deeper relationship with Him, not just turn to Him when we face an adverse situation.

So, does God's timing play a part when it comes to the conception of our children? Do we need to sit and wait until God is ready to bless us?

When it comes to the finished work of the Cross and what Jesus purchased for us, I personally don't believe in 'God's timing'. This is because it would mean you would be waiting for God to do what He has already done!

We know that when God created Adam and Eve, He created them with everything they needed to conceive and bring forth healthy children. He **blessed them** and told them to go forth and to multiply. Adam and Eve did not need to wait for God's timing to conceive — they already had everything resident inside them to achieve this.

God didn't create us with reproductive organs and then command us to come to Him and ask for a child every time we wanted one. **No! He made us fruitful** — He created us to reproduce! Birds and animals reproduce without waiting on God, plants as well, so we can too! Remember, we don't have to come and ask God for what **He has already** provided for us. Children ARE His plan and purpose for mankind. If you are struggling in this area you need to understand — it is NOT GOD WITHHOLDING FROM YOU. God is not making you sick — or preventing you from having children!

As we have already discovered, when Adam and Eve ate of the tree of the 'knowledge' of good and evil, in the Garden of Eden their eyes were opened and they knew evil. *Knowledge* means to know by observing, calculating and **experiencing**. Up until that point they only knew good. We know that the result of the fall in the Garden meant that the world was now in a fallen state (it was now cursed for Adam's sake — meaning as a result of what Adam had done). Satan was also made god of this world.

God's Solution

In the previous chapter we saw that many in the Old Testament who were struggling to conceive prayed to God for children — and EVERY godly couple who prayed received their answer! When God commanded Moses to write down the law we find several scriptures showing the PROVISION FOR CHILDREN! (i.e. **Ex 23;25–26**, and **Deut 28:1–15**).

We have seen that God never changes, so all the blessings of health and fruitfulness provided by God to the Israelites also belong to us as well. They are still God's will, plan and purpose for mankind! So even though the children of Israel under the law lived in a fallen world, God made His purpose very clear that children were still His plan and purpose.

We Have A Better Covenant!

One thing we need to remember — God dealt with people differently under the Old Covenant because they were under the law (working to earn righteousness). As New Covenant believers we shouldn't be looking to how those under the Old Covenant responded or how they came to God. The old has gone! Under the Old Covenant they were slaves or servants. But under the New Covenant we **are children** — joint heirs with Christ — seated in heavenly places **with Him**!

When Jesus died on the Cross, He paid the price for EVERYTHING that came into the world as the result of sin and the fall. Satan is still roaming the earth as the god of this world (for a time) and the consequence of the fall is still at work, and this is why sickness and disease is still operating on the earth. But, praise God, through the work of the Cross JESUS DISARMED IT ALL! He deprived it of power to harm us! He bore it ALL on His body, and He became our substitute. So ANYONE who looks to the Cross LIVES! We do not have to continue to be bitten by this fallen world and the effects of the curse of the law. If we partake of the work of the Cross we can overcome and learn how to walk in victory over what we may experience! Isn't that exciting?!

Through Jesus, God has made the provision for our healing. And this includes everything that can cause or contribute to infertility and miscarriage. We are still blessed to go forth and to multiply!

We know that when Jesus ascended to heaven — He SAT DOWN! His work was complete! We don't need to pray and ask God for what He has already provided because it is FINISHED! This means infertility and miscarriage and everything that causes it is FINISHED!

Children **are** God's plan, purpose and will for all of mankind. That never changes. You can see evidence of this all around the world. People who are not even in a relationship with God are conceiving and having children, tragically some of them unwanted and terminated, but they are fruitful nonetheless. These people are doing what God created mankind to do — be fruitful. This is how it is meant to be and how our bodies are meant to work.

The causes of infertility, sterility, miscarriage and pregnancy problems are many and varied, but remember, Jesus has already paid the price for ANYTHING and EVERYTHING holding us back from conceiving, carrying and giving birth to healthy children! So you can clearly see that God's timing has nothing whatsoever to do with conception. Jesus is sitting at the right hand of the Father — WAITING FOR YOU — to go and possess EVERYTHING He died to give to you!

- He gave us His Word (He sent forth His Word and healed you), where we find knowledge of who we are in Christ and what we have already inherited as a believer.
- He disarmed the devil.
- He disarmed all sickness and disease.
- He gave you His power and authority (so you can exercise that authority over anything preventing your victory).
- He gave you power over all the power of the enemy (**Luke 10:19**).
- He poured His Spirit in you (His indwelling resurrection life and power (see **Acts 1:8** and **Rom 8:11**)).
- His Spirit will also comfort you, strengthen you, guide you into all truth, warn you of things to come and lead you into victory!

What more do you need?!

If you are waiting for God to do something you will be waiting a very long time. I meet couples who have been waiting for years for God to bless them with a child. When they finally lay hold of this truth and apply the finished work of the Cross in every area of their lives barrenness is broken forever, and I end up getting phone calls and emails from those **same**

couples asking me how they can stop their fruitfulness because they now have too many children!

So what are you waiting for? GO FORTH AND MULTIPLY!

Where Is Your Focus?

The desire for children is natural and for a woman it can be woven into the very fabric of her being. When this natural desire is hindered, it can be devastating. **Proverbs 30:15–16** says that the barren womb is never satisfied. And it was never meant to be because God never created the womb to be barren! Facing fertility challenges and trying to conceive can be emotionally draining and often confusing. It's especially important that at these times we remember what God's Word says about the provision of children and blessings of the fruit of the womb. We also need to continue to meditate on this truth to set us free from the lies of the enemy and from how we react to the strength of the natural circumstances. If you are consumed with the desire for children it can control your life. So you will need to address this issue and change your focus from the natural circumstances to the truth in God's Word so that the desire will no longer be all consuming.

I have ministered to many women who have been so consumed with the desire for children that their life, marriage and relationship with God had lost all meaning. There can be such an enormous grief and a sense of loss associated with infertility. These are very real emotions yet if you don't allow the truth of God's Word to be established in your heart then you may not come to know the truth that will set you free. If your heart is not in the right place and your focus is not on God, it will be hard to break out of this cycle.

When I was trying to conceive, all of my energy was taken by my desire for children. My time in prayer was solely focused on this and I was consumed with trying to pinpoint the perfect time to conceive. I knew my cycle intimately. In hindsight, if I had spent that same time and energy getting to know the Lord as intimately as my cycle, I would have been a different person. My desire for a baby had become an idol. I had been serving something other than God. I was serving myself and my own plans and I became trapped and enslaved by my desire to conceive.

> *"You shall not make for yourself **an idol in the form of anything** in heaven above or on the earth beneath or in the waters below. You shall not bow down to them or worship them."* **Ex 20:4–5**

Idol worship (idolatry) is not just the worship of foreign gods but **anything** you worship or are focused on instead of God. It is therefore important not to let the desire for a baby (or for other things) come before the desire to know and serve God. There is nothing wrong with knowing how your body works and what your cycle is doing, but if you know your cycle more intimately than you know the Lord or if you are consumed with charting, timing, planning and pinpointing the perfect time for conception, then like me, your desire for a baby has become an idol.

> … *"but the worries of this life, the deceitfulness of wealth and **the desires for other things** come in and choke the Word, making it unfruitful."* **Mark 4:19–20**

Jesus said that any worries, concerns or desires can choke the Word and make it unfruitful. They are like weeds or thorns that grow up beside the Word causing you to let go of what it says and this can also choke the awareness of God's presence and peace in your life. If this is happening in your life then make a decision to stop striving in your own strength, and seek God first by obeying His commandment to *'love the Lord your God with all your heart, soul, mind and strength'* (**Mark 12:30–31**).

Overcoming Discouragement

Grief, doubt, fear, discouragement and feelings of inadequacy are all normal human emotions that may be experienced from time to time. While we don't ignore these feelings and emotions we can choose not to be governed by them. Initially this may be a constant battle until we learn how to walk by the truth in God's Word and not be subject to what our natural feelings and emotions are dictating to us.

The Apostle Paul instructed Timothy to *'fight the good fight of the faith'* (**1 Tim 6:12**). There is no doubt about it, faith can appear like a fight especially when you are trying to conceive and a menstrual cycle begins. I know the pain of an empty womb and the prospect of never having children. It's a pain that will not be easily forgotten. Initially for me, the most trying time while going through this journey was when my menstrual cycle began. I would be consumed by disappointment, failure, inadequacy, and grief. At first, all I would hear in my mind were the doctor's words that **'it was medically impossible for us to conceive a child'** instead of God's Words that said **'I would not be barren'**. Any other time I was able to stand firm on what God had said. However, at the commencement of each cycle, because I had looked to the natural, I lost sight of God's Word. Each month felt like I was on a roller coaster ride. I was living my life mainly by feelings and what I saw in the natural rather than what I knew to be the truth in the Word. Then the Lord challenged me to give up my struggle and trust Him unconditionally. As a result I made the decision to no longer live by my emotions and by what I could see in the natural realm. The Word said I was not barren and I was a joyful mother of children so that was the report I was going to believe. I had to continue to look at what the Word said about my situation and not turn away from that. This was a powerful transformation for me.

I felt a weight lift off when I gave up my struggle because I came to that place of rest. I felt a freedom, peace and joy that I had not known before. From that moment on my cycles no longer moved me from what I believed. I was able to overcome the fear and doubts and experience God's rest and peace instead. My desire for a baby was still there but my desire to serve and follow God was stronger. It was not long after this that I conceived.

How are you coping? How are you feeling? Where is God? Where is your focus? Like me you may need to make the decision to stop striving in your own strength. You may trust God with your life but can you trust Him with your womb? Remember, no matter what you go through God is for you, not against you. Cast all your pain, hurt, doubt, confusion, and discouragement upon Him so that you can be free to do what He has called you to do, to live a life of peace, fulfilment and joy.

I have noticed that many women I have ministered to have conceived shortly after giving up their struggle to conceive. When you choose to let go and place your desire into God's hands, the desire will no longer be all consuming. The desire will still be there but it will no longer take over your life!

The Empty Womb Versus The Pregnant Womb

It is difficult when you are trying to conceive and you are constantly faced with women who are pregnant. It can be even harder to cope when some of those pregnancies were unplanned. The pain of facing fertility challenges is real and to have pregnant women around you can only emphasise your own emptiness.

When I was trying to conceive I found that at first I had to force myself to make the decision to be excited every time I heard the news of someone else conceiving. I would speak God's Word for my situation and confess, 'it is my turn next'. This soon came naturally from my heart.

No matter what the situation, we have no right to harbour any ill feeling towards any woman. Who are we to judge who should or shouldn't be blessed with a child? I wouldn't want anyone to experience the heartache of an empty womb. It is a painful experience. What an awesome blessing it is for **any woman** to receive the gift of a new life. So, how much more of a blessing will it be when you experience it for yourself?

> *"Be still before the LORD and wait patiently for Him; do not fret when men [or women] succeed in their ways...but those who hope in the LORD will inherit the land [will inherit the promise!]."*
> **Ps 37:7,9**

Generally speaking, when women struggle with others conceiving it is because they don't know or understand God's plan for their own life. If you struggle in this area, remind yourself of God's Word and allow Him to help you to turn your weaknesses into your strengths. While it still may come as a shock when you hear of others conceiving, if you let the Lord help you through this, then you will be able to grow in the fruits of the spirit (*love, peace, joy, patience, long suffering and self control* **Gal 5:22**). Our God is faithful and He will help you every step of the way. You only need to ask for His help. His yoke is easy and His burden is light.

Something else which can make coping harder when you are trying to conceive, is when those who don't understand your journey make inconsiderate comments. Women who haven't experienced infertility or miscarriage will not understand your pain, so you can't hold them accountable when they take their own pregnancies for granted, or are inconsiderate towards you. There will always be someone who will say the wrong thing (whether intentionally or not). While you are not able to control what is said or done by others, you **can** control the way you react. You need to learn not to take things to heart but instead work through the pain by forgiving those who have offended you. Unforgiveness will always end in envy, resentment or bitterness and will prevent you from walking in love, consequently hindering you from walking in God's peace and joy.

Love Others As Yourself!

I have personally found that what has helped me in my journey is to pray and support someone else in their journey. This is what we encourage in our meetings and in our online support groups. I have found that those who are able to take the focus off themselves and pray for someone else have discovered how to hear God's voice and leading for others, which in turn enables them to eventually hear and be led by the Lord for their own lives. I have found that as I have received something to share with someone else, that the same 'word of encouragement' has blessed and helped me in my journey.

Strengthen Yourself In The Lord

One thing that saddens me in this ministry is when I see believers pull back from their relationship with the Lord. If you are struggling in your relationship with the Lord or are finding it difficult to trust Him, then renew your mind with the truth that **God is good all the time!** He is not withholding anything from you that Jesus has already purchased and what He has already established in His Word. If you stop fellowshipping with Him it will only prolong your situation, and the pain and emptiness you are feeling. God is not your enemy; He is for you, not against you, which means He is on your side!

> *"I WILL bless the Lord at all times; His praise shall continually be in my mouth."* **Ps 34:1 (AMP)**

King David, who wrote this psalm, is a great example to us because he knew how to strengthen and encourage himself in the Lord in tough times (**1 Sam 30:6**). He constantly meditated on and reminded himself of who God is. He often said of the Lord: 'He is my fortress, my tower of strength, my refuge in times of trouble'. The main reason why David was chosen as King over all of Israel and over all his brothers was because he had a heart after the Lord.

I encourage you to run to God and spend time with Him, getting to know Him for who He is. Remind yourself of all the attributes and benefits of God; He has forgiven all your sins and has healed all your diseases (**Ps 103:1–3**). Meditate on the truth of who He is. When you know the truth you will realise that God is on your side and that you have already been given everything you need in life to experience your breakthrough. So go forth and multiply!

PART III
The Pregnancy

chapter 14

Pregnancy
— *a Time of Blessing*

Pregnancy is meant to be a great experience, full of the joy of bringing forth a new life. However, there can be many side effects, discomforts and complications that can rob you of this blessing. I see so many women needlessly accepting the discomforts of pregnancy such as morning sickness, nausea, mood swings or blood pressure problems simply because they assume it's all part of the package. But this couldn't be further from the truth! **Isaiah 53:4–5** tells us that Jesus took ALL our sicknesses on the Cross and by His stripes we are healed! As we have been discovering throughout this book, the complete work that Jesus did on the Cross set us free from **all** forms of sickness, pain and disease, and this includes those that manifest in pregnancy.

I have ministered to many women who have felt it was easier to endure the discomforts during their pregnancy because they felt it would require too much energy to exert their authority, especially those who were feeling too unwell to do anything. However, **Hebrews 6:11–23** instructs us not to be lazy because faith, patience and endurance inherit the promises. Additionally, **James 2:17 (AMP)** says that faith without works (actions to back up what you believe) is inoperative and powerless. If you want to see a change in your situation, then you need to exercise your authority over the circumstances so that you can walk in the provision that is already

fixix

yours through Christ. Remember always that in Jesus Christ you are more than a conqueror **(Rom 8:37)** and that you can do **all** things in Him when you draw from His strength **(Phil 4:13)**.

When you first begin to walk by the truth in God's Word on healing, and exercise your authority over the situation it may seem a constant battle against the symptoms. Nevertheless if you continue to persevere and do what the Word says in spite of what is happening in the sense realm you will soon experience victory.

You will need to know how to walk by faith (in the finished work of the Cross) and exercise your authority in the areas you want to overcome. It is more beneficial to do this before you conceive than it is when you are pregnant, because once pregnant you can feel vulnerable due to mixed emotions and hormonal changes in your body. This in turn can leave you feeling emotionally fragile and weakened. This doesn't change your position in Christ or what you have already inherited as a believer, but it can affect your ability to see and apply this truth when challenged.

There were some minor things I endured during my first pregnancy because I was more focused on preparing for the delivery. But for my second pregnancy, I was more active in exercising my authority. Even so, there were still things I tolerated. By the time I was ready to enter my third pregnancy I was determined not to tolerate anything that I had accepted in my previous pregnancies. I prepared by meditating on the finished work of the Cross to remain focused on the truth and by exercising authority over sickness and disease in every other area of life.

During the very early stages of the first trimester of my third pregnancy, I began to suffer heartburn (this was probably due to carrying twins), something I had experienced in the last trimester in my previous two pregnancies. During my first two pregnancies I had tolerated it, but this time I made the decision to exercise my authority over it once and for all to obtain the breakthrough. At first it was a battle, having to daily overcome the symptoms but in a short period of time I experienced victory. From that point on, every time the heartburn symptoms tried to return I would exercise authority over them and command the acid to remain in my stomach. The symptoms would wane and my oesophagus would go numb. During my first two pregnancies (in the last trimester) I would eat smaller meals and refrain from drinking liquids after eating to help keep the heartburn at bay. By my third pregnancy I could drink and eat normally throughout the whole pregnancy without any discomfort.

I was challenged throughout all of my pregnancies, but I can honestly say that I experienced great pregnancies each time. But while my third pregnancy was more challenging physically due to carrying twins, it was definitely my healthiest and most enjoyable of the three. I feel this was mainly due to not accepting what I experienced as my lot in life, but rather exercising authority over the symptoms to lay hold of what Jesus had purchased for me. I also believed that pregnancy was meant to be a blessing and I wanted to enjoy every day of that blessing!

During part of the first trimester in my second pregnancy, with my son Aidan, I experienced fatigue. So in preparation for my third pregnancy, I specifically covered this area and learnt to draw from God's strength. I took things easy but by no means was I fatigued. I was amazed after discovering I was carrying twins! One of the first comments made by my obstetrician when he discovered I was having twins was that I must have been very sick and tired due to the double load on my body. The truth is I had not experienced any part of that at all. The only thing I did experience was an endless appetite!

I learnt that God doesn't bless us with children then leave us on our own. He anoints us to carry, deliver and care for them. Once you receive the revelation of His grace and favour you will find pregnancy and life in general much simpler, as you rely on God's power instead of your own strength and ability.

Hormones

Well-balanced hormones play a significant role in a woman's health. Hormones are chemical messengers that dictate how our body behaves. They control every function of our reproductive system and their levels constantly change throughout pregnancy, labour, birth and the postnatal period. They can also control the way we feel emotionally. During pregnancy, the placenta and unborn baby are constantly producing hormones, which result in physical and emotional changes in our bodies.

Hormones play such a large role in childbearing and in our reproductive life. For instance, they:

- Regulate menstruation and ovulation.
- Assist with implantation and preparing the body for pregnancy after conception.
- Assist in the growth, development, and maintenance of the pregnancy.
- Prepare the body for labour and delivery by relaxing ligaments, muscles, softening and ripening the cervix for dilation.
- Trigger contractions to help the uterus to contract during labour.
- Work to expel the placenta, shed the uterine lining and then continue to make the uterus contract and help the body to return to a normal state after the delivery of your baby.
- Stimulate the breasts to release colostrum and to begin milk production.

Hormones can also be contributing factors to oedema (swelling), nausea, morning sickness, sleeplessness, constipation, headaches, heartburn, blood pressure problems, mood swings, emotional outbursts and postnatal depression.

During my pregnancy with my first child Kaitlin and in the postnatal period, blood tests had shown that both my oestrogen and progesterone levels were out of balance. I experienced mood swings and I was over-sensitive. All the 'mole hills' seemed like huge mountains in my life. I took everything to heart and was easily offended. Even though some of my concerns were valid, my irrational behaviour was out of balance. In addition, I would constantly worry about different things that were said to me and I would dwell on what I imagined could happen in the future. My thought life was out of control! I believe all of these things played a major role in my progressive spiral into suffering from post-natal depression.

I soon learnt however, that I didn't have to be subject to my hormones or my emotions, because I had authority over my own thought life, feelings, emotions and body. I needed to turn things around because my body, including my thoughts and emotions, had been controlling me! I had to learn to walk by the Word and live by the Spirit — not by my flesh or feelings. I meditated on scriptures to renew my mind on who I was in Christ. I then walked that out by taking authority over my hormones, emotions and feelings, and declared the truth in God's Word instead. Praise God, my next two pregnancies were free from worry, mood swings, emotional outbursts and depression!

I used to always say 'I can't help how I feel', but in reality, the opposite is true! While we may feel a certain way, **we can choose** not to let our feelings and emotions dictate how we are going to behave! Remember, the truth is that your feelings are always subject to change — **not that you are subject to your feelings!** And this doesn't just apply to childbearing. When I discovered this truth I began to live daily in the peace of God, free from emotional stress and worry, experiencing the joy of the Lord as my strength!

Because hormones play such a large part in causing a woman's body to function normally, it will be a benefit to have them in perfect working order. If they don't function correctly then different complications can occur. However, remember that hormones, like any other part of our body, are under **our** authority. Don't let them control you; instead you control them! Command them to function efficiently at every stage; from conception through to the birth, then command them to return to normal after the delivery and birth as God intended.

Sleep, Peace And Rest

Sleep and rest are very important to our health and wellbeing, especially when pregnant. However, sleeplessness can often occur during this time. It can be as a result of chemical or hormonal changes in the body or it can occur due to unresolved conflict or stress.

"A dream comes when there are many cares"... **Eccl 5:3**

We are called to a life of peace not of stress. I recommend that you spend time in the presence of the Lord before you go to bed. His anointing will bring peace and break the yokes off your life. I battled with insomnia for years. Whenever I held onto a problem and didn't let it go I usually ended up dreaming about it or laying awake thinking about it. Once I learned to leave my daily cares at the Lord's feet, I no longer had trouble sleeping.

Hormonal changes during pregnancy and in the postnatal period can also produce insomnia. And because sleep deprivation can affect every area of your life, it is important for you to be well rested during your pregnancy, especially in the last month in preparation for labour. Plus you will also need energy to care for your newborn baby!

If you are having trouble sleeping, or are fatigued, then renew your mind with the following scriptures. Meditate on what they say so that you can come to know and experience God's blessings of peaceful sleep.

> *"I will lie down and sleep in peace, for you alone, O LORD, make me dwell in safety."* **Ps 4:8**

> *... "when you lie down, you will not be afraid; when you lie down, your sleep will be sweet. Have no fear of sudden disaster or of the ruin that overtakes the wicked, for the LORD will be your confidence and will keep your foot from being snared."* **Prov 3:24–26**

> *"The LORD replied, 'my Presence will go with you, and I will give you rest'."* **Ex 33:14**

> *"But now the LORD my God has given me rest on every side, and there is no adversary or disaster."* **1 Kings 5:4**

> *"My people will live in peaceful dwelling places, in secure homes, in undisturbed places of rest."* **Is 32:18**

> *"Come to me, all you who are weary and burdened, and I will give you rest."* **Matt 11:28**

> *... "for he grants sleep to those he loves."* **Ps 127:2**

Lay hold of the blessing of sleep, especially throughout the rest of your pregnancy so you will be well-rested and ready for your labour and birth!

chapter 15

And None will Miscarry

Before I conceived my first child I began to seek the Lord for knowledge, wisdom and revelation regarding miscarriage. Prior to this I had assumed that because I was a Christian my unborn children would automatically be safe. Yet, after struggling with infertility I knew that this might not be the case. I had been in presumption over the conception so I didn't want to make the same mistake again. I had been radically transformed by the verse in **Exodus 23:26** which said that *'none will miscarry or be barren'* and I continued to meditate on this truth and declare it over my life. I continued with this after I conceived because I wanted to keep renewing my mind on what God's Word said in relation to any concerns that I had.

It is my intention in this section to share very simply the powerful truth in God's Word regarding miscarriage, so that you too can receive a breakthrough in this area. It is not my intention to condemn or make you feel like a failure if you have already experienced miscarriage, rather I want to help you grow in God's Word so that you never experience a miscarriage again.

You will need knowledge, revelation and understanding of what has been made available to you through the finished work of the Cross to enable you to prepare for your next pregnancy. Then continue to meditate on this truth until it becomes personal and you **know** you have victory in this area. Then if you do begin to show signs of miscarrying, you will be able to walk by faith and not by sight to experience the breakthrough.

I am so thankful that the Holy Spirit had showed me how to do this when I was first threatened with miscarriage. After I had miraculously conceived my first child, during the first few months of the pregnancy I experienced period-like cramping and bleeding, and this occurred on three separate occasions. The first time this happened I panicked. I lost sight of the truth of God's Word because I was consumed with fear and overwhelmed with the natural symptoms, but I knew that this was not the time to give in or lose hope. I had to overcome the fear and remind myself of the truth in God's Word. I faced the fear head on and resisted it until it fled from me. I then continued to stand on God's truth, proclaiming 'I am not going to miscarry!' When I stood on God's Word and exercised authority over the situation I felt something break in the spiritual realm and within a couple of hours, the symptoms had disappeared. I repeated this when the symptoms returned two more times and, praise God, my baby remained unharmed in my womb.

In the twenty-first week of my pregnancy, I went into premature labour. By the time Shaun and I arrived at the hospital my contractions were one minute apart. At first the staff didn't believe me because I was calm and was not experiencing pain. It was only after a midwife attached a monitor to my stomach and saw the strength of the contractions that they believed me. I had to sign release forms stating that we understood that the baby would not survive if it were born. But the scripture in **Exodus** was in my spirit. It was mine, I knew it was true, and Shaun and I both knew in our hearts our baby was safe. We declared that *'none shall miscarry or be barren'* over our baby and commanded the symptoms to cease. When my doctor arrived, and examined me, he found my cervix was closed. It hadn't dilated at all and he didn't understand what was happening. The natural facts showed I had been in established labour, yet I hadn't even dilated!

I was given medication to stop the contractions and to help me to sleep. When I awoke, the contractions had stopped. The only remaining indication that anything had happened was tender stomach muscles. Shortly after this at a Christian small group meeting, the small group leader saw a vision of me walking above the ground. He felt the Holy

Spirit say that during this pregnancy; no harm would come to my baby because I had stolen ground from the devil!

At the beginning of my second pregnancy with Aidan, I had a continual cramp on one side. I wasn't sure what it was but I felt led by the Holy Spirit to specifically declare healing from an ectopic pregnancy. During this time I heard of a woman at our church who had been healed from an ectopic pregnancy when her baby moved from her fallopian tubes to her uterine wall. I knew if it happened to her then this could also happen for me. I exercised authority by commanding my baby to move to the correct position in my uterine wall and I continued to declare the truth in God's Word until I felt a release in my spirit and an inner peace and confidence that all was well with my baby.

However, a couple of days later I awoke with severe nausea. I also began to have severe abdominal cramps. I knew without a shadow of a doubt I would not miscarry so I assumed that I had a virus or food poisoning. I continued to declare healing over my body and baby, but the Holy Spirit impressed on my heart that I should see a doctor. I woke Shaun and Kaitlin and we went to the local medical centre. After a brief examination, I was told I was experiencing symptoms of an ectopic pregnancy, and was scheduled to have an ultrasound. The radiologist agreed with this prognosis. Fortunately, we were left alone so Shaun and I stood together and took authority over our baby and commanded him to move from my tube to the uterine wall.

At one stage, I felt a throbbing sensation in my side, which then moved down my abdomen. We also spoke to the nausea, pain and contractions and commanded them to cease and leave my body. Shaun and I felt totally at peace after our prayer, and by the time I had my scan all the pain had ceased. The ultrasound was not conclusive. I was over six weeks pregnant, but the scan showed Aidan to be barely five weeks, and the possibility that the pregnancy was not even viable was implied. However, Shaun and I both knew all was well.

By late that afternoon, all symptoms had disappeared and my poor doctor had no explanations for what had happened! However, Shaun and I both knew it was the healing power of Jesus and the truth in His Word that saved our child. After that day I didn't think about the situation again, and I didn't need any follow up ultrasounds to show what I already knew in my spirit — that all was well with the pregnancy and with our baby.

What Is Miscarriage?

Miscarriage, also known as a spontaneous abortion, is the term used for pregnancy loss — when a woman has been unable to carry her baby to the full term of the pregnancy. It is estimated that one in four pregnancies end in miscarriage, premature labour or stillbirth. A miscarriage usually begins with bleeding and period-like cramping, intensifying until blood clots and tissue are passed.

If you have suffered a miscarriage, there is more often than not a physical cause, so you may wish to seek medical advice to find out the likely trigger. Generally, tests are not performed until a woman has suffered three consecutive miscarriages However, you may be able to request specific testing through your gynaecologist.

A diagnosis from a doctor can give a name to what may be affecting your ability to carry your baby to term, but you don't have to submit to that report, because, as we have already seen, that report isn't the final authority. Instead use it to your advantage and specifically exercise authority over the condition. If it is found that there isn't a conclusive reason for your loss, ask the Holy Spirit to highlight what needs to be covered in your next pregnancy. He can teach you and guide you on what to do and on how to pray effectively.

If you have had a miscarriage, it also doesn't necessarily mean that you will miscarry again. Many women who have experienced miscarriage go on to have a successful pregnancy the next time around. However, don't leave this to chance. Begin to prepare by continuing to meditate on the truth found in God's Word regarding this area.

Is It Ever God's Will To Miscarry?

*"Worship the LORD your God, and His blessing will be on your food and water. I will take away sickness from among you, **and none will miscarry** or be barren in your land. I will give you a full life span."* **Ex 23:25–26**

This scripture is a specific promise regarding our health, fertility and the life of our unborn children. Yet, many still wrongly believe that in certain situations it was God's will that a person wasn't healed or suffered a miscarriage.

We need to understand the goodness of God, His unchanging nature and His faithfulness to His Word.

> *"Every good and perfect gift is from above, coming down from the Father of the heavenly lights, **who does not change** like shifting shadows."* **James 1:17**

> *"'For I know the plans I have for you,' declares the LORD, 'plans to prosper you and **not to harm you**, plans to give you hope and a future'."* **Jer 17:11**

Only good gifts come from God. Miscarriage for any reason is not a good gift. **Romans 11:29** tells us that the *'gifts of God are irrevocable'*. This doesn't just apply to spiritual gifts but to all of God's gifts, including His gift of children. Whenever the Bible mentions children, it says they are a gift and a reward from God (**Ps 127:3**). Pregnancy and birth are God's designed way to bring the blessing of children into our lives. Pregnancy was never designed to fail. God created all things to be good, perfect, healthy and fruitful.

Miscarriage most often occurs due to a sickness, disease or complication in the mother or baby, not because of the **will of God**. God created humanity to conceive, carry and give birth to healthy children without any complications. This was His original plan. It was as a result of the fall of Adam and Eve that sickness and disease entered the world and can now manifest in our lives. However, God's nature and character has not changed, even though we live in a fallen world. His Word and character always remain the same (**Mal 3:6**). And I believe that He will **never cause** us to miscarry or bear sick children.

We need to understand that we can't use our personal experiences to measure God's Word. By this I mean that just because we experienced (or didn't experience) something doesn't mean the situation was from God or was His will. The Bible tells us that God will not alter His promises.

"God is not a man, that He should lie, nor a son of man, that He should change his mind. Does He speak and then not act? Does He promise and not fulfil?" **Num 23:19**

If we say that it was God's will that we miscarried, we are accusing Him of killing our baby by withholding the healing blood of Jesus from us. But, as we have discovered throughout this book, healing is already our provision. So God cannot withhold what He has already provided through His Son.

There are many reasons and many circumstances that hinder us from walking in healing, or experiencing a miracle, but none are because God decided to break His Word. God is sovereign, but He has bound himself to His Word. He wants you to walk in the fullness of what Jesus has purchased for you. He has also already revealed His will on this issue. You will find it in His written Word, and within you will discover the provision for prosperity and blessings of the womb.

… "because of your father's God, who helps you, because of the Almighty, who blesses you with blessings of the heavens above, blessings of the deep that lies below, **blessings of the breast and womb.** *"* **Gen 49:25**

God has already made provision for healing of miscarriage and what can cause it. I have ministered to many women who have been healed of miscarriage, even when all odds were stacked against the survival of the baby. There have also been several miracles concerning women who were told during ultrasound scans that they had a blighted ovum or even that the baby had died. But because these women knew in their heart that it was not God's will for them to miscarry, they continued to stand on God's Word regardless of their situation. Subsequent ultrasound scans showed perfectly healthy babies with strong heartbeats! Many doctors have scratched their heads in amazement.

If you are faced with fears or symptoms of miscarriage then don't accept it as God's will, submit to what is happening and wait for the natural course of events to take place. At those times, you need to make a stand and declare what belongs to you. Instead of dwelling on the problem, focus on the solution! Focus on God and His healing power and remind yourself of who you are in Christ. Remember what Jesus said, *'If you have faith you can say to this mountain, "Be removed"!'* Don't talk **about** your mountain to God but talk **to** your mountain about what God has done! So, open your mouth and exercise your God-given authority over your body and the natural circumstances. Continue to walk by faith (by the finished work of the Cross) and not by sight, feelings or appearances (**Mark 11:20–24**).

Growth And Development Of Your Baby

"For you created my inmost being; you knit me together in my mother's womb. I praise you because I am fearfully and wonderfully made; your works are wonderful, I know that full well. My frame was not hidden from you when I was made in the secret place. When I was woven together in the depths of the earth, your eyes saw my unformed body. All the days ordained for me were written in your book before one of them came to be."
Ps 139:13–16 (KJV)

When God created Adam and Eve in the Garden of Eden they were perfect — fearfully and wonderfully made. God looked over all His creation and saw that it was very good (**Gen 1:31**). At that point in time, sickness and disease did not exist. They were introduced into this world after the fall of Adam and Eve (see Chapter Seven, Healing). This is the reason why the health, growth and development of an unborn baby can be compromised.

During Aidan's pregnancy, my second, I felt led by the Holy Spirit to declare healing from Down's Syndrome. I specifically meditated on God's Word on healing and on my baby's development. I declared that he would be knitted and formed perfectly within my womb. I continued to meditate on the truth in God's Word until I felt a peace and rest in my spirit that my baby was whole and healthy.

After Aidan's delivery, there was some commotion amongst the medical staff. They persuaded me to allow them to take him away for some tests. A couple of hours later, a midwife returned with him and pointed to the palms of his hands. In the middle of his hands, parallel to where his fingers joined the palm, he had a single straight crease line where most of us have three curved lines. This line is known as a 'simian crease' and is common in babies with Down's Syndrome. It is very rare for healthy babies to have this crease. As the midwife was explaining this to me, the Holy Spirit reminded me that I had specifically targeted this area during the pregnancy. I was overwhelmed with God's peace, as I knew my baby was perfectly healthy.

After more tests and an examination from a pediatrician my son was given a clean bill of health. I know in my spirit that Aidan was healed in my womb and I am so thankful that the Holy Spirit guided me in prayer and showed me how to walk in victory.

God's design for the human race was for us to be healthy. Yet unfortunately due to sickness and disease and living in a fallen world children can be born sick or with a disability. Disabled children are definitely precious and loved by God but we need to understand that these children are born that way due to a sickness, disease or complication, not by the will of God. God doesn't **will** us to have sick or unhealthy children. Sickness and disease happen because the world is fallen.

When it comes to the issue of hereditary and genetic sickness and diseases I thank God that the blood of Jesus is thicker than the blood of family! When He died on the Cross He took upon His body **all forms** of sickness and disease including the inherited ones. Therefore, you can exercise authority over the effect or outworking of any hereditary or genetic disorder. This way it stops at us as parents and will not pass down to our children. As believers in Jesus we can have peace concerning the development of our babies and not fear the diseases of the world.

Besides miscarriage, the potential for harm with regard to the growth, development and health of an unborn baby is the strongest fear that a pregnant woman might face. These two go hand in hand because babies can die or miscarry due to a complication with their growth and development. Praise God for His healing power and that we can claim perfect health, growth and development for our unborn children!

> *"The Lord will perfect that which concerns me, your mercy and loving-kindness, O Lord, endure for ever; forsake not the works of your own hands."* **Ps 138:8 (AMP)**

The dictionary definition of perfect is: to finish or complete, to improve, to make skilful. When God creates something He makes no mistakes! He created us to go forth and multiply and to bear healthy children. Remember the finished work of the Cross is not just for your health but also extends to your unborn baby.

Let's look at another scripture:

> *"The seed will grow well, the vine will yield its fruit, the ground will produce its crops, and the heavens will drop their dew."*
> **Zech 8:12**

As women of God we're told that we're fruitful vines within our homes and our children will be like olive shoots around our table (**Ps 128:3**). Therefore, we have the assurance that our seed (children) will grow well and will yield on the vine (not miscarry).

There have been many testimonies within this ministry where babies have been healed in the womb. Many have been born perfectly healthy even after ultrasound scans showed major deformities. Some of them were even given minimal or no chance of survival. There have also been accounts where doctors have compared ultrasound scans of the same baby showing their healing. Therefore, if you have received a bad report, don't give up, because it doesn't have to be your final report. Overcome your fears and renew your mind with the truth of what God says regarding your baby's growth, health and development. Continue to walk by faith (by what the Word says) for your baby in the same way you would for yourself!

Redeemed From Miscarriage

> *"Christ redeemed us from the curse of the law by becoming a curse for us, for it is written: 'cursed is everyone who is hung on a tree'."*
> **Gal 3:13**

As we have discovered throughout this book, through the sacrifice of Jesus on the Cross we have been redeemed from **all** forms of sickness and disease. Miscarriage is simply a form of sickness and is under the curse of the law. Remember as the scripture above clearly states, we have been redeemed from the curse of the law, therefore we are redeemed from lack, loss and miscarriage!

Preparation For Pregnancy After Loss

I believe it is important to prepare for pregnancy by spending time meditating on the truth of God's Word to help you in your journey. This is not to **try** to get the victory but to remind yourself that through Jesus you **already have** the victory.

If you have experienced the heartbreak of miscarriage and are planning to conceive again, I encourage you to prepare beforehand until you know you can enter your next pregnancy with an inner peace, and rest in the finished work of the Cross. I recommend you spend time meditating on God's Word until you come to know, beyond any doubt, that it is **not** His will for you to miscarry. I can't stress enough the importance of seeking the Lord for a personal revelation on this, because it is not sufficient just to know this, we need to **believe** and know how to apply this to our daily life.

I encourage you to make the decision to be determined to not let go of the truth of God's Word and give up or lose hope. Don't look to the natural but instead focus on the solution by meditating on and applying God's Word so you can overcome the natural and experience victory.

I have noticed that when women have prepared by meditating on the truth of God's Word for their pregnancy, they find it easier to walk by faith (not by sight or appearances). And if they are challenged in any way it is easier to overcome the fear so they can remain focused on God's truth and not on what the natural is doing. On the other hand, those who 'presume' they will have a safe pregnancy are often overcome with fear, doubts and discouragement if miscarriage symptoms arise, and they easily lose sight of the truth in the Word because they are totally unprepared. That is not to say they can't obtain the victory but generally it can be harder to exercise authority over the natural sight or appearances, during times of urgency.

A woman I met through the ministry who now has five children, had experienced six miscarriages out of eleven pregnancies. She told me that she found that the five pregnancies where she didn't miscarry were when she had spent time meditating and acting on God's Word, declaring it over her body and baby before she conceived or during the early stages of the pregnancy. She said that doing this was what got her through because whenever she was bombarded with fear or with symptoms of miscarriage, she was armed, ready and stronger within herself to stand on the Word rather than being overcome by her symptoms. The times that she was unprepared and hadn't spent time meditating on the Word she was caught by surprise when miscarriage symptoms began. By the time she felt strong enough to face the fear the battle had already been lost.

We are called to live and walk by faith, not by sight or appearances. Walking by faith by applying God's Word is meant to be a lifestyle and not something you use for a one-time event or for an emergency situation. If you know how to walk by faith then it will be easier to act on what you believe and exercise authority over the situation when you are faced with a complication. You will be able to continue to fight the good fight of faith to overcome and experience the breakthrough. And how do we fight the good fight of faith? By labouring to rest in the finished work of the Cross! This may require us to be vigilant against fear and doubt and to exercise authority over the natural circumstances. Generally speaking, we can only act on what we believe to be true or more powerful. So if we haven't spent the time renewing our mind and meditating on the truth of God's Word then the natural circumstances can very easily overwhelm us.

Suggested Prayer Points

I have listed below a suggested guide to help you to pray and exercise authority over your natural circumstances regarding your pregnancy and the health of your unborn baby. It is important that you don't view these suggestions as a formula or 'quick-fix'. Rather they are to assist you in knowing where to start and to show you some of the things you can pray and exercise your authority over.

- **The growth and the development of your baby.** Your baby needs to develop properly for the pregnancy to progress. So take authority and declare that your baby will be formed within the womb perfectly without any defect, sickness, disease or complication.
- **Perfect implantation.** Your baby needs to implant in the perfect position in your uterine wall. If a baby implants in the fallopian tube this can be a serious condition if left undetected. The baby can't survive; the tube can explode and may prove to be fatal to the mother. Another serious condition is when a baby implants low, in or near the cervix. The placenta needs to be implanted in the uterine wall so it can continue to successfully

nourish the baby. Additionally, if the placenta covers the cervix a vaginal delivery will be impossible. So command the placenta to function efficiently throughout the duration of the pregnancy and to deliver without any complications.

- **For your body to do what it was created to do.** Take authority over your body and command it to function the way God designed it to by maintaining and accommodating the pregnancy for the full duration (40 weeks).

- **A competent cervix.** Command your cervix to remain tightly shut and hold the weight of the baby until the perfect time for labour at the full duration of the pregnancy, and then for it to dilate quickly and efficiently during labour.

- **Perfect hormone levels.** Low hormone levels are another cause of miscarriage. Command every hormone in your body to function efficiently without ANY imbalances.

- **Healing of and protection from antibodies.** Another cause of miscarriage is antibodies either in the mother's body, blood or the father's sperm. Command any antibodies to be removed because by Jesus' stripes you are healed from all sickness and disease including antibodies!

Ask the Holy Spirit to guide you and show you what to pray when necessary. If you have a specific fear then face it and overcome it by replacing it with the truth in God's Word. Continue to meditate on and walk by the truth of God's Word for your pregnancy and not by sight, symptoms or appearances.

Remember The Blood Of Jesus

In the Old Testament at the time of Passover the Israelites, who were in slavery in Egypt, were instructed by God to apply the blood of a lamb over the lintels of their windows and over the doorposts of their homes (see **Exodus Chapter 12**). The blood protected all in that household from the spirit of death and destruction that came and killed the first-born of all the Egyptians. This blood was a *type and shadow* of the protection of the blood of Jesus over us in the New Covenant. Because we have faith in Jesus we have the protection of His blood! If the *type* protected God's people under the Old Covenant then the *reality* or *fulfillment* of that type will too!

Nothing Is Impossible For Those Who Believe

I have ministered to several women who were threatened with miscarriage and losing their baby seemed inevitable. Some were even told by medical professionals that there was nothing they could do, and there was no hope. But these women walked by the truth in God's Word not by sight or appearances, and were able to overcome the natural circumstances and safely carry their babies to full term. One of these women was threatened with miscarriage three times within the first five months of her pregnancy. The second time she was threatened with miscarriage symptoms, her doctor gave her a 60 percent chance of losing the baby. By the third time she was threatened, she **knew** in her heart her baby was safe. She had spent time meditating on the truth and overcoming her fear, and even though she'd been told she only had a 40 percent chance of keeping her baby, she had a beautiful little girl at the full duration of the pregnancy. In fact she was one week overdue!

Another testimony I want to share is about a non-Christian woman who had already experienced three miscarriages. I had the opportunity to share with her the love of God, His healing power and what His Word said. I explained the scripture regarding God's will on miscarriage in **Exodus 23:25–26.** She had been trying for some time to conceive and the month she received and declared this scripture over her life, she conceived. However, a few weeks into the pregnancy, the familiar period-like cramping and bleeding had begun, signaling another miscarriage. This time she turned to God. She told me she reminded God that His Word was true and then declared **'No, I am not going to miscarry!'** She spent the next hour declaring this verse and all the cramping and bleeding stopped. If a non-Christian can grasp what the Word says and walk in His healing power and receive a miracle, then how much more can we as believers! She told me later she knew her pregnancy was maintained because of God. She has since had another two children without any complications. And I recently found out (nine years later) that she and her family are now all dedicated followers of Jesus!

This woman had no knowledge of any biblical principles or how to pray. All she did was stand on just one promise in God's Word, with a basic understanding that God is good, and she received a breakthrough. It is important to note that the first part of **Exodus 23:25** reads, *'you shall worship the Lord your God...'.* This woman ran to God in her time of need and her heart was transformed. So when ministering to non-Christians, I always give them an opportunity to come into a relationship with the Healer rather than just praying for their healing or for their situation.

All of the women I have mentioned could have easily accepted and submitted to the natural course of events, but because they **knew** the truth in God's Word in their heart, they were able to make His Word their final authority. This enabled them to exercise authority over the natural circumstances and experience the healing and breakthrough they needed.

> *"For the Word of God is living and active. Sharper than any double-edged sword, it penetrates **even to** dividing soul and spirit, joints and marrow; it judges the thoughts and attitudes of the heart."* **Heb 4:12**

As I have previously mentioned, when you know who you are in Christ, where you are seated, and understand your power and authority as a believer, you can see the power of God released in your life through your words! God's power penetrates every realm: the physical, spiritual and emotional. It can bring life, health and restoration to your cells, organs and tissues. I have seen babies who have died or who have not been formed properly in the womb, and the resurrection power of God has brought healing and restored them back to life! I have seen unbalanced reproductive systems begin to function perfectly, and gene or chromosome disorders in unborn babies restored and they were born perfectly healthy. And so much more — all through the living and active power of God!

What To Do In The Event Of A Threatened Miscarriage

In the event of a threatened miscarriage it is important that you have already learnt how to walk by faith (by what you have received through the finished work of the Cross) and not by sight or natural appearances, either before conception, or during the early stages of your pregnancy. This is important because if your pregnancy is threatened with miscarriage you can continue to act on what you believe by walking by the truth of God's Word.

Over the following few pages I have listed some things that I believe will remind you of who you are in Christ and what you have already inherited so you don't lose sight of the victory. Once again it is important that you don't view these points as a formula to follow to attain your desired result. Following a formula or steps without revelation is not only powerless but also leads to frustration. As we have already discovered, we have already received the victory we needed upon salvation. We simply need to remind ourselves of this and continue to walk by that truth and not lose hope or become overwhelmed with the natural circumstances.

Remember the finished work of the Cross! *By Jesus' stripes you have been healed!* Jesus has already paid the price in full for miscarriage and for whatever causes it. Apply this truth and declare your healing and all that Jesus has provided for you.

Labour to stay in rest! When we look to the natural circumstances it is easy to lose sight of the truth and become overwhelmed. During times like these we need to continue to labour to remain in a place of rest, knowing the work has been done, and we have everything we need to walk in victory. If we lose sight of this truth we may get caught up in works and striving (doing, trying, struggling) to get the breakthrough. Instead, we need to walk by faith (by what we believe we have received through the finished work of the Cross) and not by sight — by the natural realm and senses.

Don't be ruled by fear. Overcome fear with the Word of God and declare what He says concerning that situation. Remember, you have not been given a spirit of fear but one of power, a sound mind and self-control (**2 Tim 1:7**). Remember also to not go by your feelings. I know from experience that sometimes it feels too hard when you are faced with a challenge or emergency situation. However, regardless of how you feel, remember that you are more than a conqueror (**Rom 8:37**), and greater is Jesus who is in you than our enemy who is in the world (**1 John 4:4**). In Christ, you can obtain strength for all things (**Phil 4:13**). Also know that you don't have to wait for the natural course of events to take place. Don't sit back, be passive and assume that everything will be perfect, but be active and continue to walk by faith and declare God's Word and truth over your life!

Meditate and keep focused on the truth. When faced with pain, bleeding, cramping and other symptoms it is easy to lose sight of the power of God and be overwhelmed by the natural circumstances. However, continue to meditate on the truth of what God's Word says. **Proverbs 4:20–23** tells us that when God's Word finds place in our heart it brings healing and health to our flesh and our outward circumstances. It's important that you don't base your confidence in what you see (or don't see) in the natural realm. When God's Word becomes your final authority it doesn't matter what is happening in the natural because you can see His power change and transform the situation!

Remember your authority. As believers in Jesus we have His authority, power, and person living on the inside of us! We are not trying to get power and authority, because we already have power and authority because of our position in Christ. We are seated with Christ in heavenly places, far above all rule and authority, power and dominion, and every title that can be given, not only in the present age but also in the one to come (see **Eph 1:21** and **Eph 2:6**).

You HAVE the authority to bind and loose sickness, disease, infertility, miscarriage, and barrenness from your life. If you tell it to be removed, it will be removed. If you tell it to die at the root it will die at the root. If you resist it, then it must flee! Take authority over your circumstances, symptoms or diagnosis and command any sickness in your body to leave!

Remember the power of your words. We exercise authority over any situation by our words and what we say! God released His power by His Words. If you want to see the power of God released in your life then you need to act on what you believe and use your words too. It is important to note that we don't confess or declare God's Word to make something happen. We confess what God says because of **what has already happened**! Confess **what Jesus has done** through the finished work of the Cross! Take authority and declare out aloud 'I will not miscarry', and also that 'my baby will thrive and will live and not die!'

Be anxious for nothing! Peace comes when we are anxious for nothing and can put our trust in God. *'And the peace of God, which transcends all understanding, **will guard** your **hearts** and **minds** in Christ Jesus'* (**Phil 4:6**).

Praise and worship. Put on some praise and worship music and lift up your heart and voice to God. Offer Him the fruit of your lips as a sacrifice of praise. **Psalm 22:3** tells us that God inhabits the praises of His people and **Psalm 9:1–3** says that when God comes on the scene our enemies fall back and perish at His presence. Worship doesn't change God but it sure changes you! You will need to get your focus off the natural situation and keep it fixed on God. Worship will help you to enter into the awareness of His presence where His life and healing power can flow through you.

Thank God. Give God the glory and thank Him for the finished work of the Cross and for what already belongs to you regarding your health and the safety of your unborn baby. We overcome by the blood of the lamb and the Word of our testimony (**Rev 12:11**)!

Medical help. If necessary, call your doctor or hospital for advice. Be careful to guard your mind over any negative remarks because the natural report doesn't have to be your final report. Make God's Word your final authority. Don't allow your circumstances or diagnosis to be greater than the power of God and His Word.

Remember God is good and He loves you. Regardless of what you go through, God's love is always there for you.

> *"For God Himself has said I will not in any way fail you, nor give you up, nor leave you without support. I will not, I will not, I will not in any degree leave you helpless, nor forsake, nor let you down, relax my hold on you. Assuredly not!"* **Heb 13:5 (AMP)**

Miscarriage Prayer

"Then I passed by and saw you kicking about in your blood, and as you lay there in your blood I said to you, 'Live!'" **Ezek 16:6**

Baby, in the name of Jesus I prophesy the Word of God over your life by professing that you will live and not die, proclaiming what the Lord has done.

I resist miscarriage and the symptoms of miscarriage and I command you to bow down to the name of Jesus and leave!

Body, I command every part of you to function the way God created you to function because 'you are fearfully and wonderfully made'. That means every hormone is to get into balance and function perfectly not only during my pregnancy and delivery but for the rest of my life!

Jesus is the Word of God so I speak the life of Jesus into my womb, which says I will NOT miscarry. I receive healing over any complication within my body and my baby's body.

Lord I thank you that you have given me power and authority over sickness and disease and over all the power of the enemy and that I don't have to be subject to my natural circumstances.

I take authority over fear and oppression for they are under my feet for I have not been given a spirit of fear but I have been given a spirit of love, power, a sound mind and self-control.

I choose not to be anxious for anything. I receive Jesus' perfect peace that guards my heart and mind in Him!

AMEN!

PART IV
Childbirth Without Fear

16

Childbirth Without Fear

Many women expect birth to be a complicated, fearful and painful experience where the whole process is taken completely out of their hands. While this can be the case, it does not have to be your experience! If you can put your trust in the Lord and in His Word to conceive, then take your faith one step further and continue to take Him at His Word for the safe delivery of your baby.

Children Are A Blessing!

"Behold, children are a heritage of the Lord: and the fruit of the womb is His reward." **Ps 127:3 (NKJV)**

Whenever the Bible mentions children, it states that they are a blessing, a gift and a reward from God. Pregnancy and birth were both designed by God as the way to bring forth the blessing of children into our lives. They were not designed to be complicated, fearful or painful experiences. God created us to bear children and every part of our reproductive system has been created perfectly for this task. We are not meant to fear or dread the pregnancy or birth because they are meant to be a blessing!

God's Plan For Childbirth!

Many women around the world experience straightforward, uncomplicated and painless deliveries. This is how God created us to give birth. That's the truth! However, somewhere along the line someone has sold women a lie that childbirth is meant to be a painful, complicated or traumatic experience. But I want to shine the light on the truth so you can renew your mind from a worldly point of view to God's view regarding His will and plan for childbirth.

We have already discovered throughout this book that when God created Adam and Eve in the Garden of Eden they were perfect — fearfully and wonderfully made. God had created them with everything they needed within their bodies to go forth and to multiply and fill the earth. We have also seen that when God looked over all His creation He saw that it was very good (**Gen 1:31**). Sickness, disease, pain and complications did not exist. They were introduced into this world after the fall of Adam and Eve.

Pain And The Curse Of Eve

My own understanding of childbirth before I had children was that it would be a fearful and painful experience. In fact I'd had a fear of childbirth for most of my life. After I was born again, I began to gain an understanding of who God is. As a result of this understanding I couldn't believe that my God, who was so full of mercy, compassion, and who sent Jesus to die for me, forgive my sins, heal my body and deliver me out of the power of the enemy, would want me to suffer pain and anguish in childbirth.

*"So the LORD God said to the serpent, 'Because you have done this, **Cursed** are you above all the livestock and all the wild animals! You will crawl on your belly and you will eat dust all the days of your life. And I will put enmity between you and the woman, and between your offspring and hers; he will crush your head, and you will strike his heel.' To the woman He said, 'I will greatly increase your **pains** in childbearing; **with pain** you will give birth to children. Your desire will be for your husband, and he will rule over you.' To Adam he said, 'Because you listened to your wife and ate from the tree about which I commanded you, you must not eat of it, **cursed** is the ground because of you; through **painful toil** you will eat of it all the days of your life.'"* **Gen 3:14–17**

Many read the above account of the consequences of the fall, and misinterpret it to mean that God had cursed Eve with pain and suffering during childbirth, and as a result, all women now have to suffer with the same curse. I initially believed this, and had I remained in this belief I would have suffered needlessly. However, note that while the word curse is used twice, it is actually referring to:

- the serpent (the devil) and
- the ground.

God **did not** curse Adam or Eve.

In the **NIV** Study Bible the footnotes regarding this verse explain that the Hebrew meaning of the words *pain, pains* and *painful toil* are translated as *burdensome labour* (see **Prov 5:10**, *'toil'* and **14:23** *'hard work'*). When farmers work the ground are they in excruciating pain? No! It is just labour, toil, effort and hard work. And that is what labour is — hard work! Additionally, the **KJV** translation of this passage of scripture replaces the words *pain, pains* and *painful toil* with *sorrow*. Eve was told she would have *sorrow* and *conception multiplied,* that she would bring forth children in *sorrow*. Adam was told that he would *sorrow* to eat or work the ground.

Adam and Eve were now living in a fallen world where sin had been conceived. Pain along with sickness, disease, and other complications had entered (these are also listed under the curse of the law of sin and death) and the consequence was that they were now open to experience any part of this curse.

Redeemed From Pain

As we have already seen, **Deuteronomy 28:15–65** details all of the curses under the law of sin and death. This is an extensive list of sickness, disease and complications that came in through sin, and which still exist in this fallen world. But praise God, He sent Jesus to reverse the curse and to set us free from all the effects of sin.

> *"Christ has redeemed us from the curse of the law by becoming a curse for us, for it is written: 'cursed is everyone who is hung on a tree'."* **Gal 3:13**

This means that we have been redeemed from **every** part of the curse of the law, and this includes all forms of sickness, disease, pain and complications mentioned within it such as:

- **Every** sickness, and every plague, disease, and disaster that is recorded and also those that are not recorded in the Word of God.
- **Every** sickness and disease that can be named, and those that cannot be named!
- All types of **pain**! Whether it's the pain of childbirth, toothache, headache, backache, or as a result from an injury, as well as emotional and mental pain!

For the most part, pain is the body's response to an underlying cause. But this doesn't mean that we accept it as 'par for the course'. No matter what the cause, pain is under the curse of the law, and because we are redeemed from the curse, it no longer has any legal right to afflict us!

We have been legally set free from all of these consequences of sin. Jesus took the full force of sin into His spirit, and as a result took the **fruit of sin** such as sickness, disease and pain of every kind. The price for our redemption from all of this was paid in full. Thank God for the finished work of the Cross!

Jesus Carried Our Pains Away!

*"Surely He **took up** our **infirmities** and **carried** our **sorrows**, yet we considered Him stricken by God, smitten by Him, and afflicted. But He was pierced for our transgressions, He was crushed for our iniquities; the punishment that brought us peace was upon Him, and by His wounds we **are** healed."* **Is 53:4–5 (KJV)**

The word *infirmities* in the scripture above is the Hebrew word *choli*, meaning: sickness, disease, grief, sick. The word *sorrows* is the Hebrew word *makob* meaning: pain, grief. The word *pain* is further described as sorrow (emotional), pain (physical), pain (mental).

Isaiah 53:4–5 should therefore correctly read Jesus took up all our sickness, diseases and griefs and carried our sorrows and physical and mental pains away! Jesus took all forms of sickness, disease, grief, sorrow, distress and pain upon His body on the Cross in our place!

I received a deeper revelation of the fullness of what Jesus had done on the Cross when I once experienced a bad case of stomach cramps. The pain from the cramps was unbearable. They were far worse than any labour contraction. I remember being in so much pain that I cried out '**Jesus help me**'. What happened next was amazing! I had a vision of Jesus' hand coming down and resting on my abdomen. As this happened, the awareness of pain I was experiencing left my body. I could still feel the cramping but my stomach went numb. Jesus carried all the pain from my body. He took the full force of it away! This is what Jesus had done on the Cross and this vision helped me to see that truth become a reality in my life.

Now, whenever I experience any form of pain I focus on what Jesus has done (He already took it all in my place) and take authority over the pain the same way that I had during my labour, and each time the pain wanes and disappears.

God's Word On Childbirth

There are many possible complications that can threaten the health and safety of the mother and baby during childbirth. But while these complications can manifest because we live in a fallen world, you can be assured that they were never meant to be a part of God's plan for childbearing. The following scriptures listed below talk about childbirth and show us how God designed childbirth to be:

.... *"Hebrew women are not like Egyptian women; they are vigorous and give birth before the midwives arrive."* **Ex 1:19**

"Before she goes into labour, she gives birth; before the pains come upon her, she delivers a son. Who has ever heard of such a thing? Who has ever seen such things? Can a country be born in a day or a nation be brought forth in a moment? Yet no sooner is Zion in labour than she gives birth to her children." **Is 66:7–8**

"They will not toil in vain or bear children doomed to misfortune; for they will be a people blessed by the LORD, they and their descendants with them." **Is 65:23** [**NKJV** says *labour in vain*]

If you have a fear of childbirth then I recommend that you overcome your fears by renewing your mind with the truth of what God's Word says until you know beyond doubt that you don't have to suffer or be traumatised in childbirth.

The Past Is Not Your Future!

It is vitally important that you guard what you allow anyone to speak into your life regarding your conception, pregnancy and birth.

> *"Have nothing to do with godless myths and old wives' tales; rather, train yourself to be godly."* **1 Tim 4:7**

This passage is quite clear in exhorting us not to pay attention to old wives' tales, myths, folklore or anything contrary to God's Word. There will always be someone willing to share horror stories about their own pregnancy and childbearing experiences, or of terrible things that happened to someone they know. You may also have your family sharing their history as well. But know that you don't have to submit to your family's past because the blood of Jesus is thicker than the blood of family!

It is so easy when we hear of someone else's bad experiences to become overwhelmed with fear, imagining the same things happening to us. It's important then that you don't allow other peoples' opinions and experiences, or even your own past experiences, to affect the way you view your outcome. Your past, or even their past, is not your future! Instead, meditate on the finished work of the Cross so you know what you can experience as a believer in Jesus. Declare what **you** want to have happen, not what anyone says **might** happen.

During your pregnancy, focus on what God's Word says and listen only to positive testimonies. Your faith will grow through hearing the Word and listening to examples of God's Word in action. In light of this, I suggest you choose carefully who you share the details of your anticipated birth plan with. It is hard enough to guard and renew your mind and keep focused on the truth without other people's views and negative remarks working against you. Share only with people who will support and encourage you in your journey. If there isn't anyone then keep it between yourself and the Lord!

You Can Experience A Pain-Free Birth!

As we have already discovered, God created our bodies to conceive, carry and give birth quickly without pain, trauma or complications of any kind (see **Is 66:7** and **Is 65:23**). And many women in the world are already experiencing this. We also discovered that pain and trauma in childbirth didn't come from a curse God had placed on Eve but rather was the result of living in a fallen world. And when Jesus hung on the Cross, along with our sin, He bore sickness and disease of every kind upon His body and carried the pain of it all away! When you understand this truth you will realise that you don't have to suffer or be traumatised giving birth because Jesus paid the price for this area too. So you can now apply this truth to expect a completely different outcome!

To experience labour and delivery without pain doesn't necessarily mean that you will not feel anything. Your muscles have to work hard to draw back your cervix and then to push your baby out of the birth canal. That is why this process is called labour! You might feel your muscles working hard during the contractions or you might feel nothing at all. When we work out at the gym or engage in physical activity, we can feel our muscles working. The pressure and physical exertion of the exercises can make our muscles feel tight, but, assuming we have exercised correctly, we are not left in agony. However, if a person becomes fearful, holds their breath, or tenses up then that is when the pain comes and intensifies.

I had strong contractions during both labours of my first two children. For the majority of the contractions I coped quite well and praised God for the victory, but there were also times that I had to exercise authority over pain in some of the contractions. If pain surfaced I would take authority over it and command it to leave and it would wane and ease off. In contrast, with the twins I didn't even realise I was in labour. I couldn't feel the contractions until the very end after my waters were broken. I actually slept for a couple of hours in a spa bath during my labour!

If you find that your contractions become too strong or unbearable, don't give up, but instead continue to exercise authority over the physical symptoms by resisting the pain and continue to focus on Jesus and the finished work of the Cross.

In prenatal (or antenatal) classes all around the world pregnant women are taught how to use breathing techniques and focal points to cope with their contractions during labour and delivery. Many women have found these techniques to be effective and have been able to labour and give birth without pain relief and experience a straightforward and uncomplicated delivery. If these women can experience painless childbirth without complications and without the knowledge of God's promises, then that proves even moreso God's design for childbirth!

If natural methods are effective in helping you cope with contractions during labour then how much more effective will the outcome be if you apply the supernatural! So rather than relying on focal points, panting, chanting or other natural methods, learn to focus on Jesus and His Word instead. I have had instances not just in childbirth, where my body has gone numb and the pain has disappeared by focusing on Jesus and the finished work of the Cross.

If you want to believe for a straightforward and uncomplicated birth without pain or medical intervention then go for it. However, I caution you to not fall into presumption. You will need to spend the time renewing your mind with the truth and seeking God for a personal revelation that you don't have to suffer in childbirth. Remember, it will not manifest on knowledge alone. **Information needs to become revelation** for you to effectively walk it out by acting on what you believe and by taking authority over the natural symptoms. This is done in the same way you would for healing of any sickness, disease or pain in your body.

I suggest you start to walk by faith over pain now. For instance, if you experience pain in the form of menstrual cramps or headaches, learn to exercise authority and apply God's Word to walk in healing in those areas. If you face morning sickness, heartburn, or backaches during your pregnancy, exercise authority to overcome these areas as well. If you take every opportunity to learn how to walk in healing, you will be walking by faith as a lifestyle rather than relying on exercising faith for an emergency or for a one-time event.

Preparation For Birth

Many women prepare themselves both physically and emotionally for their births by exercising and attending childbirth classes but don't understand the importance of preparing themselves spiritually. We are spiritual beings so we also need to prepare spiritually for our births as well.

> *"For physical training is of some value,* **but godliness has value for all things,** *holding promise for both the present life and the life to come."* **1 Tim 4:8**

I have often been asked why it is necessary to go to the effort to prepare for childbirth when it is only one day out of your life, yet for something that lasts a relatively short time it can leave a lasting negative impression. Many women have been left traumatised by their childbirth experience and have, as a result, decided to not have any more children in case they experience the same thing again.

In the course of this ministry I have met many first time mothers who didn't feel the need to prepare for their first pregnancy or birth. However, a large percentage of them chose to prepare for their subsequent deliveries and those who did received a better outcome the second time around, as well as receiving victory over other areas they'd been believing for. If you want an enjoyable childbirth experience then don't take your birth for granted or leave things to chance, but rather take the time to prepare.

What Happens During Childbirth?

In preparation for your labour, you can begin by overcoming your fears and renewing your mind with the truth in God's Word until you truly believe that you don't have to suffer in childbirth. Remember that Jesus has already obtained victory for you over all sickness, disease, pain or complications.

It will also be beneficial to know the physical changes that happen in the body to deliver a baby. If you understand what has to happen you can then 'go with the flow' and work with your body. It has been proven that fear produces tension, and tension produces pain in childbirth. In the 1930s, Dr Grantley Dick Read, a Christian obstetrician who wrote the book *Childbirth without Fear*, discovered that much of the pain during childbirth is due to tension, caused by fear and ignorance. Therefore, if you understand what physically occurs during childbirth and how your body is going to work, fear will not easily overwhelm you.

The Three Stages Of Labour

The following is a basic outline of the three stages in childbirth and should be read in conjunction with childbirth books. I have presented them here so you can gain an understanding of the processes of childbirth, as well as outlining how you can specifically exercise authority and overcome any fear. When you read through childbirth books remember to consider the finished work of the Cross as you read and be confident that you don't have to experience pain or complications in labour as they may be described.

During your pregnancy and especially at the commencement of labour, continue to act on what you believe by taking authority over your body and over any complication that may arise and command each part to function as it was created to work.

First Stage — Labour Begins!

This is when the cervix thins out and begins to dilate. Transition is when the cervix dilates from 7 to 10cm.

Take authority over your body, commanding that:

- The **timing** will be appropriate and that you and your family will be comfortable and ready for the birth (detail exactly what you want).
- Your **body** will function perfectly at peak performance as it was designed to, in order to bring forth this child, working efficiently because you are *fearfully and wonderfully made*.
- Your **baby** will move into the correct position with its head engaged firmly on the cervix to help with dilation, its face facing the spine, and its back to the stomach wall (anterior position and head down).
- The **umbilical cord** will be in the correct position, not around the baby's neck, body or shoulders.
- Your **cervix** will efface and dilate efficiently to the full 10cm without any complications.
- Your **hormones** will work efficiently and effectively during pregnancy, labour, delivery and recovery (see Chapter 13, 'Pregnancy, a Time of Blessing').

Second Stage — Delivery

The baby is delivered. The mother works with the contractions to push the baby through the birth canal.

Take authority over your body, commanding that:

- Your **bones and ligaments** will spread and separate to make room for the baby to pass through.
- Your **muscles** will work effectively and efficiently to push the baby out.
- Your **vagina and perineum** will be elastic and stretch as much as necessary without tearing to accommodate the delivery of the baby and that they will go numb as God designed so there will be no pain as your baby's head crowns.

Third Stage — The Final Process!

This is when the afterbirth (placenta, water sac and umbilical cord) is delivered. The placenta separates from the uterine wall and passes through the birth canal.

Take authority over your body, commanding that:

- The **placenta** will completely peel off the uterine wall in one complete piece.
- Your **uterus** will contract and push the placenta out through the birth canal and then contract (without pain) and return to its original size and heal quickly and efficiently.
- Your **body** will recover quickly after the birth.
- Your **hormones** will get back into balance and begin to release colostrum from your breasts and also begin milk production without any blockage or complication.

Be as specific and detailed as you want to be. Any time you start to tense up or become afraid, resist fear and place your body back in submission to your spirit. I know of babies that have changed position during labour, from breech (bottom first) or posterior (spine against spine) to the correct anterior (face against spine) position. This was simply done by the parents taking authority over the situation by commanding the baby to move into the correct position for birth.

God's Strength During Delivery

If there is ever a time that you will need to rely on God's strength it will be during the third stage of labour. Labour is hard work! Your muscles have to work to push your baby out. This can be both physically and emotionally exhausting. I have some friends who spent up to three hours in the second stage of labour, trying to push their babies through the birth canal. It took me nearly an hour with Kaitlin, so with Aidan I specifically prayed it would be no longer than fifteen minutes. He was delivered within fourteen minutes — my contractions were just under five minutes apart, so after three pushes he was out! Both Julie and I experienced a dramatic difference in labour when we relied on God's strength. I know women who have also experienced this and they didn't have to push at all. Their muscles did all the work for them. There is no beginning or end to God's power because His power has no boundaries. We simply need to learn to use His strength and not do everything on our own because if we do we will quickly tire.

> *"In conclusion, be strong in the Lord — **be empowered through your union** with Him; draw your strength from Him — that strength which His boundless might provides."* **Eph 6:10 (AMP)**

> *"**I have strength for all things** in Christ **Who empowers me** I am ready for anything and equal to anything through Him **Who infuses inner strength** into me; I am self-sufficient in Christ's sufficiency."* **Phil 4:13 (AMP)**

> *"He gives strength to the weary and increases the power of the weak. But those who hope in the LORD will renew their strength. They will soar on wings like eagles; they will run and not grow weary, they will walk and not be faint."* **Is 40:29, 31**

Multiple Births

When I first discovered that I was pregnant with our twins, information on multiple pregnancies and births was difficult to find. I asked my obstetrician what was involved in delivering twins and his answer was simple; that I would go through the first stage of labour once and then have to individually push out two babies.

At first, the thought of having to carry and deliver two babies was overwhelming. I was totally confident about carrying one baby but the thought of carrying two momentarily seemed like a big challenge. But God revealed to me that His Word regarding childbearing was exactly the same whether it was for one baby or for two! I had to renew my mind and rebuke any fear, and simply add another little life to my prayers. So, my prayer list grew considerably!

No matter what the world says about the challenges and complications that can come with multiple pregnancies, we do not have to experience those negative outcomes. Don't think of a multiple pregnancy as multiple troubles, but that you have been multiply blessed! I did, and my twin pregnancy was my best pregnancy! While it was more challenging physically because I was a lot bigger than my previous two pregnancies, emotionally, spiritually and health-wise it was the best!

Prayer Points For Multiple Births

Just like you would with a single pregnancy, it is important to spend time with God so that the Holy Spirit can quicken any specific scriptures for your situation. Listed below are some of my personal prayer points that I had for my twin pregnancy. I have included them here as a guide to help you to put action to your faith, and to help you to exercise authority over your natural circumstances.

Take authority over your body, commanding that:

- Your body will accommodate the growth and development of your babies without any sickness, disease or complication.
- All babies will be in the anterior position (head down and face towards your spine) for a vaginal delivery and with the head of one of the babies engaged and sitting firmly on the cervix to help with dilation.
- There will be no obstruction of delivery and that the umbilical cords are not wrapped around the neck or shoulders.
- The placenta(s) will do its/their job efficiently throughout the pregnancy, labour and delivery supplying enough oxygen and nutrients to each baby, without any failure or complications.

- Each baby will thrive without one of them becoming 'greedy', resulting in robbing the other of essential nutrition and growing conditions. Also pray that there will be enough space in the womb for both babies to grow and thrive.
- You will not miscarry or go into premature labour but will deliver safely at full term.
- Your cervix will remain closed, strong and competent until the proper time for delivery and then dilate quickly and efficiently to the full 10cm without any pain or complications.
- All babies will be perfect, strong and healthy and be able to thrive beyond the womb without assistance, with the lungs being fully developed and the sucking reflex perfected for ease of breastfeeding.
- The babies will not be in distress and the peace of God will be with them during the labour and delivery.

A Time To Be Born

"There is a time for everything, and a season for every activity under heaven: 'a time to be born'"... **Eccl 3:1–2**

There is a season for pregnancy. The predetermined season God created for a human pregnancy is nine months (38–42 weeks). When your baby is fully developed and your body is working how God created it to function then at the **full duration** of your pregnancy your labour should begin. All babies need to be in the womb for a set amount of time for their growth and development. Therefore, it is important for babies to be born at the proper time, the full duration of a pregnancy as God designed, not when it is convenient for your or your doctor's schedule.

So if your labour begins prematurely this **doesn't mean that God has brought on labour**. In the same way we don't accept miscarriage as being God's will, we don't have to accept premature labour as being God's will either. You can take authority over the situation and pray for a full term healthy pregnancy and baby.

On the other hand, if your baby is overdue and the doctors want to induce labour, you can exercise authority over the situation and pray for labour to begin, and for your body to do what God created it to do to deliver your baby safely without any complications.

It's important to note that the due date you have been given for your baby's birth is an estimated date only. As we have already seen, the 'season' for a pregnancy can be anything from 38 to 42 weeks.

> *"Whoever obeys His command will come to no harm, and the wise heart will know the proper time and procedure. For there is a proper time and procedure for every matter"...* **Eccl 8:5–6**

At eight and a half months pregnant, patience is the last word you want to hear. However, without it you can become frustrated and stress of any kind is not healthy for you or your baby. Patience is what you need to help you wait for your baby's birth.

> *"But the fruit of the Spirit is love, joy, peace, **patience**, kindness, goodness, faithfulness, gentleness and self-control. Against such things there is no law."* **Gal 5:22–26**

> *"We do not want you to become lazy, but to imitate those **who through faith and patience inherit what has been promised.**"* **Heb 6:12**

The last few weeks of my first pregnancy with Kaitlin seemed to drag on forever. Each day past my due date seemed a week long, and my frustration grew along with the size of my belly. I knew babies could go at least 14 days past their due date, but I had convinced myself this was not going to happen to me! I started to become anxious. This took some joy from the pregnancy. Thankfully after reading various scriptures on patience, I received the peace that I could wait a couple more days until my baby was ready to be born. I had also specifically prayed that I would go into spontaneous labour and not need to be induced and that's what happened just a few days later.

The week I was overdue with Aidan, my doctor commented on my change in attitude compared to when I was overdue with Kaitlin. He was sure I would not deliver for at least another week and was discussing dates for an induction. I knew in my heart I would not need to be induced. I loved being pregnant and even though I was glad I delivered two days later, I honestly wasn't bothered about being overdue. The main difference was my attitude. I had determined to focus on what I was doing, bringing forth a new life and not on my size. It is such a privilege to carry a baby and bring forth that little life. In the grand scheme of things nine months (and a couple of days) is still only a short period of time.

I experienced the opposite during my pregnancy with twins; I was constantly inundated with comments that 'twins always come early'. Apparently, this is mainly due to the lack of space in the womb. The duration for a twin pregnancy is considered to be 38 weeks, not the usual 40 weeks. I specifically declared throughout my pregnancy that I would not deliver prematurely or before the thirty-eighth week. I also declared that I would remain comfortable and each day I relied on God's strength to carry me through. The twins were born at exactly 38 weeks. I thank God for His promises because my pregnancy with the twins was my best!

Medical Intervention

Even though you may be preparing for a straightforward delivery, there are many unexpected complications that can arise. For this reason, medical intervention is required to deliver some babies safely. If this should occur during your delivery, then remember that God's grace is sufficient for you and you haven't failed if intervention is required. Continue to exercise your authority over the situation and declare that there will be no complications with the procedure, and no side effects for you or your baby.

During my first labour, my contractions were strong, but by no means painful. I remember thinking of all the breathing techniques I had learned during my pregnancy while attending prenatal classes and decided to try them, 'just for fun'. The very next contraction was extremely strong and painful. I realised that I had switched from the supernatural to the natural but didn't think to switch back because the newfound pain consumed me. My doctor advised me to have an epidural and I agreed. Once the epidural was administered and all the staff had left the room, I felt like a failure. But, I quickly shook that off and got back on track to how I started. A few days after the birth I found this scripture, confirming to me what I had done:

> *"Are you so foolish? After beginning with the Spirit, are you now trying to attain your goal by human effort?"* **Gal 3:3**

As it turned out, the epidural didn't work to its full capacity anyway. I could still feel and move my legs and feel the contractions in my body. After I had switched back to the spiritual I was able to continue to stand on the Word for my delivery and by the time it came to push, the epidural had completely worn off and I was able to push Kaitlin out and deliver her without pain.

While some consider that medical intervention is not God's best, you also need to remember that doctors are there to help God's children, not to harm them. As I have discussed throughout this book, there is a process to learning how to walk by faith and unless we are walking and living by it as a lifestyle, we may not have the confidence to apply it in adverse situations. For this reason, if you know in advance that medical intervention may be required, you can prepare by meditating on the finished work of the Cross and on who you are in Christ, and exercise authority over your body and natural circumstances before the doctors proceed with their plans.

Remember always that you have God's Spirit living on the inside of you. Learn how to hear His voice and be led by Him so that He can show you what to do and how to walk in victory.

Induction

"'Do I bring to the moment of birth and not give delivery?' says the LORD. 'Do I close up the womb when I bring to delivery?' says your God." **Is 66:9**

Induction means 'bringing on' and this procedure is mainly performed when your doctor feels that for some reason your baby should be born right away. If there is any risk to the health of you or your baby you may need to follow your doctor's advice. You can however, exercise authority and command your body to begin labour so that you will not need to be induced. I have prayed for many women who were scheduled for an induction but their desire was to go into labour naturally without any intervention. In each case, labour commenced, some just moments before the intervention was scheduled.

If an induction is unavoidable, then prepare your body by exercising your authority over it and tell it what to do so that it will be ready and will respond quickly and efficiently to the medical procedure. This applies for any other procedure you might face as well.

The Recovery

"'But I will restore you to health and heal your wounds,' declares the LORD." **Jer 30:17**

In the same way that God didn't create the birth to be a painful, traumatic or complicated experience, He didn't intend the recovery process to be that way either! Remember that no matter what type of birth you ended up having you haven't failed if it didn't go as planned. You can always prepare and learn how to walk by faith for your next pregnancy and birth so you can receive a different outcome. You achieve this by meditating on the truth found in God's Word until it becomes a personal revelation and you know you have victory in that area. Also learn how to walk by faith in every area in your life and not just for pregnancy and childbirth. You will find that as you grow in the Word in all these areas, each birth will be better than the last!

No matter what type of birth you had, there will be an element of recovery needed. There may be different degrees of swelling and bruising, even if you didn't have stitches. This can often be uncomfortable or even quite painful. God created the human body to repair itself so your body will eventually recover. However you might want to continue to exercise your authority over your body and command a quick, painless and uncomplicated recovery. Simply apply the same principles to your recovery as you did for your conception, pregnancy and birth.

I have ministered to many women who were able to experience a pain-free and uncomplicated recovery after a caesarean birth. They walked by faith and exercised their authority not only to experience a complication-free caesarean but for the recovery as well. Many of these women didn't end up needing pain relief afterwards, much to the disbelief of the hospital staff. While they were tender after their operation, they were not in pain. They were free to move around and were not limited because of their stitches or surgery. One of these women had four caesareans within four and a half years. Before her third delivery her doctor warned her not to have any more children that close together. But it was the desire of her heart to have her children close together so she specifically covered this area and prayed for the restoration of her body. During her postnatal check up after her third child, the doctor said that there was little evidence that she even had a caesarean, let alone three of them!

For all of my labours, I was given an episiotomy as a routine precaution before my body had a chance to stretch. For me personally this was not an issue so I hadn't thought to cover this area. What I had covered was that I would have a quick and simple recovery without any complications.

After my first birth, I didn't realise that there would be swelling and bruising or that I may be tender afterwards. However, I did know that I didn't need to experience a painful and complicated recovery. So, knowing my authority in Jesus, I commanded my body to return to a healthy normal condition. My body quickly responded and I received a simple, uncomplicated and painless recovery. I then added more specific prayer points to cover this for my next delivery.

After my second birth, I had more damage than my first. I was told that the size of the episiotomy was equal to a second-degree tear. I had several midwives comment on the size of the swelling and bruising. But soon after the birth I leapt from the bed and showered myself. I didn't suffer a moment of pain or discomfort, even when I sat down. I remember one midwife being in total disbelief. She advised me to take medication for the pain that I must be feeling and not try to be such a hero because it was all right for me to be in pain. I'm sure it would be if I had felt any! At the same time I began to feel some afterbirth contractions. I hadn't covered this in prayer during the pregnancy because I didn't experience them after my first birth. I prayed and applied the same principles as I did during the birth and the pain disappeared.

After the birth of my twins, my recovery was exceptional. Aaron had been delivered head-first, and then Jesse was delivered in a breech position (bottom first with legs bent back). As soon as I was alone after their birth, I prayed over my body for my recovery and for my body to get into balance and be restored to perfect health. The swelling I had was minimal and I didn't have to 'nurse' the stitches at all. I continued on as normal. There was no trace of pain or even discomfort. I also had minimal bleeding.

I had specifically prayed during the pregnancy that all the blood that lined my uterus would all come out in the third stage of labour so there wouldn't be much bleeding afterwards. I experienced no afterbirth contractions. The midwives were surprised because apparently after each subsequent delivery the contractions are supposed to be stronger. As well, with twins, there is supposed to be a longer recovery because the uterus and stomach muscles have been stretched twice as much. There are also more hormones, blood and fluid etc. Yet for me every part of the twins' birth and recovery was wonderful!

So you can see that you don't need to expect or even accept any complications in your recovery. The healing power of God can supernaturally heal and restore your body. So don't look to the natural and what your body has been through because nothing is impossible for God and His healing power!

Pregnancy and Childbirth Prayer

'Thank You heavenly Father that the work that Jesus Christ did on the Cross has redeemed me from pain and complications and by His stripes I am healed.'

'I speak to my body in Jesus' name:
Body, you will carry my baby the way God designed you to until the perfect time for birth. Then you are to function efficiently throughout the labour and delivery without any pain or complications and as God intends, you will deliver my baby free from harm.

You are then to recover quickly and efficiently to a healthy condition and be restored from all wounds!'
AMEN!

PART V
Life After Birth

chapter 17

Life After Birth

Motherhood is by far the most rewarding yet challenging role that I have ever had to face, and most mothers I've spoken to agree. The responsibility of bringing a new life into the world and nurturing that life can be overwhelming, especially if it is your first child.

Every one of us adjusts to motherhood differently. One morning you can wake up on top of the world feeling like you are on the *Love Boat*, while other days you might feel like you're the captain of the *Titanic*! Life with a newborn can be very busy but this doesn't mean that motherhood has to be hard!

I want to share with you some of the adjustments and changes that I found challenging when coping with a newborn baby to help you prepare for your own new addition.

Change In Lifestyle

The sudden change to your lifestyle can affect your adjustment to a newborn baby. The combination of feeding, changing and settling your baby can leave very little time for yourself or for your husband. While these changes may seem overwhelming at first, be assured that it gets easier as your baby grows. The newborn period is only for a short time so I encourage you to enjoy it and not wish the time away.

Change In Self Esteem

These days many women put their careers on hold or leave behind responsible positions to have a baby. The change in role may challenge their feelings of value and self worth. While the corporate sector puts mothers at the bottom of the 'food chain', God sees motherhood as one of the most important of roles. We, with our husbands, are responsible for training our children in the way they should go so that when they grow they will not depart from it (**Prov 22:6**). How awesome is that!

Change In Spiritual Life

The first couple of months after your baby's birth you may not find quality time to pray or spend alone with the Lord. Remember, your relationship with God is not one of works but of grace. He loves us regardless of what we do or don't do. While God deserves our undivided attention, there is nothing wrong with praying throughout our day if we can't seem to find the time to be alone with Him. This was difficult for me to understand at first but the Lord reminded me that wherever I go and whatever I do, He is with me. I soon learned that I could spend time with Him while feeding or changing nappies. I also found more time to pray and spend with the Lord when the children were playing, while I was preparing dinner or doing other chores around the home. The amazing thing was that God was actually being included more in my life. I learnt to walk with Him rather than limiting my time with Him for one period of time per day, and my relationship with Him was not only transformed but also strengthened!

Other Changes

There are many other factors that can hinder your ability to cope with motherhood. Regardless, the overall adjustment to a newborn is often resolved over time and in the first six to eight weeks mothers usually learn what works best for them and baby.

Caring For Your Newborn Baby

Much of the information you will find on caring for babies can be contradictory. Even in hospital when it comes time for a change of shift, different midwives can bring with them their own way of doing things. I have also found that information on caring for babies changes all the time. Over the course of having my four children, there were dramatic changes in accepted practices and opinion, even from the same sources. If we were to compare what our mothers were taught to what we are taught today, we'd find a dramatic difference. Opinions change and new methods are tried as time goes on. All of this information can be confusing and overwhelming to a new mother, but every baby is different, so what works for one may not work for another. I suggest you prayerfully apply what works best for you and your family.

God should be your first source of help in caring for your children. If you are unsure of what to do, remember that He knows your child's needs. Therefore, spend time with Him and listen for His guidance. When my twins were born, I put into practice my knowledge and what I had learnt when caring for my other two children. I also obtained a great Christian book on how to care for babies. However, nothing I put into practice seemed to work. The answers came only when I stopped striving and sought help from God. He impressed on my heart what I should do and overnight they were different babies.

Be Anxious For Nothing!

There are many things that can cause you to worry when you have a newborn baby. I remember being inundated with all sorts of pamphlets with information on SIDS (Sudden Infant Death Syndrome), immunisation regulations and on various childhood diseases. While it is very easy to be concerned about the welfare and safety of your baby, remember that the blood of Jesus has redeemed us from the diseases of the world. So do not fear and allow the cares of this world to torment you about the health and safety of your baby. Resist any evil suggestion, declare the truth in God's Word and learn to trust that God will keep your child safe.

Breast-Feeding

God created breast-feeding. It is His designed way for us to feed our babies. Our milk carries antibodies to protect our babies from sickness and nutrients to sustain them for the first few months of life. However, for some breastfeeding doesn't come naturally. There can be many complications that inhibit the ease of breast-feeding your baby.

During my first pregnancy, every mothering seminar or prenatal class I attended was pro breast-feeding. I never questioned myself about whether or not I would breast-feed. When I experienced complications feeding my first baby, every clinic I turned to for help also strongly supported the idea of breast-feeding, so the thought of changing to formula was constantly spoken of as bad for the baby's health and well-being. Because of my struggle to successfully feed my baby I was distressed and felt like a failure. The pressure I placed on myself was unreasonable; the standards I had set were too high. This left an open door for discouragement, guilt and condemnation to enter. The truth is it can be perfectly normal for breast-feeding to take up to six to eight weeks to perfect as your milk supply adjusts to your baby's needs. Reading books on feeding may be helpful. However, putting into practice what you have learned is a challenge.

To help you to spiritually prepare to breast-feed, some of the things you may personally want to cover in prayer are for:
- Helpful midwives, who can teach you the correct way to feed.
- Your baby to be a quick and efficient feeder and satisfied and comforted when fed.
- The perfect amount of milk supply for your baby, complete with enough nutrients and fat stores to sustain your baby between feeds.
- No engorgement, infections or mastitis (a blockage of the milk ducts which can be very painful).
- Perfect attachment and compatibility with your baby's mouth and your nipple, therefore decreasing the risk of sore or cracked nipples.

With my first baby, Kaitlin, I had a very low milk supply. I was given two choices, to express milk after each feed to stimulate my breasts to produce more milk, or to bottle-feed. God gave me a revelation in this area through

His Word. I found some amazing scriptures that I personalised and specifically declared over my baby and my body.

> *"'For (baby) you will nurse and be satisfied at her (my) comforting breasts; you will drink deeply and delight in her (my) overflowing abundance.' For this is what the LORD says: 'I will extend peace to her (me) like a river, and the wealth of nations like a flooding stream; (baby) you will nurse and be carried on her (my) arm and dandled on (my) her knees.'"* **Is 66:11–12**

> *"(Baby) You will drink the milk of nations and be nursed at (my) royal breasts."* **Is 60:16**

> … *"because of your father's God, who helps you, because of the Almighty, who blesses you with blessings of the heavens above, blessings of the deep that lies below,* **blessings of the breast and womb**"… **Gen 49:25**

By applying God's Word and exercising authority over my body, my milk supply increased overnight. Kaitlin almost choked on the new quantity of milk. I continued to breast-feed her for the first year of her life.

I had a perfect milk supply with my second baby, Aidan because I had covered this in prayer during my pregnancy. He was rapidly gaining weight but I had damaged nipples from his feeding. They were split at the intersection where they met my breast and it was painful to feed. I went to a lactation clinic and the lactation consultants initially could not fault my attachment. But after an examination of Aidan's mouth they found he had an extremely high palate (cathedral dome palette). This prevented my nipple from being drawn to the back of his mouth. There was no solution and the only option I was given was to wean him and bottle-feed. While initially I was discouraged, I made the decision to continue to stand on what I believed and I took authority over the situation. I began to pray for perfect compatibility between Aidan's mouth and my breast to facilitate successful breastfeeding. I declared healing, exercised authority and rebuked the pain and during the next feed the pain disappeared (just like what occurred with my labour). The attachment was also perfect! From that point on I continued to feed Aidan without any further complications. **All** things are possible for those who believe in and know their God!

Feeding Your Baby

There are many advantages and disadvantages with both breast and bottle feeding, but a mother who has made the decision to bottle feed can be made to feel like a failure, especially for mothers who are unable to breast-feed. Praise God that there is no condemnation for those who are in Christ Jesus! God doesn't condemn you if you don't breastfeed so don't allow anyone else to either!

If you are bottle-feeding you will constantly come across messages that say 'breast is best'. Even formula tins come with the message 'breast milk is best for babies'. But sometimes, due to complications, the baby can be unsettled and the mother stressed and therefore dreading the next feed. How can this be best for the baby? So, in some cases, pursuing breast-feeding at 'all costs' can be detrimental to the mother/child relationship. I have seen unsettled babies change overnight with the introduction of formula feeding.

When I gave birth to my twin boys the desire of my heart was to breast-feed. At first, my twins were fed individually until I was confident to introduce 'twin style' feeding. This is where you feed both babies simultaneously, one under each arm. It was enjoyable in hospital being waited on by helpful midwives, who would help get me into position, but it was completely different once I returned home. If the twins had been my only children, I may have taken the time to feed them individually. At the time however, I was determined to breast-feed at all costs with no thought to how this decision would affect the rest of my family. My lifestyle revolved around feed times due to the need of a large couch and a special feeding pillow. Breast-feeding became a chore and was affecting the rest of my family. Once I made the decision to stop struggling and bottle-feed, the pressure I had placed on myself lifted. And to top it off all the bottles, sterilising equipment and formula were miraculously provided to me!

I was also out and about a couple of nights per week with ministry either at the Healing School I was lecturing at or with New Life Ministries. Shaun was able to feed the twins for me on the nights I was out. At other times we would feed them together and he would often comment on how he loved being able to be more involved in the twins' lives as babies.

The Joy Of Motherhood?

What I have found with new mothers is that regardless of how they feel, many put on a 'happy face'. For some, this masks what is really happening. A mother may feel condemned and unable to ask for help if she perceives everyone else is coping and she's not. She may also feel alienated and a failure as a mother. Because of this, many new mothers suffer alone needlessly. I experienced this, but I later found that many other mothers had felt the same way, but were either too embarrassed or proud to talk about it. You don't have to 'tell all' to everyone who asks, but if you're feeling overwhelmed, it will be comforting to know that you are not alone.

Depression

Feeling sad is a perfectly normal human emotion, which we will all experience from time to time. Depression however, is very different from the emotion of sadness. Depression is when the sufferer experiences a sadness that persists for weeks or even months.

There are different types of depression but the two main forms that can occur after childbirth are the 'third day blues' or 'baby blues', and postnatal depression (PND).

The 'Baby Blues'

The 'baby blues' can occur from within a few hours, or to up to a week after giving birth. However, they usually come on the third or fourth day after the birth, when the milk supply comes in, hence the other popular name 'the third day blues'. These 'blues' are a time of jumbled emotions, and can swing between an overwhelming joy to emotional outbursts. Hormones are usually the main culprit because by the end of pregnancy, our estrogen and progesterone levels have peaked; they then drop dramatically after the birth. The 'baby blues' require no special treatment; they usually pass within a couple of days. However, rest, support and understanding from loved ones are all helpful. There is nothing to be ashamed of if you experience the baby blues, however if these emotions continue for more than a month or become severe, you could be suffering from postnatal depression.

Postnatal Depression

Postnatal depression (PND) can begin anytime during the pregnancy or up to the first twelve months after the birth of your baby. PND is unique to every sufferer. For most women it will be mild and short-lived, but for others, the depression can descend like a black cloud for a long period of time.

During my first pregnancy, I spent all my energy and focus preparing for the labour, so I didn't really think beyond the birth. I had assumed everything would come naturally. However, the first couple of months after Kaitlin's birth were chaotic. Nothing was in my control. My whole body, including my hormones and emotions, were out of balance, my thyroid gland was under-active and I gained 15 kilograms within three months. Kaitlin was also unsettled, because of my low milk supply, and I also developed insomnia. I was an emotional mess. I would go from happy to sad to angry within minutes, and was irrational over insignificant events. There was a time where I actually cried over spilt milk! I was also experiencing the same symptoms as an older friend who was menopausal. I would become dizzy and lose balance, I had hair growth under my chin and on my breasts, I experienced hot and cold flushes and skin crawls to name just a few symptoms.

Spiritually, I felt like I was in a dark pit; I had no energy and if I tried to pray, all I could put together was 'Jesus help me'. It would then feel like a lid would come down and stop my prayer. I couldn't concentrate on anything. Even when I tried to read my Bible, I would read the same line over and over. I was oppressed and depressed. I tried to cope on my own for eight weeks before seeking help. I was referred to a doctor and was diagnosed with postnatal depression. Medically there was no solution given to me apart from anti-depressants.

I praise God for what His son, Jesus Christ, did on the Cross for me! I received my breakthrough at a women's group meeting soon after. For several weeks they had prayed for inner strength for me but the week they took authority over the depression was when the victory came! I felt the oppression and depression break and lift off while I was being prayed for. Finally, the darkness was gone. Everything had been dull and dreary but was now bursting with colour again.

However, I had to continue to walk by faith and exercise my authority to maintain my healing. At first it felt like I was in an intense spiritual battle. I had to renew my mind by gaining some order and discipline in my thought life. I researched scriptures on the renewal of my mind, and on my position in Christ. I meditated on them and applied them by declaring what they said out aloud when I felt challenged. I continued to do this every time the familiar thoughts or feelings of depression started to creep in, and they would flee!

This battle was constant at first but I soon grew in the truth of what God's Word said and was able to walk by what God said about me and not by how I was feeling at the time. I discovered that even though my feelings, emotions and thoughts were real, I didn't have to submit to and live under them. Instead I began to exercise my authority over them and have my feelings, emotions and thoughts submit to God's Word instead. The stronger I grew in the Word, the more the strength of the depression abated, and in a short period of time I walked in victory. My life had turned around; instead of being a victim enslaved by my feelings, emotions and thought-life, I became the victor!

During my second pregnancy, I continued to walk by what God's Word said and exercised authority over my emotions, hormones, feelings and moods. After the birth of my second child, I was so elated I totally flew past the 'third day blues'. However, many challenges presented themselves during the early postnatal days to steal my peace. The whole family, including Aidan, came down with the 'flu, I developed a middle ear infection that nearly burst, and I was experiencing another breast-feeding complication. While it appeared that all hell had broken loose in our home, at no point did depression have a hold on me. I was able to recognise the symptoms, and that enabled me to oppose them at the onset so I was able to maintain the victory, peace and the joy of the Lord. When I was set free, I was free indeed.

During my twin pregnancy, I knew how to walk in victory so I continued on that path. I am in awe of the great pregnancy, delivery and postnatal period I had with my twin boys. It was a blessing in every way. I felt healthy, whole and happy throughout, not only physically but emotionally as well. While there were still issues that arose, I was able to continue to have victory over my emotions. I can't put into words just how wonderful this experience was.

There Is Light At The End Of The Tunnel!

One thing I noticed while I was suffering from PND is that no one talks about it. The majority of mothers I met after I had my first child appeared to be coping. I kept thinking there was something wrong with me because it seemed I was the only one with a problem. It was only after I was healed and shared my testimony that other women opened up and shared their similar experiences. I also realised, especially amongst Christians, that there was an expectation that everyone should be coping and to appear otherwise was judged as a sign of weakness and spiritual immaturity. However, this could not be further from the truth. Remember, there is no condemnation in Christ Jesus! The Bible tells us to love, support and encourage one another with prayer. Postnatal depression sufferers especially need this type of support and encouragement.

PND should never be kept to yourself because to suppress or ignore it will only make matters worse. It can be a very serious condition if left unattended. To admit you have a problem is not a sign of weakness or failure as a parent but of strength and courage. It is also the first step to recovery. There is absolutely nothing to be ashamed of if you realise you are suffering from PND. There is light at the end of the tunnel and there is nothing wrong if you need help to get there.

There is also nothing wrong if you need to seek medical advice or take medication such as anti-depressants. For some sufferers the medication helps them to cope with life again. This in turn might provide strength to some sufferers so they can focus and begin to walk by faith in the Word (through the finished work of the Cross) to overcome. It's important to note however, that when doctors treat depression with medication such as anti-depressants or tranquilisers they only numb the emotions. They cannot heal them, so the thoughts, feelings and the root of the depression will still be there. Medication can only ever reach the physical, not the spiritual realm. Also, while psychologists, psychiatrists or counselors work with the mind and help with past issues, only Jesus can heal the soul, and help you to overcome depression, unbalanced emotions or other torments of the mind.

Remember that when you received your salvation you received everything you needed for life. So if you are experiencing any form of depression or imbalance in your body know that healing is already available! The same inheritance you received for forgiveness of sins and healing in your physical body is the same healing power that can heal and transform your thought life and emotions so you can be whole; spirit, soul and body!

The Complete Work Of The Cross

At the end of the day, PND is just another form of sickness. Depression has no legal right to stay or have the victory over you any longer. Jesus took ALL forms of sickness and disease to the Cross and by His stripes you were healed!

> *"Surely He took up our **infirmities** and carried our **sorrows**, yet we considered Him stricken by God, smitten by Him, and afflicted. But He was pierced for our transgressions, He was crushed for our iniquities; the punishment that brought us peace was upon Him, and by His wounds we **are** healed."* **Is 53:4–5**

In Chapter 16, 'Childbirth without Fear', I covered the meaning of the word *sorrows (makob)*, which in this scripture is defined as *sorrow, pain* and *grief.* Pain in this context means pain in the form of sorrow, physical pain as well as mental or emotional pain.

The dictionary definitions of these words are best described as follows and show the fullness of what Jesus purchased for us:
Pain: bodily or mental suffering, distress, trouble, exertion.
Sorrow: pain of mind, grief, sadness, distress, cause of grief, to feel pain of mind, to grieve, sad, unhappy.
Grief: deep sorrow, pain, the cause of sorrow or distress.

This means that along with our sin, sickness and disease, Jesus carried the full force of our grief, sorrows, physical, mental, and emotional pain and suffering on the Cross — in our place! He provided healing of the whole person; spirit, soul and body — by Jesus' stripes you have been healed and made whole!

Satan has no legal right to torment you mentally (unless you allow it). You have been redeemed from fear, anxiety, and depression and from anything else that steals your peace of mind. We have been given a spirit of power and a sound mind (**1 Tim 4:7**). We don't have to rely on anti-depressants, medications or any tranquillisers to help us cope with life or to receive peace of mind. Through applying the finished work of the Cross to this area of your life you can overcome depression and walk in lasting victory over it.

God Is A God Of Comfort

When I first came home from hospital with Kaitlin, I had no idea what I was doing. I was physically and emotionally exhausted and my hormones were working overtime. Shaun would often come home and find me crying. He had no idea how to comfort me and I had no idea how I needed to be comforted. I found these scriptures helpful for those times:

"As a mother comforts her child, so will I comfort you; and you will be comforted over Jerusalem." **Is 66:13**

"Even though I walk through the valley of the shadow of death, I will fear no evil, for you are with me; your rod and your staff, they comfort me." **Ps 23:4** (Note here it says 'shadow'. What shadow ever hurt you?!)

"Praise be to the God and Father of our Lord Jesus Christ, the Father of compassion and the God of all comfort, who comforts us in all our troubles, so that we can comfort those in any trouble with the comfort we ourselves have received from God."
2 Cor 1:3–7

"I pray that out of His glorious riches He may strengthen you with power through His Spirit in your inner being, so that Christ may dwell in your hearts through faith. And I pray that you, being rooted and established in love, may have power, together with all the saints, to grasp how wide and long and high and deep is the love of Christ, and to know this love that surpasses knowledge — that you may be filled to the measure of all the fullness of God."
Eph 3:16–19

"He heals the broken-hearted and binds up their wounds. He determines the number of the stars and calls them each by name. Great is our Lord and mighty in power; His understanding has no limit." **Ps 147:3–5**

"Cast your cares on the LORD and He will sustain you; He will never let the righteous fall." **Ps 55:22**

To cast means to fling, throw, shed, or hurl, to **not** hold onto. Jesus cast out demons, men cast nets and we need to cast our cares onto the Lord. God didn't create us to be burdened with life or with the cares of the world. Whatever you focus on (pay attention to by worrying, analysing or thinking upon), you give it power and a hold on your life. Remember always to:

... *"Be satisfied with your present circumstances and with what you have; for He (God) Himself has said, I will not in any way fail you nor give you up nor leave you without support. I will not, I will not, I will not, in any degree leave you helpless, nor forsake nor let you down, relax my hold on you — assuredly not!"* **Heb 13:5 (AMP)**

Maintaining Your Healing

"It is for freedom that Christ has set us free. Stand firm, then, and do not let yourselves be burdened again by a yoke of slavery."
Gal5:1

If you begin to experience familiar feelings, thoughts or symptoms of depression, this doesn't mean that you haven't been healed. You simply need to exercise authority and resist the symptoms and continue to daily walk in your victory.

You Have Already Been Delivered!

"[The Father] **has delivered** *and drawn us to Himself* **out of the control and the dominion of darkness** *and has transferred us into the kingdom of the Son of His love, in Whom we have our redemption through His blood, [which means] the forgiveness of our sins."* **Col 1:13–14 (AMP)**

You don't need extensive deliverance ministry when it comes to depression. The truth is that you have **already** been delivered from the control and dominion of the enemy! You can walk in and maintain your freedom every day because Jesus has already obtained the victory over depression and spiritual oppression! Many who suffer depression have an unrenewed mind and struggle with fear, worry and anxiety. They are easy targets for Satan's torment. Always remember the truth of who you are in Christ so you can overcome your fears and the lies of the enemy.

Therefore, continue to walk by the finished work of the Cross and the fullness of what Jesus has done for you by applying this truth to every area of your life. If you begin to experience symptoms of any kind (physical, emotional or mental) resist them at the onset! Continue to declare the truth of what God's Word says about you and the situation, and continue to guard your mind and what you allow yourself to think and focus upon. While the battle of the mind and of any unbalanced emotions may seem constant at first, soon you will be strong enough to be able to recognise, face and overcome them with the truth of what God's Word says and walk in complete victory!

PART VI
Appendices

Testimonies

O n the following pages, you can read just some of the testimonies from women who have received the answer to their prayers. These have been included because as you read about other ordinary people like me who have overcome, it will encourage you in your journey. Faith comes by hearing what Jesus did through the finished work of the Cross as outlined in the Word of God. Also **Revelation 12:11** tells us that we overcome by the blood of the lamb and the word of our testimony.

I also wanted to include these testimonies to show that these truths are attainable, and how when others applied God's Word to their circumstances they too achieved results. However, I do not want to detract your attention from the scriptures in this book, because the scriptures are the foundation on which this book is built.

I pray that the following testimonies will encourage you in your faith. I look forward to reading about the future breakthroughs in people's lives, so please send in your valued testimony of how God and this ministry have affected your life.

The majority of the following testimonies are available to download or purchase on audio CD. Please write to our postal address or visit our website for ordering details. Our website is also regularly updated with new testimonies and photos of new arrivals! When you receive your breakthrough we can include yours too.

New Life Ministries — Bringing Life to Barrenness
PO Box 593, Forestville, NSW 2087, Australia
www.newlifeministries.com.au

Leanne Brooke

I was diagnosed with Polycystic Ovary Syndrome (PCOS) at 20 years of age, after suffering from painful and irregular periods for over two years. I was prescribed the oral contraceptive pill, which regulated my menstrual cycle and dealt with the symptoms. In 1999, when my husband and I decided to start our family, I stopped taking the pill and in the first month was delighted to find that my period didn't come. However, I wasn't pregnant as I had hoped and found myself on a six month roller coaster ride with no menstrual periods (amenorrhea) and no pregnancy!

Blood tests revealed that I had extremely low levels of the hormones necessary for ovulation. Scans showed that my ovaries were in fact covered with cysts and that my entire endocrine system was out of balance. In desperation, I consulted naturopaths, nutritionists and eventually a reproductive endocrinologist who stated that the only hope I would ever have of conceiving was through IVF. But because my body was not responding to the drugs I had already been given, I was told that even this option would not work.

I came in contact with **New Life Ministries** and received prayer for my situation. I stood on **Exodus 23:25–27** and meditated on **Psalm 113**, **Isaiah 49:23** and **Luke 1:37**. I stuck scriptures on my fridge and pursued God with everything I had in me. Through spending time with Nerida, I learnt to speak to my body and I commanded it to line up with the Word of God, which says by the stripes of Jesus I am healed! Over a short period of time I also received the revelation that Jesus had already obtained my healing 2000 years ago; all I needed to do was to believe it. So I did! Two weeks after this revelation, my menstrual periods returned! It was my first natural (or should I say supernatural) cycle in 18 months! I was healed! I then went on to have perfect 28-day cycles with no PMS symptoms, pain or problems!

In the fourth month (August 2000) following my healing, a home pregnancy test showed that finally I was pregnant! As I had experienced such a miracle, I had not planned on having any sickness during my pregnancy. What I had also not expected was such a ferocious attack of fear to assail me. I was terrified of losing my baby and for the first three months I threw up almost every day and could not sleep. I went for a number of ultrasounds to confirm that I was still pregnant. The first scan revealed that there was no baby, and after standing on God's Word that I would not miscarry, another scan a week later revealed a perfectly healthy baby! I also started to bleed one afternoon and I began to realise what a battle I was in. The Lord showed me that I had made an idol of my baby and as I repented I felt the fear lift. From that moment the morning sickness waned and disappeared. It was amazing to see that it was my anxieties that had caused me to be physically sick. I might add that the first ultrasound showed that I was healed from PCOS! This was such a dramatic difference from my diagnosis when my ovaries were completely covered with cysts and were also non-functioning.

The pregnancy continued without complications and on 21 April 2001, I gave birth to Joshua Isaac, a healthy baby boy. He was born after about 20 hours of labour, during which I needed an epidural. This slowed things down considerably and I required induction and many stitches! I was so disappointed. Thankfully, I had another opportunity for victory in this area, as I conceived another baby ten months later. This pregnancy was also fraught with attacks of fear. At six weeks I experienced another threatened miscarriage and doctors were also concerned about the size of the baby as I was very small. Thankfully, fear did not grip me as it had before and I was not nearly as ill during the first trimester. Kiara Grace was born perfectly healthy after a labour of five hours on 16 November 2002. I required only gas during contractions and no stitches, despite the fact that she was 3.7 kg with an enormous head! Nothing is impossible with God!

Since writing this testimony, Leanne has had two more children!

Skye Syron

In April 1996, I decided that I would like to start a family and I stopped taking the pill. In June, my menstrual cycle never came and I was quietly confident that I was pregnant because I had all the pregnancy symptoms (it is amazing what the mind can do). A blood test came back negative. In December, I underwent examinations and ultrasounds and regardless of all the negative tests, I was still convinced that I was pregnant. However, after the results of the ultrasounds showing no signs of gestation, I burst into sobbing tears. What the scan did show however was that I had Polycystic Ovary Syndrome (PCOS) and that my hormones were out of balance. I believed in the healing power of God and I decided to pray for healing of this syndrome. At this time, I had no knowledge of God's promises regarding conception. I became frustrated and begged my doctor to put me on fertility treatment. He reluctantly filled out a prescription for the drug 'Clomid'.

My periods finally recommenced in January 1997. I was totally relying on the drugs for conception, I would pray over them so that they would work. I'm not saying that God doesn't work through drugs and medicine because He can, but I had put my faith in the medication over God. I was also charting my temperature and trying to pinpoint ovulation and planning the perfect timing for conception, but to no avail.

In February, both Stewart and I went through a battery of tests. I had a laparoscopy and Stewart had sperm analysis. We were both given a clean bill of health! I was healed of all cysts on my ovaries!! They were perfectly healthy. I still keep the results showing the scans of before and after. However, when March arrived and I was still not pregnant, I begged my doctor once again to put me on fertility treatment. He prescribed 'Provera' which is full progesterone.

Two months later, I received a breakthrough. I discovered **New Life Ministries** and I contacted Nerida. She prayed for me over the phone and I felt such a peace. I mentioned that I was not comfortable with continuing the Provera and we prayed for a peace to know what to do. I prayed again once I got off the phone and felt a total peace about discontinuing the Provera. I decided to give God complete control and complete trust. Since then, my whole thinking has changed. The knowledge and strength that God placed in me gave me the ability to cope with getting my monthly period. This change had also brought peace and strength to my marriage. Instead of being miserable each month which caused tension between my husband and me it brought us closer together. Stewart said that he felt like he had a new wife.

Romans 2:11 *For God does not show favouritism.* This scripture really spoke to me and I realized that what God gives to others, He will give to me also. I might also add that God healed my hormones and monthly cycles. I no longer experienced pain, cramping and irregular cycles. I spoke to my body in Jesus' name and commanded it to come into perfect balance in every way (including my hormones). The month I began to pray for this healing, my cycle commenced exactly on the 28th day!

My faith was challenged over the next few months. I kept finding out that friends and acquaintances all around me were falling pregnant. It was a fight at times to not go back and control things but I let go and put my trust in God. A couple more months after this I conceived my miracle baby! I praise the Lord for the victory over barrenness. I am currently pregnant with our fourth child and I will have had four children within four years! I really am a joyful mother of children!

My testimony doesn't end there. Once pregnant I continued to pray and believe for an awesome delivery and recovery. I assumed I would give birth naturally. However, after eight hours of labour with my cervix not dilating and the heart rate of the baby dropping too low, my doctor told me it was too risky to continue and I would have to have an emergency Caesar. This came as a great shock. I was very upset at the time because I thought I had failed. My doctor who is a Christian told me there was no failure in having a Caesar and that it made me no less a mother, it was purely another way to deliver safely.

During the surgery my doctor discovered that not only did Mackenzie have the cord wrapped around his neck but that my pelvis was in fact too small to deliver naturally. But praise God, Mackenzie was born safely and perfectly healthy. Before the Caesar I had prayed for a natural delivery. In a split second I had I said to the Lord *'make it work for the Caesar delivery'*. Well praise God, He did!

My recovery was also exceptional. I had asked the Lord to take away all pain and discomfort and that I wanted to be up and about straightaway. The extent of the use of any pain relief was a couple of painkillers and that was for a headache caused by the epidural. I left hospital early, which was quite a surprise to the staff. They were amazed at my recovery and they said they had not come across a Caesar patient so quickly mobile and that it appeared as if it had not happened.

I went on to have two more awesome, even better caesareans and recoveries and as I write this I am only three months away from having my fourth Caesarean. I am very excited because the recovery gets better each time. After my third delivery the doctors commented on how well my stomach had healed and that it didn't even look as though I had had any Caesareans. Medically speaking, you are not supposed to have four Caesars in four years, but with God nothing is impossible. Praise the Lord that we have been blessed with facilities which will allow for a perfect delivery all the time whether natural or Caesarean.

I hope that my testimony will bring encouragement to you. I cannot explain the peace I now have in my life. It is how we cope while going through infertility (and any other problem for that matter) that counts. Where we put our trust and hope determines the level of peace. The decision is ours to make and the outcome and the way we are coping hinges on that decision!

Amy Holder

First of all, I want to thank my merciful and loving Father for being so true to His Word. But secondly, I want to thank everyone involved in this ministry, especially Nerida for writing a book that changed my life.

We started trying to conceive our first child in December of 1999, but prior to that I bought a book entitled *Taking Charge of Your Fertility*. It makes me shudder to think that for the first year of 'trying', I was relying more on that book, than the tried and true living Bible. The title alone should have put up a red flag in my devout Christian mind, but it didn't. I never dreamed that what I was trying to do was take the miracle of childbirth out of God's hands and place it into my own by scientifically calculating and charting. I was praying to God for a miracle, but doing everything to tie His hands behind His back. I mean, if I planned intercourse on a certain day depending on my temperature and cervical fluid and then got pregnant, how could the glory go to God? It would have just gone to the author of that book, and me.

After about a year of unsuccessfully trying to conceive, I came upon the **New Life Ministries**' website and it changed my life. I think in my heart I knew that I needed to be relying solely on God for my miracle, but when I read about the faith in this ministry, I knew exactly what I needed to do.

When I first came to this site, I had recently had a very painful HSG test done and my husband had undergone a sperm analysis. Although both tests came out fine and healthy, I had a sinking feeling that I shouldn't have had them done. I sort of felt like I was betraying God by seeking answers from a doctor. I had relied on pure faith so many times before, but for some reason it was harder to rely on Him so faithfully to get pregnant. However, after reading testimonies on this website, and then buying and reading *A Plan for Pregnancy*, Nerida's first book, I decided to take the ultimate leap of faith and stop 'officially' trying.

I read *A Plan for Pregnancy* in June of 2001 and it told me to believe God's promises for children. I immediately knew in my heart that this is what God wanted me to do from the beginning, trust only in Him. I filled out the back of the book with my prayer points — specific prayer points — and prayed over them with my whole heart. I learned, memorised, and believed the scriptures outlined in the book and then took my leap of faith and left the rest up to my Heavenly Father.

Last week I found out that I am five weeks pregnant. My husband was a little nervous and wanted confirmation from the doctor (I had only taken a home pregnancy test), so I went to the appointment, even though I knew in my heart what had happened. Sure enough I was a healthy five weeks pregnant with the baby in the right spot! And you know what? Last June, when I listed my prayer points, I decided I wanted a baby in the fall, because that's my favourite time of year and the time when most of my family have spring birthdays. Can you guess when I'm due? September 24th!!!!! Can you believe it! We serve an awesome God! I fell to my knees and cried out to Him the night my test came out positive because for the first time in a long time, I felt like someone special in God's eyes. I think sometimes we forget how much He loves us and how much He wants to help us... if we would just let Him!

Well thank you **New Life Ministries** for reminding me to 'let God do the work'.

Tracy Dougal

My husband was told by two doctors that he could not have children because his sperm count was weak, slow and low, and that without IVF he could not make a baby because his sperm could not make the swim and even if they did, they could not penetrate the egg. Well the Devil is a liar!! The doctors and my husband were convinced of this 'fact' but I rejected that diagnosis, prayed for healing, and believed in my heart it would be done.

We both had a strong desire for children. We previously had been through a cycle of IVF; it worked, but at 20 weeks I lost the baby. We were both devastated, I didn't want to go through IVF again. I never heard anyone teach on what God had to say regarding conception and childbirth. So after finding the **New Life Ministries** website and joining their online support group, Women In Faith (WIF) in September 2003, I began to really study and pray. Meanwhile, my dear husband (who is currently a non-Christian) was pushing me to call the fertility specialist so we can 'get started again'. But I told him that I was not ready for IVF and I also briefly explained to him that I believed that his sperm was healed and I would conceive without medical help. He backed off (out of respect), but felt that I was 'wasting time'. A few short months later I conceived!

I want to encourage those who don't have a Christian husband, to join together with other believers and stand in agreement. You can also get into agreement with God on His Word! Now I'm 18 weeks pregnant! Praise the Father!!! There is power in the Word!! Have faith, it will come to pass (April 2004).

Karon Koza

Having children had always been a great desire for my husband Edmund and myself and we were both eager to start a family shortly after we were married in February 2000. I was coming up to 38 and Edmund was fast approaching 40. We were over the moon when we conceived our first child shortly after our marriage. I considered myself to be quite a healthy and reasonably fit person but I was not feeling very healthy during this pregnancy. My prayer life was very strong at this time but my knowledge of God's Word regarding childbearing was very limited. We were both ignorant in that regard, we later established. After heavy bleeding and cramping at seven weeks we lost our baby. The weeks following were very difficult, we found it very hard to talk about and we struggled in our prayer life because we didn't understand.

Edmund and I eventually decided to move on and believed that this baby just wasn't well enough to survive and was now at home in a wonderful place with God. Our second pregnancy happened just short of three months later which was rather a surprise to us, we realised then that falling pregnant was not going to be an issue for us. Within six weeks however the same symptoms returned and the result was another miscarriage. Once again the grieving period took place and we became more anxious than anything to find answers to our problem. We sought help in every worldly capacity such as doctors, naturopath, herbal practitioners, underwent many medical tests, eating programs, you name it I tried it!

Our third pregnancy was approximately three and a half months later and I felt so much better prepared but on a medical level as opposed to a spiritual one. However, a ten-week scan revealed that our baby had died within days of this scan. Our doctor felt it might help to establish why we kept miscarrying. The test results came back and it was a genetic disorder. Had this baby survived through to birth, they would have had major problems throughout a very short life. We were also told that carrying a baby girl could be an issue and related to our losses. I had everything diagnosed from lupus to antibodies to blood clotting issues and was not really given any positive news from any of the practitioners we visited. Some even said that our age would make it very difficult to conceive as my eggs were getting on a bit, so to speak. These diagnosed complications certainly stopped us in our tracks and made us think long and hard about our walk with God. We couldn't get passed the knowledge that He was a good God and He wouldn't want us to suffer like this. I became desperate not just to find a solution to this problem but also to seek God and to know him more intimately and find out what our relationship was all about.

Having a baby was very important but the helplessness we felt and lack of knowledge we had about His will became a stronger driving force at this point in time. I prayed fervently for God to send me someone who could help us. Within about a week (under amazing circumstances) I was introduced to **New Life Ministries** and our prayers were well and truly answered. 'We suffer through lack of knowledge' is what God's Word says. How true this was in our case. This ministry was literally a God-send. The fellowship was awesome, the messages were so powerful and within a short time of attending these meetings I received many revelations in so many areas of our lives and particularly in regard to God's plan for children in our lives.

I have also received many powerful scriptures from this ministry and know without one shred of doubt that God's Word is as relevant today as it was when it was written over 2000 years ago. Every Word is true and the scripture that I repeated after every promise in the Word was **Isaiah 55:11**, *'so is My Word that goes out from my mouth. It will not return to me* *empty, but will accomplish what I desire and achieve the purpose for which I sent it.'*

That was it for us, if we had faith to believe and confessed this; it had to come to pass. **Jeremiah 1:12** *'The Lord said to me, "You have seen correctly, for I am watching to see that My Word is fulfilled."'* **NOT NEGOTIABLE**, how powerful the scriptures, His promises had become. Edmund and I also thoroughly read through *A Plan For Pregnancy* and it became our compass for our exciting journey with this new knowledge. Nearly six months after our most recent loss we had conceived our precious gift from God.

However, at nine weeks I experienced cramping and bleeding. Edmund and I felt weak for all of about ten minutes and grabbed Nerida's book, the Word and more specifically the scriptures we had which related to God's promise for us in this area and started to pray and confess these out loud. One scripture that spoke to me very clearly, was the scripture in **Ezekiel 16:6**: *'Then I passed by and saw you kicking about in your blood…and I said you will live and not die.'* Nerida and Julie came over and joined us together in prayer. They stayed quite late that night to support us in prayer and left when we all knew that we had the victory. I felt so much at peace and very strong; the support we received was overwhelming. Edmund and I knew all would be well even though the circumstances didn't support this at this moment in time. The next day everything returned to normal. The remainder of the pregnancy we continued in prayer, standing in agreement and confessing God's promises over our baby. We really had a very close and intimate relationship with our Father during this journey. At the full duration of the pregnancy we received our perfect gift from the Lord, after what can only be described as an incredibly joyous pregnancy. Our precious, beautiful and perfect gift Abbye Elizabeth Koza was born exactly 40 weeks to the day on 11th of April, 2002.

I have delivered this same message of hope to many couples, through prayer, Nerida's book and CDs produced by Nerida and other women involved in this ministry. I have received many wonderful testimonies from friends who had difficulty conceiving children or had some other major complications during pregnancy. Many have been blessed by the knowledge of God's Word and the promises He has for each and every one of us in this area, and those children are here as living proof today.

In closing I would like to emphasise the importance of knowing God and His Word. Don't be ignorant as we were. Stand strong and united with your husband or anyone who can agree with you as the scripture says in **Ecclesiastes 4:9**, *'Two are better off than one, because together they can work more effectively. If one of them falls down, the other can help him up…'* Two people can resist an attack that would defeat one person alone. A rope made of three cords is hard to break. Also have faith to believe that with this knowledge, what you hope for will come to pass. **Hebrews 11** *'Faith is being sure of what you hope for and certain of what you do not see.'*

God Bless you Nerida, Julie and the **New Life Ministries** team for your love and support. Praise God for He is always faithful, and all the Glory goes to God. AMEN!!

Deb Mcintyre

In 1999, I was pregnant with my first child. Several weeks into the pregnancy, I was woken in the early hours of the morning with what I can only describe as excruciating cramps in my abdomen. I was initially filled with fear about losing my baby, and could not pray anything; it is the times when we need to pray that we often aren't able. So there I was in my lounge room groaning in pain and unable to pray. Praise God that I had recently bought *A Plan for Pregnancy*, a book full of scriptural references.

I opened the book and began to read aloud some of the relevant scriptures. As I was doing this, the fear began to leave but the pain remained. I paced around my lounge-room, reading scriptures, becoming bolder and stronger and faith was stirring in me. Within half an hour, the cramping had left. Praise God! The rest of the pregnancy progressed without event and on October 17 1999, our beautiful Aimee Elizabeth was born.

I became pregnant again two years later. However, six weeks into the pregnancy the familiar painful cramping and bleeding began. I began praying the scripture, *'worship the LORD your God, and His blessing will be on your food and water. I will take away sickness from among you, and none will miscarry or be barren in your land'.* (**Exodus 23:25–26**) Over and over, I repeated this trying to muster faith. I then experienced a tremendous bleed. Fear and panic took over before I could take hold and begin again meditating on the scriptures. We rang our doctor who said there was nothing I could do and suggested I had probably miscarried.

I also rang Nerida and she prayed with me immediately on the phone, building faith and hope.

A couple of days later I saw my doctor who arranged an ultrasound. He was already talking about a curette. By six and a half weeks, there should be some sign of a baby and a heartbeat but during the ultrasound the radiographer said she could see some evidence of where the beginnings of the embryo had begun to form but that there was no baby. Before having a curette, they said they would perform another scan in one week's time. We were obviously upset by the ultrasound. I rang Nerida and again, she prayed with me and we continued to agree together and stood on God's Word that I would not miscarry. The next week, much to the surprise of the radiographer, the ultrasound showed a healthy baby with a strong heartbeat. God performed a miracle! On July 15, 2002 Allie Rose was born, perfect. Praise be to God!

Two years later we were blessed again and while I did experience another threatened miscarriage with a few days of bleeding and cramping I continued to stand on the Word as before. Once again I contacted Nerida and she also stood in agreement with me. God's Word and the power of prayer continued to bring faith and peace and I knew that my baby would be safe. A few days later an ultrasound scan showed a healthy baby with a strong heartbeat and on 26th February 2004, our son, Jesse James Harris was born perfectly healthy.

One thing the Lord showed me during my last threatened miscarriage was the importance of the Armour of God. While meditating and praying about this, the Lord showed me that you need to be clothed with the armour before the battle. We should not allow ourselves to be off guard and have to then put on our armour if we do experience a complication. While I felt that I did enter the battle unprepared, God showed me that His grace was sufficient for me and I was able to clothe myself and obtain the protection and victory I needed. I now don't take things for granted but I am sure to clothe myself daily with the Armour of God.

Gillian Robson

My husband, Alan, and I had tried for years to conceive and after seven long years we conceived fraternal twins. I bled for the first twelve weeks and the doctors thought that I had lost one of the twins. However, Alan and I had set ourselves in agreement and we looked up all scriptures in God's Word relating to children and we began to speak it over my body and over the children in my womb. So to the surprise of the doctors one of the placentas had tried to come away from the uterine wall but ended up re-attaching itself.

At 21 weeks I was rushed to hospital to have my cervix stitched up because it had opened up and twin number one had her head coming through. After a week in hospital I went home. The next day I noticed I had a funny pain in my back. It kept getting more severe and it felt like I was constipated. After arriving at hospital they hooked me up to all these machines and told me that I was in labour. They then hooked me up to all these drugs but to cut a long story short they couldn't stop the labour. I ended up labouring throughout the Saturday night and on Sunday morning at 8:15am I gave birth to the first twin. Then fifteen minutes later I gave birth to the second twin, another girl. They both died five minutes apart.

After the twins had died the first thing I thought was that I can never have a baby again, I can never go through a pregnancy or go through this pain of delivering a baby again. There was also the fact that the doctors had told us that the chance of us ever carrying a baby to full term was very slim. Alan told me later that when he got in the car to go home the first thing he heard was **John 10:10**, *'the thief comes to steal kill and destroy'*. The Holy Spirit quickened it to his spirit. We both knew that this was not the will of God or the plan of God for our lives. It was also not the plan of God for our future. So we knew that this was an assault from the thief to totally crush us and to crush our faith.

Once I got home I felt like I was in a barrel and someone was churning it and I was going around and I had no control of what was going on. I couldn't cope with what I was feeling because I was so distressed. One day as I lay in bed I remember crying out to the Lord and saying to Him 'what am I going to do?' 'How am I going to get out of this?' I knew the Word and what it said but I didn't know how to get it to work. It's okay for people to say 'the Word of God says this or it says that' but when you are in a situation how do you get it to be a reality? So I picked up the Bible and I turned to **Isaiah 53** and read. The scriptures jumped out at me from the page. In the Amplified Bible verses four and five say *'Jesus had delivered me from distress.'* That was exactly what I was going through because I was distressed and traumatised. God said that Jesus took my distress and He took my grief. So I realised that I didn't have to feel like this or suffer in this way. The Holy Spirit showed me that I could take His Word and start to work it to get out of the circumstance. All of a sudden it was like I got a shot of life. I had been so perplexed but that Word became so alive to me. It hit my spirit.

I got up the next day and I felt the same but I took that Word and began to speak it out. I professed that Jesus had taken my distress so it no longer belonged to me. I also spoke to the grief and told it to go as Jesus had taken my grief as well. I could now walk free of this. So I began to confess this morning, noon and night. Every time I felt like I was going back into that kind of mode of being really distressed I would speak out the Word of God. At first it was a battle but it soon became real to me. I actually felt when the grief left my spirit. And I felt the Word of God begin to rebuild and heal my wounds. Even though it took some time, what I found most astonishing was that by taking God's Word as mine I began to walk in a spirit of victory.

Another key to our victory was that every time Alan and I felt the heavy burden of grief try to oppress us we would begin to praise and worship God. During these times we would feel the heaviness lift and a spirit of joy and peace would flood over us.

Isaiah 61:2(b)–3 (AMP) *To comfort all who mourn. To grant consolation and joy to those who mourn in Zion — to give them an ornament a garland or diadem of beauty instead of ashes, the oil of joy instead of mourning,* **the garment expressive of praise instead of a heavy, burdened, and failing spirit** *— that they may be called oaks of righteousness lofty, strong, and magnificent, distinguished for uprightness, justice, and right standing with God, the planting of the Lord, that He may be glorified.*

We are to 'put on' the garment of praise. There were many times where we didn't feel like it but we knew that we had to put it on and break through in worship. We would sing, meditate on God's goodness in His Word and worship Him because of who He is. So we had to throw off our grave clothes and actively put on the garment of praise. It was in the **doing of the Word** that we were blessed and became victorious.

A couple of weeks after the funeral I met Nerida. I had seen her testimony about **New Life Ministries** on the Christian Channel and through that we were able to meet. I then began to come to the meetings. I didn't come with a defeated spirit. I had explained what had happened to me but I didn't feel defeated. Because I was walking in a spirit of victory it was like the circumstances couldn't come and crush me anymore. I put a stop to it by God's Word. It wasn't me but it was by working His Word and wielding God's Word in my mouth and speaking out and believing it and by acting on it. When Satan would come and say 'you will never have another baby', I would open up the Word of God, read it and say 'listen devil it is written blessed is the fruit that comes from my womb and my body and there will be neither male nor female barren in my house.'

I also had to overcome the fear of having another baby. It wasn't just the fact that the twins had died but I had this monumental thing in front of me where I was literally terrified to get pregnant again and of giving birth because of what I had experienced in the past. But I learned that you cannot take your past into your future. You've got to put closure on the past because you can't change yesterday you can only deal with now. The Bible says that **now** faith is (**Heb 11:1**). So I began to deal with the now. I began to speak to my body and speak to my emotions and tell myself that God did not give me a spirit of fear but I've got a spirit of power, love and a sound mind. I was also not double minded. I was not going to say one day 'I want a baby' and the next day say 'I'm too scared'. So I began to be very decisive in my choices and I made a decision that come hell or high water that I would have another baby. I had also decided that I would not be traumatised by another delivery again because God's Word has promised me certain things. So I made a concrete decision and stuck with it. I knew that I had to go with my decision because when you are double minded you get nothing.

Around eighteen months later I conceived again. While I was threatened throughout the first trimester with miscarriage, I continued to stand on the Word of God against fear and against miscarriage and at the full duration of the pregnancy I had a wonderful birth and delivered a beautiful baby girl and experienced everything that I had believed and specifically prayed for.

Another thing I want to cover is my healing of strep B. Strep B is just a bacterium that sometimes women can harbour in their vagina. If you are pregnant it can cause your babies to be sick. When my twins were born they examined the placentas and found that both were infected with strep B. This was what had brought on premature delivery. The doctor had said that it couldn't be cured because it is just there and that I may be able to take antibiotics but that is about it. There was also the chance of it bringing on premature labour in any future pregnancy. When I first came to the meetings I told Nerida about it and how I hated it with a vengeance. I was being tested regularly and all the tests showed up positive to it. However, I came to the point where I got indignant against it and I said 'if God's Word says that He took my infirmities and my diseases and by His stripes I am healed then I am laying claim to that and I believe that today is my day of healing.' I then stood my ground. I went back for several more tests and they all still showed up positive for the infection. But I did not care what the tests said because I believed I received my healing when I prayed for it. A year and a half went by and I just stood my ground and I kept thanking God and professing that I was free from strep B. When I became pregnant a routine check showed up no traces of strep B! They had said that when I became pregnant again I would be on antibiotics right throughout the pregnancy. I wasn't! It was awesome to know that while there was a fight, I got the victory. AMEN!

Margaret Viliamu

I believe with all my heart that God answers prayer. If I didn't believe that, then my faith in God would be in vain. Sometimes the answer to prayer is fought with a battle and sometimes whether we realise it or not we go into that battle unprepared. Why this is so in some cases and not in others is still very much a mystery to me, but one thing I have learnt is that for the things I really want, I must not take them for granted but apply the Word of God and pray them through until they are attained.

With the birth of my fourth child Claire, I went into the battle unprepared. Having delivered my second and third children easily, I assumed it would be just the same for the fourth, and doctors seemed to back up that belief. Moreover, why shouldn't it be the same was my thinking? Fourth labours are usually quick and finished in no time. So I guess you would say I took a low-key approach to believing for my fourth labour. Unfortunately, I found myself in the middle of a crisis situation when ready to deliver the baby, her position turned and there was no way she was going to come out. I felt very unprepared for that eventuality, but God was faithful and she was born healthy and strong. I, however, was left traumatised after hours of pain and had many fears of the same thing happening again.

While pregnant with my fifth child, Michael, I knew I had to do a lot of preparation to take me from a position of fear to faith. I didn't leave it to the last minute, but began by reading the Word and praying. I went to the prayer group run by Nerida and Julie. God doesn't expect us to fight the battle alone, and I was very grateful for the prayer support and encouragement they gave me. I went there on a weekly basis 'bathing' myself in prayer and the Word. I also wanted to give in this area by praying for other women. I soon began to get built up in my faith; *'faith comes by hearing the word'*, and took every concern and detail I had to the Lord and prayed it through. I began to believe God for a very positive and joyful birth medically and emotionally. I prayed about everything. I did this for the last five months of the pregnancy. I also prayed to get into a private hospital, because I had left it too late to apply. I wasn't even on the waiting list. I kept ringing the hospital believing God that I would get in. They kept saying no. But God answered my prayer two days before the due date and I was admitted as a full private patient. On the day of the delivery, Julie and Nerida supported me in prayer. As far as deliveries go, you couldn't get any more perfect than this one. With a textbook 'pain free' delivery, our beautiful baby son, Michael, came into the world. The peace of God was over us and I had a strong sense of His abundant grace given to us for that birth. It was a joyful and beautiful experience. God is a rewarder of those who diligently seek Him!

Julie Cantrill

When my husband Graeme and I decided to start a family, we stopped using contraception and I became pregnant that first month. What a blessing! My pregnancy progressed well and my husband and I attended pre-natal classes. After seeing a graphic video of a woman giving birth, I promptly burst into tears and decided I could not do that on my own. I knew I needed God's help to do it. At our small group the next night, I asked the members to pray for God's strength to be with me during my labour. The small group leader had a Word of Knowledge for me that since I had asked for strength, it would be given to me. I had had a fear of pain in childbirth since my early teens so I prayed about this, and covered the pregnancy, labour, birth and my baby in prayer. I also prayed for a quick and easy delivery. When I went into labour, I arrived at hospital nearly fully dilated and my son, Levi was born 90 minutes later. My husband can bear witness to the strength with which I gave birth. The only pain relief I had was gas, which was totally ineffective, and local anaesthetic.

My second child, Jack, was born four hours after I had the first twinge of labour. At first the contractions felt like very mild wind pain but when I realized I was in labour, I rang the hospital. I had to talk them into letting me come in because I wasn't in pain and I had only been in labour a couple of hours. Jack was born 90 minutes after arriving at hospital and again I only used local anaesthetic. The scripture that was my *rhema* for this birth was **Isaiah 66:7–9**.

With my third child, my daughter Holly Elizabeth, as soon as I knew she was on the way, I was off to hospital. The contractions disappeared at one stage, or so I thought. They were still happening according to the monitor but I couldn't feel them. From the first twinge of labour to her birth was about six and a half hours. My *rhema* for this birth was that *'God inhabits the praises of His people'* (**Ps 22:3**). When I could I escaped to the ensuite bathroom to praise Him. This made all the difference. There was one point where I felt that if the labour got any more intense, I wasn't sure if I could handle it. But I made a conscious decision to go for it and stand on the promises of God. My midwife broke my waters and Holly was born 30 seconds later. My doctor arrived about five minutes too late. I see now the significance of the decision I made about standing on God's promises; Holly was born within 15 minutes of making that decision. The Word says *'that what you decide on will be done and light will shine on your ways'* (**Job 22:28**). I was told later that such a quick birth after the breaking of the waters was dangerous but we had no problems, our God protected both of us.

When I prayed to conceive Holly, I specifically prayed about the timing of her birth. I preferred not to have the baby after I turned 35 and I preferred not to have a newborn in winter (we had a cold house). This meant that I had to have the baby in September. Holly was born on 27 August, one month and one week before my 35th birthday and when I took her home, it was September, the first month of spring in Australia. Also, I wanted her to be born after the Tuesday, as I needed to go to the dentist on that day. Two minutes after Tuesday had ended, Holly was born.

Three years later came a little surprise, another son named Finn. Finn was born 75 minutes after arriving at hospital. I had a similar labour to the others and again, the doctor didn't quite make it in time. While I was pregnant with Finn, thoughts kept coming to mind about my age. I gave birth to him when I was 38. The world will tell you that this is old to have children and there is a great risk of problems, especially with the baby. It was like an oppressive fear that came on me. I got hold of one scripture *'fear not for I am with you says the Lord'* and every time a negative thought came I spoke the scripture to that thought. The Word says that we are to renew our minds and take every thought captive to the obedience of Christ Jesus (**2 Cor 10:3–5**). After a few weeks, these thoughts no longer had any influence on me. I knew that I knew the baby would be fine.

Another surprise awaited me about 18 months later when I became pregnant again. I prayed the usual things for labour, that my body would stretch and accommodate the birth of this child, without pain, no need for a Caesar, no induction, no forceps, no drugs etc, no problems or complications.

I felt something happening about 3.30 one morning and could not get back to sleep. There was no pain and the contractions weren't growing in intensity. I couldn't even say they were contractions at the time. At an appointment with my doctor later that day at 12.30pm, I was two cm dilated and was told I would probably not deliver until the following day. Graeme and I prayed in agreement that I would deliver our baby before five pm that day! On our way to hospital at three pm, I asked Graeme to agree with me again that I would be nine or ten cm dilated and that once we were in the delivery suite the baby would be born in less than half an hour. We got into the delivery suite at four pm and I was nine cm dilated. Axel was born at 4.28pm, after two pushes. The Word says that Hebrew women are vigorous and give birth before the midwives arrive (**Ex 1:19**) and I prayed that I would have this strength (and I did!).

The *rhema* I had for this birth was *'I will perfect that which concerns you'*. God answered so many of my prayer points, even the trivial ones such as the location of my hospital room. I took the book *A Plan For Pregnancy* into the birthing suite with me and the midwife (who wasn't a Christian) had a good look at it. She also told me I should come in and witness some other births so I know how the other half does it! Each time I became pregnant, I made a list of prayer points. These points were quite detailed and included such things as perfect development and growth of the baby, enough time to get to the hospital, a short, quick and easy labour, etc. During my pregnancy with Jack, the prayer points expanded as I began to learn more about God's will for me in this area. By the time I was pregnant with Holly, I had learned of the term 'supernatural childbirth', and my prayer points expanded even further. My faith matured in many areas. With each of my children's births, for the best part of labour, I experienced pain free contractions, most of which I prayed through. While they did get uncomfortable towards the end of labour with the last three or four contractions having some degree of pain, being able to push was wonderful, and hard work took the place of any pain. I did tear or have an episiotomy with all five children but I didn't feel it at the time. The stitches were not a problem and the other problems that usually come with tearing and stitching did not eventuate.

During the nine months of pregnancy, I spent time in prayer and I had the prayer support of Nerida as my prayer partner as well. Having my prayers answered was great but just having the time with God was wonderful and helped me to get closer to Him. I also found it was great to have my husband beside me during my labours to agree with me in prayer and support me. Thank you Graeme. I felt such joy at giving birth to my beautiful babies and I encourage any woman to study the knowledge given and the scriptures noted in this book because they are God's promises for you to experience the best He has for you.

Katrina Woolcott

I've been friends with Nerida for many years and when I first read Nerida's book I was pregnant with my third child Liam. I utterly devoured it from beginning to end. I ended up having the most amazing spiritual experience in the delivery room. For the first time in my Christian walk I felt the tangible presence of Jesus. It was amazing.

Anyway, a few weeks after Liam's birth I was diagnosed with Postnatal Depression. I was put on medication and after three weeks, my symptoms subsided and I began to feel better but I was pregnant again (Liam was almost five months old). The doctor took me off the medication and believe it or not, ALL the signs of PND disappeared for the duration of that pregnancy. Three weeks after the birth of my fourth child, Clare, my doctor called me in because he was very concerned. The symptoms had returned with a vengeance and he put me back on medication. Six months went by; I was coping okay but we were living away from all our friends and church family. We made the decision that if I was to get better we had to move back to Sydney so that I could go to **New Life Ministries** meetings and get some prayer. I was in a VERY dark place and unable to help myself out of this despair despite being on medication.

Two weeks after attending the meetings God healed me. I discovered that time that the symptoms of PND were only a trigger for something far deeper that I needed to hand over to God. Postnatal depression and other sicknesses like it can be simply signs of a broken heart for which there is always a wound. I had lost my mother when I was 16 years old and later my father at 21 and the Lord revealed to me that I had not fully dealt with that grief.

But praise God, He sent his Son to heal us; mind, body and soul. I came home from that prayer meeting a changed woman. I decided that in order for me to see the fruit of my faith I would obviously have to go off the medication. I wisely did this gradually, so that by the time Clare was nine months old I was medication free and completely healed in **Jesus' name!!**

I emphasise in **Jesus' name** because it is in His name that I am healed and it is in His name that to this day more than four years and another child later that I have maintained my healing.

During this process I spoke many scriptures but what got me through times of attack from the enemy was the name of Jesus. I would just say His name over and over again. When people around me would question my healing I would speak His name, when I would **feel** symptoms returning I spoke the name of Jesus. I am living proof that in ANY situation there is power in the name of Jesus!

How to Receive your Salvation

"For God so loved the world that He gave His one and only Son that whoever believes in Him shall not perish but have eternal life." **John 3:16**

God loves you so much that He sent His son Jesus to come and take the sin of the world (including yours) upon His body so that you can receive forgiveness, have a relationship with Him and experience eternal life. Without receiving Jesus we can't experience that relationship with God.

"For all have sinned and fall short of the glory of God." **Rom 3:23**

Sin separates us from God and separation from God will lead to judgement and death.

"For the wages of sin is death, but the gift of God is eternal life in Christ Jesus our Lord." **Rom 6:23**

Since sin is the problem that separates us from the love and acceptance of God then we need to get rid of it. Simply making the decision to start doing the right thing does not achieve this. God sent His Son to die in our place.

He put on a human form and as Jesus He became *'God in the flesh'*. Because Jesus was sinless, He suffered on the Cross in our place for our sins so that we can have a right standing with God and be reconciled back to Him.

The very moment that you accept Jesus as your Lord and Saviour you receive an inheritance from God and eternal life. You also received the forgiveness of all your sins.

"If we confess our sins, He is faithful and just and will forgive us our sins and purify us from all unrighteousness. If we claim we have not sinned, we make Him out to be a liar and His word has no place in our lives." **1 John 1:9–10**

We can only have a right standing with God through the atoning death of Jesus Christ on the Cross. When **anyone** believes in and receives Jesus' sacrifice, God declares them cleansed from all unrighteousness and in that moment we experience peace with God.

> *"Therefore, being justified by faith, we have peace with God through our Lord Jesus Christ."* **Rom 5:1**

When you become a Christian you are no longer just born of your mother here on this natural earth but you are now also born into the kingdom of God! You become a child of God.

> *"As many as receive Him to them gave He the right to become the children of God, even to them that believe on His name."* **John 1:12**

You receive so much more as well! You will have acceptance, love, joy, peace, patience, kindness, goodness, faithfulness, peace, joy, fruitfulness, and self-control. The restoration of your soul is deep, satisfying and lasting! The joy of the Lord will become your strength!

Doesn't Being A Good Person Make Me A Christian?

Being a Christian is not about good works or about being a good person. You cannot work or earn your ticket to heaven!

> *"For it is by grace you have been saved, through faith — and this not from yourselves, it is the gift of God — not by works, so that no one can boast."* **Eph 2:8–9**

Going to church, reading the Bible, praying, and being a giver are all 'things' a Christian **does**; they are not what earns their way into heaven. The **only** way into heaven is through Jesus. Christianity therefore, is not about going to church and doing the outward things but about a personal relationship with God our Heavenly Father!

> *"Jesus answered, **'I am the way and the truth and the life. No one comes to the Father except through me.** If you really knew me, you would know my Father as well. From now on, you do know him and have seen Him'."* **John 14:6–7**

Salvation is not about what you can do for God but about what **God has done for you!** Therefore, it does not matter who we are, what we have been, or what we have done in our past, because our eternal destiny lies with one truth and that is whether we have (or have not) received Jesus!

So, What Will You Do With Jesus?

If you have never received Jesus, then you now have a decision to make. Your response determines where you will spend eternity. God has given you a free will to make your own decision. It is up to you what you want to do. But if you choose to refuse to receive Jesus, there is nothing else you can do that will make you right with God.

How To Receive Jesus!

"everyone who calls on the name of the Lord will be saved."
Rom 10:13

Do you want to accept God's provision of His gift of eternal life right now? If so, this is simply done from the moment you say, 'Yes' to Jesus Christ.

*"That if you confess with your mouth, **Jesus is Lord,** and believe in your heart that God raised Him from the dead, **you will be saved**. For it is with your heart that you believe and are justified, and it is with your mouth that you confess and are saved."* **Rom 10:9–10**

If you are ready to say **'Yes'** then say this prayer out loud right now...

Salvation Prayer

Father, I thank you for sending your Son Jesus Christ to die on the Cross for me. I turn away from my old life and I ask you to forgive me for going my own way.

I receive you Jesus, as my personal Saviour and I choose to follow you and make you Lord of my life. I ask you to minister to my heart and fill me with your strength, joy, peace and to fill me with your Holy Spirit. I also ask you to guide and help me on how to follow you.

I receive your perfect will for my life and everything that Jesus died to purchase for me!

AMEN!

Welcome to the family of God!
Your life will never be the same again!

Resource Information

New Life Ministries has a range of audio recordings, DVDs and books available to help you to walk by faith in your personal journey. These resources are specifically designed to establish the truth in God's Word on healing and on every area of childbearing, and contain detailed information on how to apply it to your life.

We have received many letters and emails from all around the world about how our resources have blessed the lives of those who have received them. Many couples have experienced breakthrough and now have their miracle babies! We encourage you to share these products as an outreach to others.

Details on where to order our resources are on the **New Life Ministries** website www.newlifeministries.com.au. Below is a list of just some of our resources. All new releases will be added to our web site as they become available.

Books

God's Plan for Pregnancy

Discover God's plan for conception, pregnancy, childbirth and beyond; and how to apply it to your life. This fully comprehensive book is designed to help you to overcome fear and walk by faith for all areas of childbearing. It also teaches how to pray effectively, and contains testimonies from women who through God's Word overcame incredible odds and received their children!

God's Plan for Pregnancy — Pocket Companion

A companion to **God's Plan for Pregnancy** which has been specifically designed for you to pop into your handbag so you can have relevant scriptures and teaching at your fingertips. The **Companion** is a practical guide to help you to mix God's Word with faith and to act on what you believe, so you can see the power of God released in your life to change your natural circumstances.

Visit **www.godsplanforpregnancy.com** for more information.

Coming Soon

IT IS FINISHED!
Transforming your life through the finished work of the cross.

The price has been paid and the victory won for you!
As Jesus breathed His last on the Cross His final words were, "*It is finished*" (John 19:30). Three simple words, but so very powerful in their meaning!

Through reading this book you will discover how to:

- Walk in the fullness of everything that Jesus purchased for you through the finished work of the Cross
- See God's Word come to pass in your life
- Walk by faith, not by sight or appearances
- Overcome doubt and discouragement
- Replace fear with faith
- Renew your mind and gain victory over your thought life
- Overcome your past
- Walk in victory over all sickness, disease, pain and depression, as well as poverty, debt and lack
- Exercise your authority in Christ over your natural circumstances
- Walk in the fullness of God's Kingdom and what you have ALREADY inherited as a believer!

When you discover the truth behind these three simple words and the fullness of what Jesus purchased on the Cross, you will see God's power released to transform every area of your life!

Visit **www.itisfinishedbook.com** for more information.

Audio Messages

God's Plan for Pregnancy
4 Disc Audio Set
God's Plan for Pregnancy, Created for Fruitfulness, Positively Pregnant and Childbirth without Fear.

Audio messages also sold separately:
- God's Plan for Pregnancy (updated 2008)
  - Created For Fruitfulness
  - Positively Pregnant
  - Childbirth Without Fear
- God Is Into Increase Not Decrease!
- Stepping Out In Faith
- How To See God's Word Come To Pass In Your Life
- Victory Over Loss — Testimony By Gillian Robson
- Overcoming Infertility — Testimony By Leanne Brooke

DVD Messages

God's Plan for Pregnancy
2 Disc DVD Set
These messages were recorded in Ps Joseph Prince's New Creation Church in Singapore on 5th & 6th November 2008. Nerida shares the truth about God's Plan, purpose and will for your Conception, Pregnancy and Childbirth. You will discover how through the finished work of the Cross you can lay hold of everything you need to overcome any sickness or disease that causes infertility, miscarriage, pregnancy health issues and complications with the growth and development of your baby so that you can now go forth and multiply!

Please feel free to write or email to let us know how these resources have personally ministered to you. We look forward hearing from you!

About the Author

Nerida Walker is the mother of four miracle children: Kaitlin, Aidan, and twins, Aaron and Jesse. In 1994, Nerida's husband Shaun was diagnosed as sterile, but through the truth in God's Word they conceived and had four children, within four and a half years. Based on her own experience, and with a passion to help others struggling through infertility, Nerida founded **New Life Ministries** — *Bringing life to Barrenness*. New Life Ministries is a non-denominational Christian ministry catering to couples who need prayer, encouragement, and the knowledge of God's will in any area of childbearing.

Following the conception of her first miracle baby, Nerida wrote '**God's Plan for Pregnancy**', a book detailing the truth in God's Word regarding all areas of childbearing. It was written for couples needing truth and encouragement in the areas of infertility, miscarriage, pregnancy, birth and postnatal issues. The book is accompanied by '**God's Plan for Pregnancy — Pocket Companion**' — a practical guide to help you to mix God's Word with faith and to act on what you believe, so you can see the power of God released in your life to change your natural circumstances.

Since the first edition of God's Plan for Pregnancy in 1997, among the thousands of letters and testimonies received were many from husbands, single friends and grandparents. While they weren't necessarily in need of miracles in the areas of fertility and pregnancy, they were blessed by the chapters and Godly principles shared in The Foundations Section of these books, Nerida's way of communicating the truth in God's Word, and the simplicity on how to apply it to their lives. With this in mind, and with a passion to see every believer cross the line from barrenness into fruitfulness in EVERY area of life, Nerida wrote **It Is Finished**, a book revealing how to see God's power released to heal and transform every area of life through the finished work of the Cross.

Nerida has also co-written a course on the scriptural principles of healing, and lectured for over 5 years at a Healing School in Sydney Australia. Since moving from Sydney to the NSW Central Coast, Nerida has become the Director of the **Woy Woy Healing Rooms**, and alongside her husband Shaun, is Senior Pastor of **RIVER Christian Church** Kariong.

Since 1995 Nerida has ministered to people around the world, though the **New Life Ministries** website, online support group (**Women in Faith**), through her books, and ministry by email and over the telephone. She has seen many healings, and many babies conceived and born into the world, at times against incredible odds. Nerida also ministers internationally and at conferences by invitation, most recently in London and Singapore.

In Nerida's heart is a passion to see believers living in the *fullness* of their salvation in every area of life, and to cross the line from barrenness and miscarriage into fruitfulness, from sickness and disease into health, and from lack into the abundance of the work of the Cross and into all that God has provided. Nerida has seen many come to know Jesus, and many believers fall in love with Him all over again, being healed and transformed by the power of God in every area of their lives.

About New Life Ministries

New Life Ministries — Bringing Life to Barrenness is a non-denominational Christian ministry supporting anyone who needs *prayer, encouragement, and the knowledge of God's will in any area of childbearing*. That means if you need support with overcoming infertility, pregnancy health issues, miscarriage, childbirth complications or in the postnatal period, then we are here to help you!

We aim to reach those who are struggling to conceive and/or carry a baby safely to full term, as well as those who are not experiencing complications but want to gain knowledge of God's Word (His will) for these areas, and practical information on how to apply it to their life.

We have a passion to teach God's truth in these areas. We desire to see everyone receive revelation on who God is and what He has provided for them, and to see them lay hold of the fullness of the Cross, and receive their breakthrough.

New Life Ministries — Bringing Life to Barrenness
PO Box 593 Forestville NSW 2087
Sydney, Australia.
Email: contact@newlifeministries.com.au
Web: www.newlifeministries.com.au

Partner with New Life Ministries

How to help continue the work we have begun...

If you have in any way been blessed by this ministry, and believe in what we're doing, then we invite you to be a part of it by becoming a **New Life Partner**.

Our vision is to reach those who are in need of this ministry, and as a **New Life Partner** you will be joining us in the fulfilment of this vision and purpose. **New Life Ministries** is a not-for-profit organisation, and we rely on the Holy Spirit to lead people to sow into this ministry. We ask that you would allow yourself to be led by the Holy Spirit in your giving, so that we can continue the work we have begun. Your contribution will enable us to continue the work of teaching the promises of God for all areas of childbearing to others, and in proclaiming the Gospel to the lost.

New Life Ministries is 'fertile ground' in more ways than one and we know your family will be blessed by supporting this ongoing work. We love the words of the Apostle Paul, *'that each man should give what he has decided in his heart to give, not reluctantly or under compulsion, for God loves a cheerful giver'* (**2 Cor 9:7**).

On partnering with us you will receive a partner pack and the address for our exclusive **New Life Partner** web site. For more information, please visit our website.

Your gift, no matter how big or small is greatly appreciated and we look forward to the opportunity to pray over your gift and prayer requests, and believe for increase, prosperity and fruitfulness to follow you in every area of your life.

You can become a **New Life Partner** through a regular monthly contribution or you can make a one-off donation at any time. Visit our website and complete the Partnership form, (found on the New Life Partner's page). Alternatively, you can email us or write to our postal address for a brochure (previous page).